Palmer Ellen

Heroes of Ancient Greece

Palmer Ellen

Heroes of Ancient Greece

ISBN/EAN: 9783337196509

Printed in Europe, USA, Canada, Australia, Japan

Cover: Foto ©ninafisch / pixelio.de

More available books at **www.hansebooks.com**

HEROES

OF

ANCIENT GREECE.

HEROES

OF

ANCIENT GREECE:

A

STORY OF THE DAYS OF SOCRATES
THE ATHENIAN.

BY

ELLEN PALMER,

AUTHOR OF "THE FISHERMEN OF GALILEE," "CHRISTMAS AT THE BEACON,"
"NONNA," "THE STANDARD-BEARER," ETC.

WILLIAM P. NIMMO.
LONDON: 14 KING WILLIAM STREET, STRAND;
AND EDINBURGH.
1876.

EDINBURGH:
PRINTED BY M'FARLANE AND ERSKINE
(late Schenck & M'Farlane),
ST JAMES SQUARE.

PREFACE.

IN gathering together some of the memories of Socrates, which have been preserved by his pupils, Xenophon and Plato, I have endeavoured also to present a picture of "Living Greece," as it existed during the later years of the illustrious Athenian sage.

"The children also of Judah, and the children of Jerusalem, have ye sold unto the Grecians, that ye might remove them far from their border."

These and other words of prophetic warning, against the sins of the Phœnician cities Tyre and Sidon, were uttered some three hundred years before the battle of Salamis; they must be my authority for the introduction of Asahel into Athens.

As the "Standard-Bearer" was written to illustrate the position of the Christian Church, when in the first throes of its emancipation from heathenism, and to point out some of the blessings for which we are indebted to the sanctions of Christian law, so has this book been written as an attempt to illustrate the position of "The Church Expectant," during the sway of Grecian Art, Heroism, and Philosophy; when captives and exiles preserved that true light of Revelation, which enkindles all who approach it with holiness, truth, love, and that Righteousness, for lack of which, to use the words of Byron :

> "Rome decayed, and Athens strews the plain,
> And Tyre's proud piers lie shattered on the main."

CONTENTS.

CHAPTER I.
The Thalamos—Asahel—The Herb-Garden—Hygeia—The Wanderers—Farewell, ... 1-14

CHAPTER II.
Sparta—Nausicaa—The Eastern Veil—Herodotus—The Hebrew Captive—Platæa—The Guest-Friend—The Herbalist—The Heart of Greece—Hyllus—The Pythoness, ... 15-37

CHAPTER III.
The Eurotas—Spartan Outposts—True Friendship—Athenian Injustice—Androclea—The Redeemer—Spartan Youth—The Reciter—The Skias—Timotheus—Nausicaa—The Ægis of Athena—Opis—Farewell to Sparta, ... 38-66

CHAPTER IV.
Sunrise—The Everlasting Father—Attica—Attic Hospitality—Sparta or Athens—Hebrew Melody—An Anxious Mother—Desolations of War—A First Sight of Athens—Asahel's Letter, ... 67-88

CHAPTER V.
Athens and Sparta—A Blessing—The Parthenon—The Agora—The Thracian Dance—Euthydemus—Socrates—The Glory of Athens—Neptune Unveiled—"Iron Sharpeneth Iron"—Faith, ... 89-111

CHAPTER VI.
Home Duties—Position in Society—Charity—The Leschæ—Retrospect—The Palladium—A Falling Meteor—The Midnight Cry, ... 112-127

CONTENTS.

CHAPTER VII.

The Lesson of the Portent — From the "Paralus"— Alcibiades—The Foolish Virgins—The Reward of Faith — The Council — Retribution — The Vows of Youth, ... 128-143

CHAPTER VIII.

The Power of Light—Artemis—Earth or Heaven—Leda— Victory—The Spartan Muster—Hope Extinguished— Forethought—Asahel's Farewell—Fostered by Sparta —Faithful Friendship, ... 144-166

CHAPTER IX.

King Agis—The Allied Camp—Dion's Banquet—The Sibyl of Theseus—The Song of Hyllus—Terms of Surrender—Love me, Love my Dog—Thetis—Victor and Vanquished—National Sins, . . . 167-188

CHAPTER X.

Exile—Contemplation—Artemis or Hera—Self-Service— Immortal Love—The Isles of Greece—Whence art Thou?—Compensation—Unransomed—Resurrection —Glaucus—Salem—Teaching of Prophecy—Reunion —Athena Promachus, ... 189-219

CHAPTER XI.

The Death of Theramenes—Sunrise—Bridal Preparations —Herds and Herdsmen—Restoration—Triumph of Apollo—The Bride—The Bridal—Home—A Father's Heart, ... 220-239

CHAPTER XII.

A Wounded Heart—The Sacred Ship—Return from Exile —Socrates Impeached—Self-Examination—A Spartan Noble—Athena Assailed—The Victim—Judged by Works—Time's Verdict, ... 240-259

CHAPTER XIII.

Bountiful Earth—Harvesting—Explanations—Victorious —The Herald—The Laws in Hades—Euchidas—The True Light — Harmony — Church Expectant, . 260-280

HEROES OF ANCIENT GREECE.

CHAPTER I.

> "Clime of the unforgotten brave,
> Whose land from plain to mountain cave
> Was freedom's home, or glory's grave."
>
> —*Byron.*

RATHER more than four hundred years before the Christian Era, the sun of a bright autumnal day was shining into the large low-roofed thalamos of a substantial country villa in Attica. The radiant beams shone brightly upon the glistening veil of a lovely maiden, who was busily engaged in examining the workmanship of a rich piece of embroidery in the loom which stood upon one side of the room. At length the silence of the room was broken. "Come, my Thetis, come! and help me to decide. Shall I fill up this foreground with a field of flowers, or shall I picture our pet doves sipping water from the fountain? With what design shall I fill up this vacant space?"

> "Fill it up with roses,
>   With roses, red and white;
> Fill it up with eagles,
>   With vulture, crow, or kite."

"It will be all one to Cimon, my beloved Penelope. He will care nothing for the design, but will weigh it by the minutest hair balance to find out its value. If it weigh less than his favourite Persian robe, he will honour you with a message by his favourite slave, and a nosegay gathered by his own hands. Should it prove too weighty for his taste, however, he will buy a pennyworth of nettles in the Agora, and send them to you by some old crone, as a thank-offering for your year's labour. My own darling Penelope, why do you spoil your beautiful eyes over work which you well know Cimon will never prize as he should?" As the younger sister spoke, she threw her arms round the elder.

"You do not understand Cimon, my Thetis. You are too young to appreciate his lofty intellect. But see, my question is answered. I must emblazon that lovely dove. Pet him, my Thetis, while I sketch him in that position."

Softly untwining her arms, Thetis advanced to the pet dove which had flown in through the open window, and alighting upon the loom, was now busily engaged in cooing over the radiance of colour upon the silken robe it contained. Thetis spoke to the pet in gentle murmuring tones, while her sister lightly sketched out the form of the lovely bird upon her work. When the sketch was completed, the young girl opened an alabaster cruse of perfume; and sprinkling the liquid lightly over the plumage of the bird, she took it upon her hand, repeating the operation until its feathers were drenched with the fragrant liquid; then lightly shaking it from her wrist, said gaily, "Fly, birdie; fly to my mother! and refresh her with the odours of Elysium."

The bird, which seemed to understand every word spoken, immediately flew to the upper end of the thalamos, where a noble-looking matron reclined upon a crimson-cushioned, carved ivory divan. The bird hovered over the head of the lady, fluttering his wings softly as he did so, and thus scattering the exquisite perfume in a soft refreshing shower.

"Many thanks, my little Thetis. The sun shines so fiercely that I am grateful for your perfume."

"You need me to fan you again, my mother," was the reply, but the words were scarcely spoken when the lively speaker, who had approached the window, cried out in an altered tone, "Fly, Thratta, fly, summon the men. Here comes Lysippus down the hill side; he has two strangers with him, as well as our own men; and look, they have a deer, and a burden of other game. Oh, leaden-footed Thratta, fly," she cried, to the slaves at the other end of the room.

The excitement of Thetis soon brought her mother and sister to the window, where, looking out, they saw displayed one of the loveliest landscapes in Greece. Bright in the west, instinct with living beauty, lay the blue waters of the Gulf of Ægina, while far away rose the purple mountains of northern Greece. Nearer home a gentle acclivity rose from the other side of the valley which the house overlooked. This hill, crowned with myrtles and laurels, was clothed almost to its feet by carefully-tended orchards and vineyards. The boughs of the trees were laden with luscious fruit, while the long festoons of vines were trained over every graceful support which the art of Greek gardeners could suggest. The rich clusters of purple and white grapes clothing the hill side, the glistening of the transparent stream in the valley, the pure sapphire sky overhead, formed a lovely picture for the eye to rest upon, but the mother's eye saw only her youngest son, whose quick eyes had already discovered her at the window, and who was now waving his bow in triumph, now pointing to the splendid deer hanging over the back of his horse, and again racing down the hill impetuously with his two splendid dogs.

In less than a quarter of an hour the young hunter was standing in the outer court of the house eagerly displaying his spoils to his mother and sisters, who had descended from the thalamos to welcome him. "It is a noble stag, and your father will rejoice over your skill when he hears of it, my bright boy," said the mother gently, "but you have not yet introduced your companions."

"Forgive me, I forgot," said the youth quickly; then turning round, he led forward the elder of the two strangers. "Redeem my promise for me, dear mother, and, if you care for me, show gratitude to Asahel, who is, it seems, herb-gatherer for Menares of Athens. I had shot my stag, but he was still so swift of foot that neither Hipponicus nor I could have secured him alone. Our good friend here saw him in full flight with the arrow in his side, and secured him before we could possibly have reached him; and I have promised them a peep into your herb-garden, with any spare slips of herbs which your bounty may bestow for their ready help to me, my mother."

"I thank you for your kindness to my son," said the lady courteously; "but as you have already come far out of your road, you will rest and refresh yourself with food, I hope, before you gather such herbs as you may care to have from my store."

"Your son, in his desire to show gratitude for a very trifling service, soon discovered what would be very acceptable to me, lady, for there are few herbalists in Attica who have not heard of the Lady Androclea's garden. We cannot linger, since we have a long journey before us; but I shall be very grateful if you permit us to view some of your treasures."

The speaker was a man about forty years of age, tall, erect, and of a singularly composed manner. His complexion was of a light olive, his eyes black, but his features at once marked him out as an alien; a large, prominent, and slightly-hooked nose proved him to be of no Hellenic race.

"You must not tempt me to outrage the sacred demands of hospitality," said Androclea. "Rest here for a short time with your son; my servants shall bring you food, and when you have refreshed yourselves, you must, if you please, come to me in the flower-garden, where I shall be glad of your opinion concerning some rare herbs which my husband has procured for me from Italy. You seem to know me!" the lady continued, "and if so, you must know that I have long made herbs and their medical virtues my study. I am therefore always glad to meet with any one who can help me to fresh knowledge."

"There is no study more interesting than the study of the works of the Almighty Creator," replied the stranger. "Yet I have not hitherto met with any lady in Greece, who cared to devote her time to it; while in my own country many noble matrons love to study the knowledge gained by the wisest of our native kings."

"Ah! you are from some tyrant state?" said Androclea, inquiringly.

"From no tyrant state, lady," said the stranger. "The glory of our kingdom has passed away, yet was it—while it lasted—the glory of the noblest freedom upon earth." The lip of the strong man quivered as he spoke, and Androclea, turning towards the son, saw the eyes of the youth flashing with suppressed emotion. The lady felt that she had touched some tender chord, and, with a simple apology, turned to Thetis and bade her hasten the coming of the refreshments; then with a few courteous words she left her guests with Lysippus, and, as she passed on into her flower-garden, bade him see to the comfort of his friends, before bringing them to her in the garden.

The flower-garden into which Androclea entered was one which would have excited feelings of admiration in the breast of even the most highly cultivated English gardener. So scrupulously was it kept that an air of perfect purity and peace pervaded every nook. There, clumps of noble trees fenced off the eastern winds and glaring sun. Here lonely glades bloomed with bright blossoms, and filled the air with perfume. The verdure was refreshed by running streamlets issuing from several fountains, each of which was guarded by its presiding Naiad, sculptured with rare art from the pure white marble of Pentelicus. Androclea passed beds of blooming roses, lilies, geraniums, and those myriad flowers which were so carefully cultivated in Greece for festal garlands, as well as for their native beauty and odour. Then passing through an avenue of acacia she entered a sort of paddock, very carefully shaded upon one side by a fence of ilex, while on the other it rose in sharp acclivities or sloped down to the banks of a clear mountain stream.

This space was the garden specially devoted by Androclea to the cultivation of beneficent herbs; and here in soil specially prepared for each, flourished the rarest, as well as the most common, of all the herbs known to the Grecian herbalist of the day. There grew the native Attic thyme, valerian, hemlock, and melilot, once so highly valued for their qualities received from the pure air and porous soil of Attica, that they were regular articles of export to other lands; while the Arcadian liquorice-vetch, celebrated all-heal, and other exotic plants, were planted in spots carefully prepared for their reception. The lady passed on among the fresh, health-inspiring herbs, and at length seated herself upon a rustic bench beneath a plane-tree. There the air was filled with pure incense from spikenard and rosemary, from cytisus and vervains. The bank of the little stream was brilliant with various coloured pansies, and other violets; while beds of saffron and iris filled the lower grounds with radiance, and the air was filled with music from colonies of sweet singing birds in the surrounding trees.

Exactly opposite to the seat upon which Androclea was seated stood a fair statue of Hygeia, and before it a small altar. Through her marble veil the calm, majestic features of the goddess could be clearly discerned, and the eyes of Androclea were soon raised in devout reverence to the beloved face. At length the lady arose; and plucking a few sprigs from some of her rarest plants, wove them with dexterous fingers into a garland, with which she encircled the goblet in the hand of the statue, saying reverently while she did so:

> "Let others weave a crown for Mars,
> Or bind the brows of Bacchus bright,
> My hands shall twine a wreath for thee,
> Hygeia, sprung from heavenly light.
> O raise thy veil, disclose thy love,
> Teach me the wisdom I adore."

A slight rustling caused the lady to turn quickly, when she found Thetis with the strangers standing by her side. "I did not intend to interrupt your devotions, my mother."

"Nay, Thetis, you have not interrupted. I was but raising my oft-repeated prayer. I have finished." Then turning to the herb-gatherers, the lady said, "To you as men the divine Æsculapius appears unveiled; but to our weaker apprehensions, Hygeia but reveals herself through a veil, yet I believe that I at least love her none the less for this. Though her veil be of marble, so also is the rugged crust of the beautiful earth; yet as there are times when I perceive the glory of the radiant goddess gleaming clearly through her veil, so also do I sometimes perceive, in fuller light, the marvellous beauty and power of those secrets which, imprisoned and veiled by the rugged earth, yet force their way upwards, and blossom for our benefit in these simple herbs with which the earth has crowned herself. It seems to me that when our bodies become diseased by their separation from the source of life, they are healed, and renewed by returning once more to the simple gifts of our bountiful mother, and the veiled Hygeia is our guide to the mystic treasury. Surely of all the deities, Hygeia is the most merciful, the most adorable."

During this speech of Androclea's, a strange change passed over the face of the stranger. At first he listened with eyes averted from the statue, and closely fixed upon the ground. As the lady proceeded, however, he raised his eyes, and fixed them upon her face; and having thus looked upon that pure, noble, spiritual face, it would have been strange if they had not rested there in admiration. Gradually, however, the stranger followed the direction of the matron's eyes, and looked up to the fair white marble statue, so exquisite in its perfection of artistic workmanship, where the simple, clear-eyed womanly face looked through the marvellous texture of her marble veil straight into the eyes of her worshipper. In one hand she held the mystic serpent, in the other the health-inspiring bowl. When Androclea ceased speaking, the stranger stood silent for a few moments, then spoke, "Lady, your speech sounds to me as the voice of one who tells some midnight dream. For me, there is but one Lord and giver of life, health, strength, and all other good gifts, even the Eternal Uncreated, who made the heaven and the earth, and who revealed His holy law unto my fathers."

The strangers bowed their heads reverently when the name of their God was thus mentioned, so that not one thought of any irreverence could be imputed to them; yet their words sounded very strangely in the ears of Androclea.

"I do not understand you," she said. "Is it possible that you belong to some barbarous race to whom the beneficent Hygeia is unknown?"

The stranger raised his head proudly: "Lady, one thousand years before Solon or Lycurgus were born, centuries before Hesiod taught or Homer sung, my forefathers had conquered some of the most civilised nations in the world, nations whose brazen statues and pictures might have equalled even yours. We had a code of written laws nearly one thousand years before Solon and Lycurgus strove to bestow the same blessing upon you. Ours indeed were divine, proceeding audibly from the Divinity, while yours were but the faint copies, the fruits of expediency. And as to barbarism, while your greatest poet, Homer, was celebrating the deeds of a hundred petty kings, our sovereigns ruled over a country which, in its prime, stretched from the shores of the Mediterranean far away to the river Euphrates, while our inspired singers and prophets penned hymns of grateful adoration to the one holy God, which you, lady, I feel assured, would love to hear. Forgive me if I have spoken ungraciously, lady."

"Nay, rather forgive me," said Androclea, sweetly, "I spoke but in ignorance. I know nothing of those eastern lands from which so many strangers visit our shores. To me they are all connected with the barbaric Persian, and the merciless invasion of our beloved Hellas by his savage hordes. You, then, are not connected with the Persian?"

"No, lady, save as an unwilling tributary. The conquerors of my beloved country were in their turn enslaved by the Persian Cyrus, and thus we are subject to the power which you Greeks repulsed. Alas, alas, the destruction of our liberty was but the natural result of our desertion from our God and His holy law. This is, however, a theme of no interest to you, lady, and you were kind enough to promise us a few spare cuttings from some of your rare herbs. We must not detain you by our private sorrows."

The faces of his auditors seemed to assure the stranger that the narration of his history would be far from unwelcome, but the evident pain from which he had spoken of his native land forbade any return to the subject; so turning at once to her beds of herbs, Androclea pointed out with no little pride her rare and valuable collection, and was amply rewarded by the evident pleasure the stranger took in the careful rearing and healthy appearance of the exotics. There bloomed rare spikenard from the Ligurian Alps, the Sardinian seseli, famed for its sedative power over an aching tooth; Italian hyssop and madder, the perfumed Illyrian iris, Macedonian rue, rha from the shores of the Black Sea; and, amid a hundred other varieties, one carefully cultured stood out pre-eminent. This was the marvellous Æthiopis, transplanted from Mount Ida, in the Troad, and used by enchanters to open locks, and stay the course of rivers.

Even in an English country-house, the visit of one who understands and sympathises with the object in which we are interested is always a welcome event; but in Attica, at that time partly in possession of the hostile power, it was doubly so. Androclea kept her guests far on into the evening, and pressed them to remain all night. "If you pursue your journey so late," she said, "you are sure to encounter some of the marauding Spartan host from Decelea; and remember you have rare treasures now in your wallet."

"The herb-gatherer is sacred in Greece," replied the stranger; "and if it were not so, I have a talisman which would restrain the cupidity of the boldest of robbers from the camp of King Agis."

"Then remember," replied the lady, "that you have promised to visit me upon your return, and display your spoils from the Arcadian hills; and since you will persist in going, I suppose that I must 'speed my parting guest.' May you travel under the protection of Ceres herself; may Diana give you free passage through her woods and forests; and may the bountiful Hygeia unveil the fairest treasures of earth for your inspection."

The setting sun brightened the delicate white veil which hung from the head of the noble lady, forming a radiant halo, as she stood between her two lovely daughters to bid the strangers farewell. Lysippus was preparing to show his guests the nearest path to Eleusis, when, to his surprise, as his mother's voice ceased speaking her farewell, the elder stranger left his side, and returning to Androclea, bowed in graceful reverence, then kissing the hem of her purple stole, he spoke once more. "Lady, may the God of my fathers, the only One whose protection I seek, guard you and yours for evermore. May His holy angels watch over you, and keep you true in your love for His marvellous works; and may He in His own good time reveal Himself to your faithful eyes!"

Before Androclea or her children recovered from their surprise, the strangers were almost out of sight.

CHAPTER II.

> " Is Sparta blest, and these desiring eyes
> View my friend's son?"
> —*Homer, Pope's translation.*

ABOUT a week after the events narrated in the last chapter, the two herb-gatherers were travelling upon the road which led from the Isthmus to Arcadia and the picturesque city of Sparta. When they approached the banks of the Eurotas they changed their route, and, instead of entering the city by the bridge Babyx, they followed the course of the river until they at length approached the defile which terminated the ancient street Skias; here two temples stood, one dedicated to Ares the Destroyer, the other to Æsculapius the Healer; and towards the precincts of this latter temple the strangers approached, with the confident air of those who are entering upon well-known paths, and with the cheerfulness of those who feel assured of a hospitable reception at the end of their journey.

The city of Sparta was perhaps more strongly fortified by nature than any other in Greece. Surrounded by rugged mountains, and enclosed by the confluence of its two rivers, the Tiasa and the Eurotas, the five villages, or rather small cities, set apart for the five Laconian tribes, were united by four principal streets, and one common government. Thus securely built upon the gentle acclivities and slopes of her mountain-girded valley, Spartan patriotism might be excused the boast, "Sparta needs no walls."

The part of the city towards which the herb-gatherers were approaching was not within the river boundary; it stood outside the sacred Eurotas, and the noise and hurry of the populous city scarcely reached its seclusion. The hills around were covered with vineyards irrigated with the greatest care; farms well cultivated by the industrious Helots gave an air of comfort to the scene, wherever the marshy banks of the river permitted any cultivation. In the immediate neighbourhood of the temple a change became apparent; villas and more stately buildings appeared, the residences of the more wealthy citizens; and at length gaining the street itself, the strangers passed on unquestioned, until the houses once more became far apart; and at last leaving the high road altogether, they ascended the rocky eminence which rose above the temple of Æsculapius, and opened a gate which led them into a small plantation. Passing through this, they entered a lovely flower-garden, in which stood a small well-built mansion, evidently ancient; the architecture was simple and unpretending, yet well fitted to withstand the fierce heat of a

Spartan summer, or the biting cold of the winter. The strangers who entered the garden so unceremoniously, had no need to announce themselves, for the master of the house was seated upon a bench outside reading, and when they approached, he at once started to his feet with a cry of joyful welcome!
"Asahel! and you never sent me word that you were coming."

"Our journey was suddenly arranged, I had no time to send you word, but trusted to finding you at home. If you had not been here, I should have visited you upon my return from Arcadia."

"Thanks, ten thousand thanks, my friend; but who is this?"

"Only my little Gershom, grown up to be a staff for my old age."

"What, that Gershom! Nay then, Asahel, my friend, we are old men, and must now join in the chorus of the elders: 'We have been.' It is no longer, 'I am,' or 'I will be,' but alas! 'I have been.' And you, Gershom, what is your 'Will be?'"

The youth looked up with a bright sunny smile in his deep eyes, while he answered in the true Laconic fashion:

"Whatever ye can do or tell,
I hope one day to do as well."

"Welcome to Sparta, dear boy; you have not forgotten old friends or old pastimes, I see. But do come into the house, you must be famishing, I am sure."

The room into which Hyllus led his guests was

much better furnished than most Spartan dwellings, and displayed far more of the ancient luxury which reigned supreme under Menelaos and Helen, than the bare severity which Lycurgus had introduced. A rich Asiatic carpet covered the centre of the floor, curtains of crimson silk hung round the open door, which served as a window; many curious tripods and tables, some of carved ivory, were placed round the apartment, and upon some of these stood vases not only of Greek workmanship, but of that rare Eastern and Etruscan porcelain, only found in those days in the houses of those who had travelled beyond Sparta, and whose rank and authority enabled them to defy the censorship, which proscribed foreign luxuries — a censorship very lightly executed in those days, when Sparta, by her close alliance with Persia, was gradually swerving more and more from the rigid discipline which had lasted over four hundred years. The crimson cushions upon the couches, the rare cabinets for the safe keeping of parchments and scientific instruments, all told not only of other than Spartan tastes in the owner of the mansion, but also of the determination and power to cultivate them. The refreshment spread before the travellers was very simple; their customs were too well known for any time to be wasted in the preparation of meat for the repast. Fresh sweet milk, barley bread, excellent cheese, with a plentiful supply of fresh and dried fruit, a salad of fresh vegetables with eggs, a cruse of oil, and flagon of old wine, sufficed for the refreshment of the guests. Nausicaa, the young daughter of the host, presided over the arrangement with a quiet dignity which was rare even in Greece.

"You were surprised by the change in Gershom: what shall I say about Nausicaa? She was but an infant when I saw her last, and now she must be——"

"Fourteen springs last Xanthicus. I almost wish I could say but four; she is almost a woman, and must soon leave me, yet I cannot bear the thought of losing her!"

"She is precisely what her mother was—in form and face. I can therefore easily understand your feelings; but have you been able to preserve her from the public discipline, as you intended?"

"It has been hard work, my friend; but she was my only child, and I was determined she should not grow up as one of the Amazons around us. I had seen other Greek states, and other Greek women, and, although the struggle has been hard, I have succeeded in keeping her as I wished her to be—my own home-bird, my own home-child; not the public property of our iron state. She has true Spartan blood, and I have trained her body well, according to a liberal interpretation of our lawgiver's code; but I hope some day to see the barbarisms of that code repealed, and woman what she is in Athens, or in your own native land, Asahel."

"I am thankful to hear this, for I was not likely to forget the vow you took when I last saw you."

"When last you saw me! Ah! Asahel, do not re-open old wounds."

Asahel was silent for a few moments; and as Nausicaa re-entered the apartment he lightly changed his tone, and questioned her concerning the news of the city; then opening a small leathern wallet, which was suspended by a belt from his waist, he took from it a cocoa-nut. "Open it, my child; it is yours, if your father permits."

The young maiden vainly tried to find an opening in the rough rind, until Gershom, taking it from her hand, displayed a hidden spring; when this was pressed, the husk opened, and discovered itself to be a casket lined with sandal-wood, inlaid with gold and gems, and fragrant with aromatic perfume. Inside this casket lay a roll of snowy muslin, closely folded.

"I have brought you an Eastern bridal-veil, if you will accept it," said Asahel; then turning to Hyllus, he continued: "I shall be happy if you will permit Nausicaa to wear it in remembrance of our friendship; it was brought from Persia by my grandfather, although I fancy it was manufactured still farther east than Persia even."

While Asahel was speaking, Nausicaa was unrolling the muslin; fold after fold was displayed, until the apparently inexhaustible store at last ended. Nearly thirty yards of the finest and most delicately-woven muslin had been rolled up within the small compass of an ordinary cocoa-nut shell.

"What marvellous workmanship," said Hyllus.

"It is finer and more delicate than aërial gossamer."

"I may keep it, my father?"

"Most assuredly, my child, since Asahel has brought it for you; but, indeed, that is a present for some Eastern princess, not for my simple Spartan maiden!"

Nausicaa had now twined the delicate muslin round her lithe and graceful figure, in a myriad fantastic draperies; then throwing the silver-embroidered end in a light wave over her head, she looked out with bright laughing eyes from a perfect sea of pure snowy drapery, something like the pink pearl-shells which lie embedded in their nests of sea-foam, after a rising tide retreats for one moment from their home.

"Yes, my nymph! you can think of nothing but how to display your treasure to the best advantage; but I am overwhelmed by the marvel of its manufacture."

"I have heard," said Asahel, "that when such muslin is washed, and lies on the grass to dry, it is absolutely invisible, so fine is the texture; and yet it is strongly woven and durable. I am glad that it pleases you, Nausicaa."

"Pleases me! I shall wear it at Elis two years hence, when we go there to the games. Yes! my father has promised me that I shall go and hear the contests of the poets. Oh, that there were another Herodotus to read another history!"

"We must first act another history worthy of the pen of Herodotus, if we are to have another historian; and yet I for one have no wish to see another Thermopylæ, or another Salamis."

"I am told that Thucydides the Athenian is collecting materials for a history of the present war, which he intends writing during his exile in Thrace."

"And who does he expect to read it, I wonder?— the history of a war between members of one family," said Nausicaa. "Surely, my father, such a history could never be read at Elis?"

Hyllus did not reply, but Asahel spoke in a half sad tone:

"The child recalls to our memory those early days of boyhood, Hyllus, when we heard the Halicarnassian read his history; how well do I remember the whole scene, it was the only time your father could gain permission for me to accompany you; and when the hardly wrung consent of your king was gained, my own father (very wisely, I admit) prohibited my witnessing any of the contests, but those of the votaries of your Muses."

"Can I ever forget it, Asahel? Boys we were both then; but you rose up with the rest, and your plaudits were almost louder than mine, when the story of Salamis was told."

"Plaudits! Hyllus. I am not ashamed to say there were as many tears as plaudits that day—surely there never was so stirring a sight as that grand majestic man, when he told the history of the fathers' struggles and sufferings for freedom to their assembled children. We were obscurely placed, but young Thucydides the

Athenian attracted the attention of the Halicarnassian himself, you remember, by his tears and passionate emotion. I suppose it is the memory of that scene which has impelled him to write history also."

"Ay, ay, we Spartans had great need to be proud that day, and the men of Athens looked enviously, even in the midst of their plaudits, when the story of Thermopylæ and Leonidas was told, until their turn came with the sea-fight of Salamis, and we were all reunited at last in the glory of Platæa, and the final expulsion of the barbarians."

During these reminiscences of their elders, the young people had been standing in rapt attention, Nausicaa, still enveloped in her foamy drapery, looking like some radiant statue, but when her father's voice was silent she at once moved forward, and kneeling before him with clasped hands, said, with deep emotion, "O father! my father! this was Greece when you were a boy, and now—and now——"

"And now! Ah, my child, what would I not give that it should be Greece still; but who can reunite the shattered tree? The shoots may thrive, but can never be reunited."

Still Nausicaa knelt, her face bedewed with tears, while she looked up to her father from earnest, sorrowful eyes.

"My father, I saw our gardener reunite the branch of citron which had been torn from its stem by the Etesian winds, and now the wound is so perfectly healed that you cannot perceive the fracture. May it not be so with our troubled Hellas. The wounded branch was swathed in clay, and bound with cords. Suffer me to devote myself to the service of Apollo, when, day and night, I will offer prayers and sacrifices for the return of harmony to our beloved Greece, our unhappy Hellas."

"Child, child! you know not what you say; never even dream of such a plan, which would be utterly useless. See, let me help you to refold your lovely veil, and then summon Doris. The lamps have been lighted far too long for my young maiden to be still out of her nest."

The veil was soon restored to its casket; and the eyes of Nausicaa once more free from tears, she advanced to Asahel and Gershom to bid them "Good night;" then bending low before her father in reverent Spartan fashion, he laid his hands upon her head, and implored a blessing from heaven upon his motherless child, then kissing her affectionately, he led her to the door of the apartment, where a young slave stood ready to convey her to the care of her aged nurse.

Safely sheltered in the thalamos, into which no male was ever permitted entrance, Nausicaa was soon eagerly questioning her nurse concerning her father's guests, and delighting the old woman's heart by displaying her splendid present.

"Remember Asahel, the young Hebrew? Why, my child, he and your father were like brothers together when they were boys, only Asahel was not permitted to attend the Gymnasium or schools; he

studied at home, and learned (your father used to
say) far more than he did. Asahel was always kind
and gentle to those who were in trouble, and altogether different from our people. You must know
that long before the Persian war, and the invasion of
Attica, long, long ago, the Persians, or some of those
barbarians, had conquered Asahel's people, and carried
them away captive to a country called Babylon, I
believe. Well, some of Asahel's family escaped, and
were not in their city when it was burnt, but were
taken prisoners by the army outside, who sold them
for slaves to some Tyrian merchants; these sold them
again in Athens, and they were slaves in Athens for
many years. Asahel's grandfather was born there,
but when his people regained their freedom from
Cyrus, the great Persian king, he went home, and
married, after a while, a young Greek, who had determined to worship his God (for they only worship
one, my child). Well, I do not know how it was exactly, but the people, when they returned to their own
land, were determined to obey their law very strictly;
and it seems they are forbidden to marry any but their
own people, unless they will submit to the same law.
Now Asahel's grandfather's wife was anxious to submit to the law, and had quite given up her faith in
our gods; yet some of his enemies, who wanted his
inheritance, persuaded the rulers to order him to
divorce his wife. He would not do this, but left his
own country, and went back to Athens; but when
Asahel's father was born, he thought, for his sake, he

must set matters right, so he took his wife home once more, took her to the priests, and explained; then they were married freshly, after the Hebrew fashion, and all was made right as to the inheritance conveyed to Asahel's father; but, after a while, his old enemies made his life miserable, and so he returned to Athens as a sojourner, for he had bought his freedom long ago; then his wife died, and then came the Persian invasion of Athens, and the sojourners helped the Athenians, as well as the natives themselves. Now Asahel's father was but a boy at the time when the battle of Platæa was fought; and it was then your grandfather first saw him."

"Was he fighting for Greece then, nurse?"

"Not exactly fighting, child. He understood the Persian language, and many another Eastern tongue, and had been very useful to the Greeks in many ways —but indeed it is time my darling was asleep."

"I shall not sleep until I know about Asahel's father, nurse."

"Well, child, I have heard, I believe, that there were some of Asahel's people in the Persian army, for they were then, and are still, Persian subjects; but I am not sure about that; I only know that the Greeks trusted Asahel's father entirely, and he passed through the whole army as he pleased. Well, it was just before the great battle, when the Persians had driven the Greeks back from the Asopus, and the fountain of Gargaphia was choked up; there was no water in the camp, and scarcely any food, for the armies had then been lying opposite to each other for ten days, without doing anything but sacrifice and search for favourable omens. Your grandfather bore his hunger and thirst as——"

"As a Spartan should, nurse."

"Yes, child, as a Spartan should; but even Spartans are mortal—he had been three whole days without tasting liquid—and I have heard him say that a fever was raging in his veins, as though madness was coming on; but he had lost all real feeling of common thirst, when one of his Helots brought him a small flask of milk, which he had bought for a large sum of money from a camp-follower. Your grandfather was just about to drink the milk when the general of the Æginetæ came up. 'Oh! how daintily you Lacedæmonians are faring,' he said. 'I have only tasted muddy waters, and still muddier wine, for the last week.'"

"Of course grandfather gave him the bottle?"

"The small flask, my child. Of course he did. Asahel's father, who had just come up on a message, saw the whole, and left the place; but he never rested until he had been to the temple of Ceres, which stood not very far off; here he had a friend among the priests, and from her he obtained water and some fresh melons. When he returned your grandfather was already delirious, but the good Hebrew nursed him so well that he was able to take his part in the battle, when it was fought, and afterwards to receive the commendation of King Pausanias."

"And that was Asahel's father, was it, nurse? I could not tell why I seemed to like him so much, long before he gave me the veil."

"Yes, child, that was Asahel's father—Barak he was called. Your grandfather took him to King Pausanias, after they returned home; and in consideration of his services to a descendant of Hercules and the cause of Greece, the Ephori, under the king's influence, granted him certain privileges in the city—not its freedom exactly, but permission to enter and remain here unquestioned; permission to buy and sell if he chose (which of course he never did), and all the privileges of a 'Guest-Friend,' for himself and his children. Barak lived here for some years with your grandfather; then he returned home and married one of his own people, and Asahel was born. At last your grandfather went to see him, for Barak had often invited him; he reached Syria just after the whole country had been terribly shaken by an earthquake. Barak's wife and new-born baby had died from terror and exposure to the open country during the shock, and Barak himself was so overpowered by grief that he seemed utterly helpless, but so glad to see your grandfather, who remained with him nearly a year. Very soon after your grandfather's return he received a letter from Barak, begging him to take charge of his son Asahel after his death. Your grandfather went over to him again, as he could not believe that he was so ill as he imagined. He brought him over here with Asahel. I remember it quite well, although I was but a slip of a girl then. Asahel was a bright merry boy of about seven years old; his father did not live long afterwards; and that was how it came to pass that Asahel and your father were brought up together. Your grandfather thought as much of the fatherless orphan as he did of his own son, and they were brought up as brothers, excepting in religious matters. Your grandfather was wise beyond most men, and knew well all the rights (and the wrongs, we should say) of the Hebrews, and so he never let the boy go to any of our temples, or pour a libation to any of our gods; and when he was twelve years old he took him to his father's home himself, and left him with the priests, to be initiated in their mysteries."

"And how long did he stay away, nurse?"

"Oh, he just came backwards and forwards as he liked; and after a while he married there, but his wife did not live long; they were unfortunate in their wives—all of them. Poor Asahel did not look like himself for many a long year after her loss, but he brought Gershom here, and trained him as he had been trained himself when he was a boy."

"Nurse, how was it you never told me this before?"

"You have heard me speak of them surely, child, and it never came into my head to tell you the whole story. You see Asahel has been away this time for nearly ten years, and I am growing old—nearly sixty years of age. I was not likely to think of him."

"I am very glad they have come, and I hope they will stay a long time; but, nurse, where is Opis?"

"None but Hermes can answer that question, child. I have sent Doris with some of the men to see if she can have gone off to Leda; that girl will bring me to my grave long before my time."

"Poor dear, nurse, do not fret over her so much. She is sad and sorrowful, but you know she is never mischievous, she is ever gentle. Kiss her for me, nurse, when she comes in; and now, good night."

Very soon after Nausicaa had left the public-room, Gershom retired to the chamber which had been prepared for him, and the two old friends at last found themselves alone.

"Come to the roof, our old happy consultation-room," said Hyllus. "I scarcely dare ask how long you mean to stay?"

"And I grieve to answer, but this one night."

"I saw it in your face, and yet I have not deserved this. Why should you leave me so soon?"

"Hyllus, let us make the most of the few hours we have together. I am thankful for those few hours, believe me—thankful to see you once more—thankful to see how happy you are in your child."

"And so I must rest contented without any reason. Tell me, Asahel—you used to prize truth as a Persian professes to prize it—why must you leave me so soon?"

"Briefly, then, Hyllus, my time is not now my own.

I have undertaken to collect some rare herbs for Menares, the physician at Athens, and can spare no time from my quest."

"Asahel, is this right or kind? Are you to go about the land as a vagabond and to serve those whom you should command, while my purse is too heavy, alas! since I have but one daughter to dower? You know well that my father's shade will reproach me with the deepest ingratitude if I permit you to suffer penury."

"You need fear no such reproach, my Hyllus. I have but to return to my own country, put aside old grudges, forget old heart-wounds, and I should be as rich—yes, as rich as you, my friend. I sometimes wonder whether I ought not to do so for Gershom's sake; but there are some wounds yet too sore to bear the touch of old scenes and old associations. I cannot return yet, and I know well that my boy is learning good lessons in hardihood, endurance, and temperance, while we live as we do. Moreover, it is a happy life. I am frequently able to feel that healing and strength follow where we pass. We have brightened many a sick couch, lightened many a suffering heart, by the good hand of our God upon us; and surely it is a happiness to know that our lives are not useless to others. No; if I need your help, Hyllus, I will ask it; but I do not. Gershom is happy; he is my constant companion, and I am happy in perceiving the gradual growth of his soul in all manly vigour. Some day I must take him to the home of our ancestors again, but not yet, not yet."

While the two friends conversed thus, they had gained the roof of the house, and now they seated themselves upon a low seat which was placed close to the stone balustrade which surmounted the roof. A brilliant autumn moon was shining in the clear bright sky. So brilliant was the moon, that the light of every star seemed extinguished as in renewed daylight. A sacred, peaceful hush of silence seemed to rest over the city which lay beneath them, where even the smallest and most remote buildings were clearly visible in the pure white moonlight. There stood the Acropolis on the summit of an eminence, and beneath this was the Agora, the celebrated market-place, whose fame had tempted the haughty Persian monarch to declare that he felt no fear in encountering a nation which kept one place in its city sacred to swearing false oaths and cheating. Yet how lovely the Agora and its surrounding temples looked by moonlight.

"Surely the Persian Gate is finished since I was here," said Asahel.

"Yes; the spoils from the camp of the routed barbarians have been well laid out. You cannot see it properly here, but it is a glorious portico; pure white marble columns support the entablature, upon which appear faithful representations of all the principal events in the war, with correct likenesses of all the chief warriors. How sorely would the tyrant Persian lament if he could see the immortal record of the defeat of his barbaric hordes, enriching the beauty of the market-place he despised."

"The Agora was very beautiful without the Persian Gate. It will equal some of the Athenian buildings now, I suppose; and how lovely the pure white theatre looks in the quiet moonlight. Then there is the dear old Skias; that umbrella-shaped roof would recall Sparta to my mind anywhere; and the old palace of Menelaos has not tumbled down yet, I see. You Spartans preserve the records of the Past; Athens creates new marvels for the Future to preserve."

"Yes! Sparta was, Sparta is, and Sparta shall be, as we say. The heart of Greece does not change."

"No, not in some respects. Yet I, as her well-wisher, often pray that the heart of Greece would throb in more kindly unison with the rest of the body. Athens is still confident of final success, but she has suffered terribly, and I can but pity her."

"My dear Asahel, on this subject I can but think and speak with my people. The arrogance of Athens must be humbled. Is there one Greek state she has not insulted in her prosperity? Not contented with being Athens, she has sought only to assume the sovereignty of Greece to erect an Athenian tyranny over the free-born states of all Hellas. I say, as more than twenty years ago our far-seeing ephor Archidamus said, 'How we ought to deliberate when we have been wronged, let no man pretend to inform me. It would have better become those who designed to com-mit such wrongs to have deliberated a long time ago.'"

"I do not wish to excuse Athens altogether, Hyllus; but I feel for her. I look upon that completed Persian Gate, the glorious trophy of united Greece; I hear your patriotic speeches in remembrance of the valour of your fathers; yet when I turn to see how Spartan soldiers are now employed, I find them uniting with the Persian to humble Athens, which shared with Sparta the glory of saving Greece from the yoke of the barbarian."

"As Athens would now gladly unite with the Persian to humble Sparta if her alliance was considered as valuable by the great king as ours."

"Times have changed since the scene was enacted which your grandfather and mine witnessed in the temple of Athena Chalciœcos yonder, when Pausanias, the victor at Platæa, was denied the privilege of sanctuary, and starved to death within the sacred precincts for the sin of too close an alliance with Persia."

"Times change, and our duties change also, my Asahel. You would not have us at perpetual war with Persia. I thought that you loved peace, and would have shuddered to recall the terrible memories connected with Pausanias."

"I love a peace founded upon righteousness, but not a false peace with Persia, and a fratricidal war with Athens. I loved the peace which produced a united Greece listening to the inspiring memories of Leonidas and his royal ancestors. I can but say as your lovely daughter said to-night: Is it impossible that such a scene could be reproduced—such a glorious scene of united sympathy? Is Sparta really determined to crush her sister state down into the very dust? You spoke to me as though you feared the reproach of your father's shade for fancied ingratitude to me. Has Sparta no fear of the reproach of Leonidas?"

There was a long pause. Asahel looked far away over the valley in which the sleeping city looked so bright and peaceful, upwards to the heights of Mount Taygetos, where every variety of silvery light and floating shadow was passing over the pine-clothed heights. Hyllus sat with his elbow leaning upon the parapet, his eyes shaded by his hand. At length, he raised his head, and spoke:

"Asahel, I beseech you to remain with me for a few days, your words are like oil upon a sore wounded limb—some precious balsam or soothing narcotic for a delirious patient. I cannot tell you how hot and fierce are the passions now raging in the city. The affair of Arginusæ has done much to increase the bitterness of feeling; and I greatly fear that when Athens is fully conquered, small mercy will be shown to her: those who would obtain mercy must first have shown it. I am sorry. I wish with all my heart it were possible for Greece to be reunited; but the struggle has now continued so long, that, to secure the liberty of the rest of Greece, Athens must submit."

"O yes! Athens shall submit;
I see her bent, and lowly,
I see her walls so holy,
Shattered, lying on the strand,
On the white Piræan strand.
And I see the Theban rising,
Epaminondas uprising;
O'er the Isthmus he is surging.
Hide it! Spartan blood is flowing.
The Heracleidæ are weeping
O'er the King of Sparta sleeping;
And the Macedonian creeping,
Through Thessalian pass is sweeping.
Weep for Hellas, for Laconia,
For her glory gone for ever,
For her freedom lost for ever,
For Apollo fled for ever."

"Silence! cease your ominous blasphemy," said Hyllus, sternly advancing to the opposite end of the roof, where a young girl simply robed in white, with hair flowing wildly over her shoulders, stood like one entranced, while she uttered the warning doggerel. Hyllus attempted to seize her, but eluding his grasp, she vanished as swiftly and silently as she had appeared.

"Who is it? What can she mean?" asked Asahel.

"Do you not remember Opis, the babe I picked up from the steps of the temple of Helen; you must remember her, for it was by your advice I took pity upon her, and brought her up as a companion for Nausicaa."

"True, true, my friend, I had entirely forgotten her;

but what has produced this frenzy, has she been ever thus?"

"Not always, not for many years. Still I must say that never was pity so misplaced as mine. She was rational and cheerful enough for many years, but lately, since the affair of Arginusæ and the reappointment of Lysander, she has seemed half crazed, and is evermore singing some doleful prophecy of evil. A false prophet she must be, for Hagias has promised us a victory, final and complete, through Lysander before the year is out."

"Let me see her to-morrow. I have, as you know, some skill in such cases, I will use it to its utmost extent, you may be well assured; but now, my friend, the moon is already setting behind Taygetos, and we have but discoursed of public matters, you have not yet told me anything of your own studies, your private interests of late."

"Stay with me over to-morrow at least, Asahel; you speak of mercy, surely you must see that it will be merciful to stay with me for one day at least. There is strife and a sword in the very air. Lysander sways everything at his own will, and the peaceful quiet of your soul seems like breath from Elysium. Stay! surely that mad girl must have proved to you that I have some heart-sorrows still."

"Say no more, my friend, let us retire to rest now, if you please, and I will not leave you to-morrow at any rate."

CHAPTER III.

"I have been formed by Nature, not to join in hatred, but to join in love."—Antigone, Sophocles.

WHEN Gershom awakened the next morning, the grey dawn was fast reddening into daylight. A very few minutes sufficed for his toilet, and he was in the garden before the sun had fully risen over the eastern hills. Two splendid Spartan dogs bounded forward to meet him; they were the children of an old hound, which last night had so completely recognised his father, as to ensure a welcome reception from every member of her kennel. The young hounds fawned upon Gershom, as though he was still a child, and they the playmates of his boyhood. Accompanied by his canine friends, Gershom passed through the gate, and mounted the hill above the villa, where he could gain a full view of the city below. The rosy flush of an autumn morning was brightening every white marble temple, statue, and trophy in the valley, and deepening the glory of the red-tinted hills upon which the villa of Hyllus was built. It was a lovely scene, and Gershom stood absorbed in reverent admiration of the beauties of nature and of art outspread before him; long and wistfully he gazed until he was recalled to active life by the restless baying of the dogs. Descending to the high road, Gershom now directed his steps towards the banks of the Eurotas, passing on his way well cultivated farms, and fruitful vineyards. The wheat harvest was over, but rich crops of maize stood ready for the reapers, and the hill sides were glowing with purple grapes, ripe oranges, and citrons, dusky pomegranates and figs, with a profusion of nuts of almost every European species, while the carefully cultivated gardens of the Helots, showed a plentiful supply ot melons, lettuces, and other household luxuries. Walking swiftly along, and noticing everything he passed, Gershom at length reached the banks of the Eurotas. Pure and clear, this celebrated stream rolled on towards the sea, through banks bordered with rose laurels on the eastern, and with reeds tall and bristling on the city side. Some beautiful white swans were sailing down with the current, but when the dogs plunged in, they rose fluttering and screaming, to take refuge upon the opposite shore.

Nothing could exceed the beauty of that lovely morning. The air was filled with perfume from a hundred scented flowers, and with melody from the joyous throats of a myriad soaring song-birds. Very soon, however, this harmony was interrupted. Discordant sounds were heard, and harsh voices rose upon the air. Gershom's quick eye detected a purple cloak, hanging upon the rose laurels. He took it down, and rolling it up into as small a compass as was possible, placed it on the ground under an olive-tree. Then beckoning to one of the dogs, he pointed to the cloak. The well-trained animal understood at once, and covering the parcel with his body, lay basking in the beams of the morning sun, as lazily and unconsciously as Gershom could have desired. Followed by the other dog, Gershom now approached the scene of disturbance. A bend in the river brought into view a party of Spartan youths taking their morning's exercise in and upon the banks of the river. They were indulging in a perfect saturnalia of riot, previous to a general forage for food. Upon the banks some were engaged in friendly wrestles for mastery; others were competing in the water, and all the air was filled with sounds which might have proceeded from barbarians rather than from free youths of Laconic birth.

As soon as Gershom appeared in sight, walking leisurely with the dog by his side, he was surrounded by a band of about eighteen youths ranging from the age of about twelve years to sixteen. A noble looking group it was, and Gershom gazed with admiration on the supple limbs, upright forms, and fearless faces, by which he was surrounded.

"Your name?" questioned the leader of the band as he approached.

"Gershom."

"A foreigner?"

"Free in Sparta."

"Prove your freedom."

"Assail it."

The youths looked puzzled, when Gershom with a bright light in his eyes suddenly turned upon his questioner.

"Who are you?"

"Leon, the son of Theopompus, the son of Callicratidas, the son of Brasidas, the son of Eurycrates, the son of Agesilaus, the son of Archias, the son of Menelaos, the head of the noble tribe of Pitanatæ."

"One word too many, unless the Pitanatæ have declined so low as to need a trumpeter for their nobility," said Gershom gravely.

A glad shout of approval greeted this retort of Gershom's, and under the guidance of their leader, the youths now joined hands to form a close ring round the stranger.

"Free of Sparta it is evident; now free yourself from her sons."

"I do not struggle with naked men." Before the words were well out of his mouth, or the ring strongly formed, Gershom had perceived the only weak place in his adversaries' leaguer, and running full tilt, burst through the chain, then calmly seating himself upon a hillock at a short distance, he awaited his opponents; he was soon followed, and once more a contest of words commenced, in which Spartan wit and ingenuity were vainly taxed to force the stranger to declare his tribe and place of residence.

"He is from Athens! a spy, a spy!" cried one or two.

"No Athenian would have had patience to follow a Spartan pedigree," said another.

"I am no Athenian; but you are mistaken in supposing that Spartans alone possess pedigrees; and now shall I prove my claim to Spartan teaching?" said Gershom at last.

"Shall you obey your masters? Forsooth, do you not see that we are eighteen to one?"

"I deny that I am only one; for, according to your own belief, the ghosts of your hundred kings hover over the head of every suppliant guest of Sparta for his protection."

Again a puzzled look passed from youth to youth, and the silence was unbroken until Gershom said, "Robe yourselves, and I will tell you my history."

The youths, half laughing, but eager to solve the mystery which surrounded the young stranger, who was evidently so familiar with their customs, returned to the river for their robes. Very soon there was an outcry. A cloak was missing. Loud and fierce were the denunciations hurled against the robber, and a Helot, who had been seen passing a short time before, was at once accused, and devoted to destruction upon the first opportunity.

"You must take me as I am," said the owner of the cloak, as he seated himself by Gershom's side.

"I believe I can provide you with a robe," said Gershom whistling.

The whistle was at once answered by the dog, who carried the cloak, and laid it before Gershom.

"Will this prove my freedom in a truly Spartan accomplishment," said Gershom, returning the cloak to its owner.

"There was small skill needed for that theft, a Helot could have accomplished it as well," was the sulky reply.

Gershom, however, was not to be daunted by any display of ill-temper; he was determined to make friends of these young warriors. So simply, and in their own unadorned Laconic fashion, he told them the history of his grandfather's adventure at the battle of Plataea, dwelling fully upon the bravery and self-denial of the Spartan and but slightly upon his grandfather's services. This was just the story to suit the temper of his auditors. They listened eagerly, applauded heartily; and when Gershom rose to return, he had invitations to the houses of members of almost every tribe in the city from one of its young sons, who each and all assured him, that while the Eurotas ran to meet the Tiasa, he and his would ever be welcome guests at every Spartan hearth.

Hyllus and Asahel were seated at their morning meal when Gershom returned, and all traces of despondency seemed to have passed from the face of Hyllus, who was busily planning an excursion through the city, and deciding upon the visits to old friends which it was absolutely necessary Asahel should make.

"Anaxander is with King Agis at Decelea, and Eumolpus, Eteonicus, and Diomedes, are at sea with Lysander; but Leon will be rejoiced to see you, and your old friend Archytas is ephor this year; you cannot go without seeing him."

"If he can spare a few moments from his official duties, I shall be very glad to see my old playfellow. I little thought to hear of his attaining the dignity of ephor when I saw him last."

"Then there is Philoctetes; you must say nothing of your sojourn in Athens if you go there, for he lost two sons with Callicratidas at Arginusæ, and his wounded heart is sore yet. Callicratidas might comfort himself with the thought that 'Sparta would be no worse governed even if he should die,' but we at home have been compelled to wish that he had governed his fleet so well that we might have seen it and our old friends once more."

"Yes, I had some hopes that there might have been an opening for peace when the news of the total loss of your fleet reached Athens."

"Sparta has never relied upon her fleet. We had but ten galleys of our own engaged, and one of these escaped; the sixty taken by Athens were those of our confederates."

Asahel looked up into his old friend's eyes. No! there was no sign of shame. It was really true that so perverted had his sense of right become during the protracted war that the defeat at Arginusæ, with its terrible loss of life, was measured by the loss which

Sparta individually had sustained; her allies were not worth thinking about.

"Hyllus, my friend, your relations with your Helots seem to me to influence all your relations in life. You speak of the loss of your allies as though you were speaking of your Helots. Surely it was this spirit which induced the first revolt against Spartan supremacy after the Persian war, and led to Athens being appointed receiver-general of Greece, and eventually to her supremacy, which you are now contesting. It seems to me, that unless you Spartans change your character and become more conscious of the rights of others than yourselves, the confederates will reject your alliance again; and even if you should conquer Athens, you must yourselves be consumed in the fire of your own overbearing spirits. Forgive me, Hyllus, if I speak too plainly."

"You cannot speak too plainly to me, Asahel. It is refreshing to hear some one who can speak on the other side, for we are all one now in Sparta as regards the war. You see our faults very clearly, but seem very blind to those of your new friends. What do you say to the mob-law of Athens, and the execution of her six admirals, because, after destroying the fleet commanded by the heart of Greece, they were unable to destroy the gods who took toll from the victors? Is there any nation upon earth capable of such ingratitude as the Athenian?"

"It is too true that Athens is too much under the influence of popular clamour. That sentence was carried by mob-law, and repentance followed immediately. Socrates, the son of Sophroniscus, was the only one who had courage to vote against the sentence of death upon the admirals. But I cannot see, my Hyllus, that the faults of Athens excuse yours."

"Then we will amend together, and when Athens sends in her full submission to Sparta, I will seat myself at the feet of Socrates for instruction in wisdom. I hear that Apollo has declared him to be the wisest man in Greece."

"And I, as a reverent worshipper of One far above all Delphian oracles, can assure you that he is a most sincere searcher after wisdom; but where did you hear about him? I scarcely expected that his fame could have surmounted the iron barriers of your hatred of Athens."

"About four years ago. I sent Nausicaa to spend some months with her mother's relatives in Arcadia, and having gained permission to travel, visited Italy, among other places. I wanted to know more of this Rome, of which we are now beginning to hear so much, and also to visit the north of Italy. That lovely vase which stands under the window is one of my spoils from Etruria. Well, to return to Socrates. Before I reached Rome, I spent a few days at Herculaneum and Pompeii, two towns built upon the side of an eruptive mountain something like Etna. I found plenty of amusement and interest there, both in the towns themselves and the lovely country by which they are surrounded. One day I set off with guides to ascend the mountain, and on my way overtook a gentleman and his wife, Greeks evidently. I never felt so sorry as then for the wretched broils of our Hellas. At first, when we discovered that one was Spartan and the others from Athens, we kept apart; but the lady was irresistible. She was utterly unlike any other woman I ever saw. Now she stooped to collect some rare herb and place it in her wallet, again she was attracted by a passing fly, and her husband secured it for her inspection. He seemed as devoted to her as she was to him and to Nature. At last, after toiling up separately for some time, the husband slipped in reaching over the precipice for some flower. The guides lost their senses, and so it fell out that his misfortune was my opportunity. I assisted him, and received unbounded gratitude for my trifling service. After this, we agreed to forget that we were born in separate states. The lady improvised an imaginary Elysium in which all true sons and daughters of Hellas might meet, and for a week I lived in that Elysium. Ah, me! I only wish I could transport it here. But we were compelled to part at last; and it was during that week I heard enough of Socrates to make me long to see him."

"And the names of the husband and wife were Aristarchus and Androclea?"

"How in the world could you find that out, my Asahel?"

"Because there is but one Androclea in the world, and I know she was in Italy four years ago; her husband has property there. I saw her in her country villa a fortnight ago, and promised to visit her on my return from Arcadia."

"Asahel, I am almost tempted to renounce my ancestors and go with you. Athens lost her presiding deity, when she sacrificed her six admirals. The end must soon come, and then I shall be enabled to fulfil the desire of my heart in renewing the acquaintance with my Elysian friends, and learning from Socrates."

"You say that Athens has lost her presiding deity! Believe me, she has in Socrates that which will immortalise her, when the glory of Sparta has vanished into air."

"His pupil Alcibiades does not do him much credit. He contrived to stir up more mischief here than most men could have done in twice the time, and he has embittered the war by infusing personal hatred into it."

"Alcibiades would have had the same faults anywhere, and under any masters. He is one of those who are too self-willed and proud to be taught. They say that the cakes destined for sacrifice to the gods must not only be kneaded with clean hands, but the flour, the oil, and the frankincense must be clean also. I do not say that the hands of Socrates are clean, as our holy law would have them; but I do see that he wishes them to be so, while Alcibiades purposely seeks out the mud with which to soil himself, and no warnings can repel him. If I, having been taught by a holier law than Socrates, can see where his human wisdom fails to reach the truth it seeks, I can yet see plainly that he is not responsible for the faults of Alcibiades."

"Well, Asahel, you know well that I have always said, I long, I pray for the day when some one of your people shall come to us filled with the spirit of a true prophet, one who would emblazon the ten holy commands of your law upon the washed-out code of our own lawgiver, and compel us to obey it. Such a man would regenerate Greece."

"The law is dead without the Spirit of Life, Hyllus. We have had that law for one thousand years, and we pray daily now for the advent of Him who has promised to pour down that Spirit, not upon us only, but upon you Gentiles, and even to the uttermost ends of the earth. If you do hear Socrates, you will find that he speculates upon the nature of the Deity, and to him duty is an open question—the moral law, a law which man must ordain for himself. We believe, as you know, that the moral law, already revealed to us, can never alter, and have no curious speculations concerning the nature of the Deity, since we know that He has revealed himself already, as a holy, pure, and merciful God, but a truly living one, ever present. The advent for which we long has been predicted, and must surely be approaching. He has promised to visit His people, when His reward will be with Him, and His work before Him. He has promised to call the Gentiles to the brightness of His light, and having seen of the travail of His soul, He shall be satisfied."

D

"Yes, I remember that sublime book of prophecy which you let me read when I visited you last. We must wait His time, I suppose, for I can see well that any attempt upon your part to teach your truth would be useless; no one would listen to you here, and you would be sacrificed at Athens. As you truly say, there must be a fresh descent of the Divine Spirit if our life is to be renewed. But, enough of these matters. Will you dine with us at the public table to-day?"

"Not if Nausicaa will bestow her hospitality. We shall be a long time in the city, I fear, and then I must see your unhappy Opis; and to-night we must retire early, as I wish to start at day-dawn."

"Let it be as you will, my friend; Nausicaa will be delighted to entertain her guests; but, Gershom, you must come with us, and be introduced to your father's old friends."

The whole morning was spent in paying visits to such old friends as still remained in the city, and in inspecting the many improvements which had been made since Asahel's last visit. The Persian Gate was duly admired, although Asahel could not but compare it unfavourably in his own mind with the marvels of genius with which Phidias and Pericles had enriched Athens. The old well-preserved memorials in the Gymnasium and the Platanistas were, however, joyfully greeted by both father and son, and every association belonging to them affectionately recalled. Gershom lingered in the Dromos, after his father and Hyllus had left it. He was interested in watching the exercises of the Spartan youth, under the eye of their Pædonomus, who was no easy slavish pedagogue, as in Athens, but an officer appointed by the State from that class from which the chief magistrates were chosen. The elder youths were his assistants and scourge-bearers, thus learning betimes the duties of obedience and the responsibilities of command. Gershom stood for some time enjoying the feats of strength and agility in which some hundred youths of all ages were engaged. Tight ropes were stretched across one part of the Gymnasium, and here a sharp contest was kept up, with naked foot and carefully balanced body. In another part, a rope was passed through the top of a firmly-fixed post, and here two youths were engaged in trying their strength by attempting to raise each other to the cross beam above. Leaping, wrestling, and all the usual feats of the gymnast, were here taught as the essential duty of every Spartan youth, and all around was displayed the quiet energy of those who are engaged in the ordinary duties of their lives. Just as Gershom was turning to leave the Dromos, he was touched upon his shoulder by one of his acquaintances of the morning, who at once carried him off to see the sports in the Platanistas. This was a lovely island formed by the converging waters of the Tiasa; it was bordered by ancient platane trees, and covered with the softest verdure; no spot could be better fitted for those contests of strength—those essays in the use of arms in which the life of the Spartan youth was passed. No public contest was proceeding on the day when Gershom saw it, but the youth of the city were simply engaged in voluntary practice and friendly contests. In one part of the island young archers were shooting through the rings, emulating the skill of Ulysses; in another, a knot of youths, lightly armed, were learning to thread the mazes of the martial Pyrrhic dance, advancing and retreating to the sound of flutes, and enacting a mimic battle with the grace and dignity as well as the impassioned fervour of a sacred dance. Again, others were employed in throwing the javelin, others in the lighter contest of hurling the discus, while the fathers, mothers, and sisters of the youths stood watching the various groups, and encouraged their skill by affectionate commendation. Nor, indeed, was the sport confined to young men alone, their sisters were also engaged in various parts of the same ground in healthy, active exercise; many parties of ball-throwers were occupied in games which have now become obsolete; but there were also young maidens engaged in those exercises against which Hyllus had rebelled. There might be seen a group of young girls boxing or wrestling like men, and with equal publicity; in another group, amid some really graceful dances, might be heard the boisterous laughter of the bystanders, while fair young maidens were employed in the dance whose chief object was to enable the dancer to strike her back with her upraised heel. Gershom turned away with a feeling of horror; he had not seen any such sight as this in all his wanderings, and to the surprise of his companion, he begged to be allowed to leave the island.

"What has shocked you?" asked Leon.

"Seeing young maidens, who should be respected for their modesty, courting the laughter or applause of a crowd of strangers, by their monkey tricks."

"Have you no such customs?"

"Our maidens would be stoned to death most likely, if they were to venture upon such an exhibition."

"That accounts for the freaks of Hyllus; he is a friend of your father's, and has taken up these notions from him. No one has ever seen his daughter Nausicaa in the Dromos or the Platanistas."

"And yet Nausicaa is as agile and nobly formed as are any of those maidens we saw down there."

"That may be; but if Hyllus were not of the race of the Heracleidæ, and Nausicaa his only daughter, and he as strong-willed as his great ancestor, he would be obliged to do as other people do. Nausicaa is compelled to take her part in the sacred dances; and I assure you we all long to see her under the same discipline as our sisters."

Gershom laughed merrily. "I have no doubt you do; but I am thankful she has Hyllus for a father."

The youths had now passed the bridge from the island, and were approaching the statue of the fettered Mars; here a large crowd was gathered round a venerable man, who was reciting to his attentive audience the verses of Homer—young and old, husbands and wives, brothers and sisters, all were intently listening; and Leon, pushing his way through, brought Gershom to the front row immediately. Thus surrounded it was not possible to avoid listening; and as Gershom listened to the clear well-trained voice of the public reciter, he scarcely wondered at the rapt attention of the audience. The words to which he listened were those immortal words which tell the story of the final contest with Penelope's suitors — when her disguised husband receives the long cherished bow from his son:

> "And now his well-known bow the master bore,
> Turned on all sides, and viewed it o'er and o'er;
> Lest time or worms had done the weapon wrong—
> Its owner absent, and untried so long.
> While some deriding: 'How he turns the bow;'
> 'Some other like it, sure the man must know!'
> 'Or else would copy: or in bows he deals.'
> 'Perhaps he makes them, or perhaps he steals.'"

Gershom listened with breathless interest until the reciter ceased speaking, then, heartily joining in the applause, he dropped a few oboli into the hand of the old man, and once more sought out some object of interest.

"Come to the Skias," said Leon. "A lyrist, said to be a pupil of Timotheus, is performing to-day, and every one will be there; we shall just be in time. We Spartans care nothing for sophists, or for philosophers, but we love men of action—and in music no state of Hellas can beat us. A good musician is sure of a welcome in Sparta—as sure of it, as is a good talker of a welcome in Athens."

"But why is he performing in the Skias, instead of the theatre?"

"Through favour of Pausanias, our sole sovereign at present. The Skias is said to be better adapted for the performance; but hasten, or we shall be too late."

Gershom hesitated, he was passionately fond of music, but scarcely knew whether his father would approve of his entering a building, in which he might possibly be compelled to witness ceremonies, and listen to hymns addressed to some idol; and yet how could he refuse? "I will not bow my knee to Baal, let the consequence be what it will," he said, inwardly; and then surrendered himself to the guidance of his new friend.

The Skias was a very ancient building, in which the assemblies of the people had been held for more than three hundred years. It was circular in shape, with a singular roof shaped like an umbrella, and this peculiarity of construction had led to its selection by the lyrist, for his exhibition, since no building in the city was so well fitted to assist his musical skill.

When Leon and Gershom entered the seats assigned them, the Skias was already well filled, and crowds were hurrying from all parts of the city to fill the vacant spaces which remained. A blast of trumpets announced the Ephori, who entered in all the dignified state which belonged to the most powerful officers of Lacedæmon. In a few moments afterwards the flute players announced the entrance of King Pausanias, and immediately the whole assembly rose to its feet, and remained standing until he was seated in his regal chair. The Ephors alone remained in their seat, as being in their official capacity absolved from all deference to the kings. By the side of King Pausanias stood the empty chair of King Agis, who was with the army which had invaded Attica and fortified Decelea. The king looked round for a few moments upon the well filled building, where not only the noblest and wealthiest Spartans then in the city were assembled, but artisans and free men of the manufacturing classes. One moment had scarcely elapsed when the signal was given, then there was a buzz of restrained excitement, and in another moment the lyrist appeared upon the stage prepared for him. The musician was a man in the prime of life, and held in his hand a lyre. In one moment he saluted the kings, Ephori, and audience; in the next his fingers were moving over the strings of his instrument in a soft, sweet prelude. A soft melody, which recalled woodland scenes, and the happy notes of the feathered songsters of the forest,—these sounded sweetly from the vibrating strings of the Milesian lyre, but this strain was almost insensibly changed, and soon the spectators were listening to the broken tremulous cadence which recalled the rippling of summer waves upon a rocky shore. Again the accents changed to the murmuring sobbing of a winter's wind, and the dash of angry waters beaten upon a rock-bound coast, sounding in passionate melodious harmony from the wondrous lyre; then the minstrel seemed impelled by some passionate impulse to add his voice to the inspiration which seemed to vibrate from his instrument, and thus the lyre sank into a mere expression of the emotions which swayed its master, and the air vibrated with a grand heroic pæan. Every heart throbbed in unison; every thought was absorbed in the strain, which rose in triumphant melody, such as mortals are seldom permitted to hear. The ancient building was filled with a strange vibrating harmony, which entered into the heart of every one, and united in one indissoluble bond, the kingly sons of Hercules with the rugged artisans and stern soldiers of Sparta. For one half-hour Gershom forgot where he was, forgot his own existence while listening to the lyre and song of that marvellous master of harmony, Timotheus the Milesian.

"It must be the master himself, and no pupil," said Leon, as he led Gershom from the building, but Gershom was too much excited to answer. Dazed and bewildered, he scarcely knew where he was, when suddenly he found himself standing by his father, who had also been in the building with Hyllus. This was an intense relief to Gershom's mind, especially as he saw at once from his father's face that he also had been mastered by the rapture of the lyrist. After speaking a few words to his father and Hyllus, Gershom turned, expecting to find Leon, but he had vanished. "The youths are having a battle with the Hippocrætæ in the street Aphetæ," said Hyllus, "and no doubt your young friend has gone to work off his excitement in the pleasure of a street fight. And now, Asahel, will you not come to the public table?"

"Not this time, Hyllus; I must see Opis."

"Then, farewell for a short hour; I will return home as soon as I possibly can."

Nausicaa, who advanced to meet her father's friends when they entered, was in every respect different from other Spartan maidens. Her figure was tall, lithe, and singularly beautiful; but the comparative seclusion in which she had been nurtured, had imparted a gentleness and simple modesty of expression, which was not characteristic of her fellow-maidens; while her father's care, in the cultivation of her intellect, had heightened the intelligence of her singularly beautiful countenance. The dress of Nausicaa was in some respects different also from most Spartan ladies, for a robe of soft white muslin fell in full folds to her ankles; this was an addition to the usual simplicity of the Spartan chiton, which Nausicaa wore over her robe. The chiton, a sleeveless dress of fine woollen material dyed purple, reached to the knees, and was fastened upon each shoulder by a brooch; a zone, of rare workmanship, studded with jewels, confined the chiton round the waist. Nausicaa also wore sandals of fine scarlet leather, which were girded by thongs crossed over the instep, and carried up until they were lost beneath the folds of her robe. Her hair was simply banded round the head, and a garland of freshly gathered rosebuds crowned the fair young face, with an added beauty.

The meal, which awaited the small party, was very simple, yet, to Nausicaa, a strangely happy one. Asahel's singular and varied experience had but strengthened his love for all pure childlike enjoyment, and he entered into every detail of the young girl's interests and employments, as he had done into the graver trials and interests of her father. Laughter, merry and hearty, sounded cheerfully through the room during the meal, and, when it was concluded, Nausicaa felt sorry that she had no excuse for prolonging it.

At length Asahel inquired for Opis.

"She ought to have been with us," replied Nausicaa; "but as she said she was tired, nurse advised her to lie down."

"If she is not really sleeping, I must beg nurse to let me see her. I promised your father to see if I could do anything to help her."

A change instantly passed over the bright happy face of the young girl. "Oh! if you can but help poor Opis, we shall all rejoice. She suffers terribly after her inspirations, and to-day, after last night's attack, she has been silent and sorrowful, not speaking one word even to me—and she used to be so merry and so loving; but ever since the news of the defeat at Arginusæ reached us, and then the more terrible story of the Athenians' execution of their own admirals, she has been subject to these fits."

Asahel, like all truly wise men, was glad to receive knowledge from any source. How did she hear the news? and why should the ingratitude of the Athenians to their own citizens affect her?

"Why, you see, poor Opis had only known a short time before that she was not really my sister—and she heard it very unkindly, for some of our young companions taunted her with her birth. And when our fleet was defeated, and so many families in the city were bereaved of sons or husbands, the girls called Opis a spy, and said she was no true Spartan, but the child of some captive Athenian. She felt it very bitterly, and at last, I believe, she came to think that they spoke the truth. Then she began to dislike those who had taunted her, and listened eagerly for all news from Athens; and at last she heard the story of the admirals, then it was that she began to speak those strange words which sound so much like curses. Nurse and I did all we could to keep her quiet; but now, not even my father can stay her. Nurse watches her constantly to prevent her going out into the city, as she fears that she will be cast into the Apothetæ. Oh, do help poor Opis if you possibly can."

"I will do what I can, dear child, but the soul of man is not subject to mortal remedies or control. One alone, He who formed it, can heal its wounds, or restore it to its habitation. He has, however, given power to His children to act as His ministers, and I pray that I may be permitted to be of use. I will do what I can, for your sake, and for your father's; but you must let me see nurse."

"When you know Opis, you will love her for her own sake, not for ours; but I will go and see if she is awake."

In a few minutes Nausicaa returned with her nurse, who led Asahel to a small chamber which opened out from the thalamos. Before leaving him with his patient, the nurse gave him all the information she could concerning the state of Opis—answering his inquiries with the intelligent good sense which proved that her patient had occupied a large share of her thoughts and affections. One item of news Asahel gained from the nurse. Opis seemed to be most undoubtedly of Athenian birth. Of this the nurse seemed perfectly assured, although she had never dared to show her master that which led her to believe so—as she knew well his embittered state of mind respecting Athens, and all connected with her. But Asahel and the nurse were old friends, and she knew well his pitiful, gentle heart; thus the robe, in which the little foundling had been wrapped, was at once brought out for his inspection. There could be no doubt that the nurse was right. There was the sacred shield—the Ægis of Athena—upon which every Athenian mother loved to place her new-born infant. It was there beautifully embroidered upon the soft delicate woollen material, which formed the shawl or blanket in which the child was found. The fine material, and delicate embroidery of the linen dress, proved also that loving fingers must have spent long hours upon the work, or wealthy parents have purchased it.

"My master never noticed the child's robe; and I never dared to show it to any one before; he took for granted that the babe was the child of some poor Spartan freeman—as it was upon the steps of the temple of Sparta's queen—and I never contradicted him, for the babe won my heart at once as she had done his; it was some weeks old when he found it, and looked so grave and quiet out of its pretty eyes, that I little dreamed what trouble it would give us, when I promised the master to bring it up with Nausicaa."

It was with renewed interest that at length Asahel found himself alone with his patient. Opis was reclining on a couch when he entered, but rose hastily, and, drawing forward a chair, waited until he was seated, before seating herself and preparing to answer the questions of the new physician, as nurse had called him.

Asahel felt slightly embarrassed before this young maiden; for, young though she was, Asahel was wise enough to know that some mighty power must be working in the heart of the delicate creature before him—an influence which he was unable to fathom, unable to reach; and he felt that, without the aid of his patient herself, he should be as unsuccessful as her former physicians had been. He began with the usual inquiries, felt her pulse, which was, as he had expected, very feeble; he then inquired as to the seat of the pain; this also was as he had expected—starting from the heart to the left side and upwards to the head.

These were just such symptoms of feverish disturbance as he had expected to find; and opening a small case, he at once gave his patient a few grains of a rare narcotic, reduced to powder, which would, he felt assured, give present relief to the nervous system, which had been so unduly excited last night. This was, however, but a temporary resource; what was really needed was something which should enable the young girl herself to resist these attacks and ecstasies—if, indeed, it were possible.

During his preliminary inquiries Asahel had been carefully studying his patient, and had at once noted the singular eyes, which he had learned to associate with the priestesses of those oracles which were at once the curse, and the great bond of unity, to the great Hellenic nation. Asahel had seen such eyes in a servant of the temple of Ceres first, and had since noted them among his patients; and now he was called to prescribe for this young delicate creature, and saw at once that she also was subjected to the same sensitive organisation. Very gently and cheerfully Asahel led the conversation to Nausicaa, and soon found that love for her was the one absorbing feeling in the breast of his patient. Knowing her history, as he now knew it, he was enabled to understand this, when he knew that the poor girl was living among those whom she felt were waging deadly warfare against her kindred, and Nausicaa alone had sympathised with her. And yet as Asahel pondered over her case, he felt that this isolation of spirit was in itself sufficient to account for the excitement under which she laboured.

Once more Asahel changed the subject, and spoke of Athens, told her at last that he lived there; a quick flush passed over the pale face at once, and Opis looked up with eager eyes waiting for the next word. There was something about this lonely orphan wh... touched the heart of Asahel; he felt as though in presence he was acting under the impulse of a po... apart from the rules of his daily life; he looked d... upon the thin worn features, the eager eyes upon his with an appealing gaze, and acting u... impulse he could not explain or resist, he said:

"Would you like to come to Athens i... would permit you? It would do you good.

A deep sigh, as though relief had arrive... sounded from the heart of poor Opis. another word was spoken, and yet Asahe... once that his work was accomplished. which had troubled the maiden, what now appeased, and was no... exhaust the weak fra... soft happy tears Opis; and w... seemed to... every a...

her mind with gods hostile to the gods of her own people; but Nausicaa, her own beloved sister, it would be hard to part from her. Asahel was not sorry that there should be this sorrow in the prospect of parting; it was a human feeling over which he rejoiced as a certain token of returning humanity. When Hyllus returned, and heard such a report as Asahel thought right to give, he at once acceded to his request, trusting entirely to his judgment, since it was a case where the best physicians of Sparta had failed to give relief. It was agreed that the journey should be spoken of as a visit to Asahel, for although her new friend felt that it would be very unwise to permit Opis to return to the scene of her suffering, yet at present Nausicaa also must be considered and permitted to look forward to the return of the happy days of their untroubled childhood. The next morning Asahel and Gershom, accompanied by Opis on a mule, and one female attendant, were passing through the gates of the villa. Before the sun had risen over the hills Nausicaa was there to bid her friend farewell, and there was a strange mingling of tears and hopeful anticipation on all sides. "Leda corresponds with the priestess of Artemis Brauronia; so you must be sure to write to me often through her," were Nausicaa's oft-repeated words.

"You will see the noblest lady in Hellas, Opis. Be sure you speak well of me to Androclea. You will crave her protection for the child, Asahel," said Hyllus.

In the midst of all the hurry of preparation, and of the sense of ingratitude to her kind protectors which would intrude upon Opis, and which had led to a passionate outburst of self-accusation, with prayers for forgiveness to both Hyllus and her long-suffering nurse, she had at last given herself up to an intense feeling of joy in the prospect of her release, a joy in which the pain of parting from Nausicaa shrank into obscurity, and the thought of freedom arose more vividly before her. There were tears and fond embraces for all she left behind, but deep in the heart of Opis lay the newly-found rest and happiness of knowing that she was at last going where the sins of Athens would not be the subject-matter upon every tongue—the destruction of Athens, the prayer upon every lip and every heart.

CHAPTER IV.

" Mist! mist! beautiful mist!
Feathery, floating, tremulous mist;
Fair, pink, empurpled, golden light—
Angel of morn and herald of night.
Breath of the earth, ascending to heaven,
Floating, freed from earthly leaven;
Full flushed with glory, by sunbeams kissed,
Praise God in thy beauty, marvellous mist."

SAHEL was not proceeding directly to Athens. He must first visit Arcadia, there to fulfil the prime object of his journey, in procuring some of the pure Arcadian all-heal, which (although it could be procured in Athens since it was largely exported) was always most pure when collected on the spot. Hyllus had quite agreed with Asahel's opinion that a fortnight's ramble among the Arcadian uplands would of itself do much towards strengthening the nerves of Opis; and, indeed, Hyllus had longed to accompany them, and had proposed a united expedition, in which Nausicaa might join. Asahel, however, knew well that the presence of Hyllus would of itself destroy all the good which change of scene might effect, since he was so intimately connected, yet so unconsciously, with the sufferings of the ever excited Opis. Thus, when the friends parted at the gate which led over the high road to the Eurotas, and thence over the bridge to the Arcadian uplands, Hyllus regretted the hasty departure which had prevented his accompanying them, while Asahel, for the first time in his life, was rejoicing in the departure of his friend.

Very slowly the little procession passed on to the second bridge over the Tiasa, and then upwards to the wild tableland of Arcadia. The sun had not fully risen, and the city was shrouded by the morning mist which filled the whole valley. The air was chill, and Asahel turned to ask his young charge if she felt the cold too keenly; when thus turning he saw one of the loveliest sights which man can witness. Very hastily he turned the head of the mule from the upward path, and, putting his arm round Opis, pointed out to her the glorious scene which lay beneath them.

The pure white mist which entirely hid the city and the valley in which it lay, was now rolling and heaving in soft foaming billows; it was a new-born ocean of the purest white vapour. The rocks above rose on every side clear and sharply defined; the dark forest trees which clothed Taygetos casting a solemn grandeur over the scene; while on the other side of the mystic ocean the vineyards, with their trellised vines just brightening into colour under the rays of

…RLASTING FATHER.

…your physician, Opis, I must act …rough your mind. Are you con… …you as my own child?"
…our own child! Why should you …out one who only escaped from the …ounty of Hyllus?"
…k, dear child; although my grand-…n Greek, I am a Hebrew, and hope …you my own land, where we have …n Sparta; no Clytra, with its living …tcast babe, as in Athens. We wor-…ose gods whose terrors appal you. …m we worship is a God who has …will surely execute, vengeance upon …ice children, and upon those who see …tted, and yet forbear to punish the …God whom we worship is the Eternal …formed every living creature, and …e work of His own hands. If I can …ind to a full faith in this Heavenly …will be no more tortured by the terrors …hens, for the Most High will be your …your strength, a very present help in every …uble."
…ou say that your God is a Father? Is He …r of all mankind?"
…Creator of all living beings—a loving Father 'ce." Asahel…ho become members of His family by faith …d then con…dience." Asahel looked upwards for a few …s, and then continued in reverent, yet half-

'A cry of delight escaped from the lips of Opia. She gazed entranced ... As the mist arose, Sparta was revealed.'—HEROES OF ANCIENT GREECE, p. 69.

the rising sun, the rich autumnal tints of their ruddy golden-hued leaves glistening against the clusters of purple grapes, produced an effect which was almost unearthly in its beauty. A cry of delight escaped from the lips of Opis; she gazed entranced, while as the sun rose higher and higher above the eastern hills, the mist changed from white to opal, and then to purple, until at last it seemed to dissolve into an aerial pink and golden cloud, which gradually floated away, disclosing the city which it had hidden. And thus, as the mist arose, Sparta was revealed, the blazing sun glistening upon every brazen statue and Parian temple, and shedding an ineffable splendour over all.

Opis gazed wistfully at every well-known object, the beauty of the scene seeming to awaken a regretful feeling, Asahel thought, until turning her eyes towards the western side of the valley, her attention was drawn to the terrible Apothetæ, the cave at the base of Mount Taygetos, into which every new-born babe, condemned by the elders of its tribe as unworthy of life, in their opinion, was ruthlessly cast—the terrible Apothetæ where rumour said that the two thousand Helots had been cast, who had served Sparta so well in the war that they were considered dangerous to their iron masters; and after having been led through the city crowned and garlanded, had disappeared, none but the guardians of the Apothetæ knew how or where. No sooner did the eyes of Opis rest upon the terrible spot than she shuddered.

"It is a city full of blood," she cried, in a low moaning tone. "Apollo has but to shine, and all the blood is revealed, although night and darkness may hide it for a time. There is blood, blood everywhere," she murmured. "Oh take me away, as you promised that you would do." Opis spoke so pitifully that again Asahel was touched to the heart with her misery; and Gershom, who knew nothing of the cause of her illness, looked on in wonder while he noted the gentle care with which his father soothed her, and the evident sympathy he felt with her trouble. For some minutes the whole party walked silently up the steep rocky path, but the silence was soon broken, for Asahel's voice rose in firm, clear tones upon the morning air, and Gershom instantly responded. The father and son were chanting the alternate verses of the sacred psalm—chanting the sweet Hebrew melody, as it had been for centuries, and was still chanted in the temple at Jerusalem:

"The Lord is my light and my salvation; whom shall I fear?

"The Lord is the strength of my life; of whom shall I be afraid?"

While Asahel sang thus, his arm was round Opis, supporting her upon the mule; and when the psalm ceased, she turned towards him with soft, tear-filled eyes.

"How beautiful that was! I did not understand one word, and yet I am sure it was a hymn to one of the gods."

"If I am to be your physician, Opis, I must act upon your body through your mind. Are you contented that I treat you as my own child?"

"Treat me as your own child! Why should you trouble yourself about one who only escaped from the Apothetæ by the bounty of Hyllus?"

"I am no Greek, dear child; although my grandmother was a Syrian Greek, I am a Hebrew, and hope some day to show you my own land, where we have no Apothetæ, as in Sparta; no Clytra, with its living burden of an outcast babe, as in Athens. We worship none of those gods whose terrors appal you. The God whom we worship is a God who has threatened, and will surely execute, vengeance upon those who sacrifice children, and upon those who see the sin committed, and yet forbear to punish the sinner. The God whom we worship is the Eternal Creator, who formed every living creature, and delights in the work of His own hands. If I can lead your mind to a full faith in this Heavenly Father, you will be no more tortured by the terrors of the heathens, for the Most High will be your refuge and your strength, a very present help in every time of trouble."

"Did you say that your God is a Father? Is He the Father of all mankind?"

"The Creator of all living beings—a loving Father to all who become members of His family by faith and obedience." Asahel looked upwards for a few moments, and then continued in reverent, yet half-pleading, tones, "Hast Thou not, O most holy One, suffered Thine holy prophets to give the Gentiles this assurance? Hast Thou not, by the Holy Ghost, declared that they also have permission to plead with Thee, and say, 'Doubtless Thou art our Father, though Abraham be ignorant of us, and Israel acknowledge us not; Thou, O Lord, art our Father, our Redeemer; Thy name is for everlasting.'"

These last words were spoken in Hebrew, and Opis did not seem to notice that Asahel was speaking, but kept repeating, "A Father! a Father!" At length she turned to Asahel. "You will teach me how to sacrifice to your God; for a Father is what I have been longing for, ever since I knew that I was not the child of Hyllus."

"From you, my child, He will need no sacrifice, but a humble and a contrite heart. Obedience, He has declared, is better than sacrifice; but I will teach you how He loves to be worshipped, for you have been given to my care by Him, I can well perceive; but now you must alight from your mule, and join us in eating our morning meal."

Doris the Helot, who had been given to Opis as nurse, soon arranged a comfortable seat for her, beneath a chestnut-tree; and in a short time every trace of despondency had passed from the face of the young maiden, and Asahel commenced his instruction of his young charge, by pointing out to her notice the lovely wild-flowers which were growing in such profusion around them; while Gershom very soon charmed her from her seat to follow him in his search for the rarer species, and aid him in their collection.

Rather more than three weeks after Asahel and his charge had left Sparta, Penelope and Thetis were walking with their mother upon the high road, which led from their own villa to Eleusis; the day had been unusually hot for the season of the year, and now that the sun was setting, a fresh pleasant breeze had tempted the ladies to prolong their walk. Androclea had just decided that they must return home, to avoid being overtaken by the darkness, when Thetis exclaimed: "Behold them, my mother! The herb-gatherers; but who can they have picked up on their way?" Then, as the travellers drew near, and Androclea quickened her pace to meet them, Thetis again exclaimed: "My mother, who is it? Who can it be? Surely it must be Diana herself, with a broad-brimmed Arcadian hat hanging back upon her shoulders. The young girl upon the mule is lovely enough, and ruddy enough, to be the huntress goddess herself—she needs but the bow to confirm my faith in her."

"Do not be so irreverent, my Thetis; that surely must be the daughter of my friend."

"An herb-gatherer's daughter in a purple chiton!"

"She is not veiled, and is therefore not a lady of noble birth; but they will hear us," said Penelope.

In a few moments Androclea had met Asahel, and her greeting was so cordial, her welcome so sincere, that the heart of Opis responded to the gentle lady at once. In a short time Penelope and Thetis had carried the young stranger off to the thalamos, where each tried to outvie the other in hospitable attentions to their guest, while Asahel, in the room below, was recounting his adventures to Androclea.

In scarcely any other house in Greece could Asahel have found a more sympathising listener, while he narrated not only the history of Opis, but sufficient of his own, to enable the lady to understand the reason of his affection for Hyllus; while he condemned the present war, and sympathised so deeply with the affliction of Opis.

Androclea listened eagerly, and at once remembered Hyllus, and the happy week they had spent together in Italy; but all her thoughts seemed centred in Opis; the interest which she took in the care and cure of disease would alone have been sufficient to secure a welcome for the unfortunate orphan; but when to this was added the patriotic sympathy with one whose malady was so evidently connected with the misery of Athens, it was no wonder that tears started to the eyes of the happy mother, who thus listened to the sorrowful history.

"You must leave her with me, my friend. Trust me. She will recover at once under the brightening influence of my Thetis and Penelope, and you can surely trust my judgment as regards other matters."

"It is utterly impossible," replied Asahel, with deep emotion. "Already my heart is so entwined with hers that she is as my own child. I cannot leave her with you, lady, although I thank you for your kind offer. No, she is not like the same being who left Sparta. Already she calls me father, and my son brother. Her nerves have been strengthened by the pure mountain air, and her tanned face is but the outward sign of the mighty power which has changed the wretched Pythoness I saw in Sparta to the maiden you see. There is another reason, lady, which will, I know, commend itself to your judgment, even more than my affection. Opis still loves Hyllus and his daughter as I would wish her to do, and I have already perceived that any conversation with those who would call for vengeance upon Sparta outrages her sensibilities almost as much as the cry against Athens, which tortured her in Sparta. In my home at Athens she will hear nothing but prayers for peace and unity; and I will, if I find it necessary, take her to my own land, where she would be free from all sight and sound of this terrible war. I am well convinced that rest for the mind, with healthy and womanly occupation, is alone needed to complete the cure of my child."

"The last requisite she would have here, with abundant love," returned Androclea, " but then," she added, sadly, " as to the first, I can answer for myself, my daughters, and my only son at home; but how can I assure you that the free men and women around me, whose lives are embittered by their losses, and the rapacity of the invaders, the treachery of Sparta, and her allied Persian paymaster—how can I assure you that they will always be able to stifle their indignation?"

"Nor dare I ask you, lady, to persuade them to do so. To each is given our separate task. To me has been given an unexpected treasure, and I dare not throw it away or lose sight of it."

"And I suppose that you are right," replied the lady, sadly, "but you will at least stay with us to-night."

"Very gratefully; the rest will refresh my Opis, and I have found some rare species of the liquorice-vetch upon the Arcadian hills. I have put away a few roots of each rare species of plants I found, as well as some seeds which I was happy enough to collect for your garden."

In a short time Androclea and Asahel were fully occupied in examining the treasures of his wallet, and time flew insensibly while they were thus happily engaged. Lysippus was in the meanwhile entertaining Gershom with an account of his last hunting expedition; and in the thalamos the foundations of a lasting friendship seemed to have been laid between the sisters and their young guest. They soon discovered that not only would Asahel never consent to be separated from his adopted daughter, but that no inducement would avail now to part her from him. When it was known that Opis could but remain with them for that one night, the two young Athenian ladies felt it incumbent upon them to enlighten her upon some points of

Attic morality. "You cannot possibly ride into Athens unveiled, and in that dress. You will have all the boys and young men in the city following you with derision."

"Yes, and perhaps rather more than that, my dear," said Androclea, who had just entered. "You will be certainly known as a Spartan, or from Sparta, and you may meet with rough handling, and perhaps expose your friends to danger on your account."

"Wear a veil before I am married? They never do so in Sparta," replied Opis.

"Oh, no! We are all perfectly aware that Spartan maidens are not what we call modest," replied Thetis, quickly.

A cloud passed over the brow of Opis, and she looked forward in her old, anxious, troubled manner. "Nausicaa is modest, and she wears no veil, and walks in the public street when she will."

A glance from her mother restrained Thetis, while Androclea, seating herself by the young girl, drew her close to her side. "All true daughters of Hellas are modest, be they born in Athens or in Sparta, my child; but we have different fashions in our different states. If you love the Spartan fashions best——"

"Oh, no, no, no! Do not speak of them. I forgot. I only thought of my beloved Nausicaa. No, no! tell me what I must do to be unlike a Spartan," and as the young girl spoke she stood up, and, with trembling fingers, attempted to unclasp the zone which fastened her chiton.

"My dear child, sit down and rest. See, you have startled my poor Penelope by your energy! There, rest your head upon me. To-morrow I will myself give your nurse such instructions concerning your dress as will relieve you of all thought about the matter. Do not trouble your mind any more just now, but tell me of Arcadia. Asahel, your father, has promised me that you shall visit us when we return to Athens for the winter, so we had better begin to exchange confidences now."

"Oh, I am so glad that I shall see you again," said Opis, simply; and Androclea saw at once that all danger of the return of her malady was averted for the present.

Opis spent a very happy evening, and when she had narrated some of her Arcadian adventures, both Androclea and her daughters expressed their longing desire to visit the sublime scenery which she described, and to see for themselves the picturesque life of the hardy mountaineers. Opis dwelt long upon the charms of the Arcadian music. She declared that it had seemed to her as though every Arcadian was a born musician. The flute sounded from among the rugged rocks where the peasant boy was tending his goats, and in every village through which they had passed they had heard children chanting in unison melodies sweeter than any she had ever heard; while the lyrics and pæans sung by the men at their village festivals and exercises of mimic warfare, were far nobler and more spirit-stirring than even the far-famed Spartan music. "Their hymns to the gods were nobler and more devout than any others, excepting, indeed, those which my father Asahel sings."

"My son Lysippus heard our friends singing when they left us after their first visit. He described the song as very peculiar. I should much like to hear them sing. Do you think you could induce them to sing for our amusement."

"Oh! no, no," replied Opis, gravely, "their singing is a sort of sacrifice of devotion to their God. My father is always very reverent when he sings, and I dare not ask him to amuse us by thus singing."

"Their God! Do they not worship our gods then?" asked Thetis.

"Not any of ours. Only the Heavenly Father, the Eternal Creator. They say that He is in heaven, and in earth, and in Hades, and is ever present; that He never had a beginning, and will never cease to exist. Asahel has taught me to sing one of their hymns; he translated it into Greek for me, and if it will give you any pleasure to hear it I shall be very glad to sing it;" and as Opis spoke she turned to Androclea with something of the simple Spartan reverence for age, in which she had been nurtured. During this revelation of the teaching of Asahel, Androclea felt rather uneasy. Was it possible that he could be luring this young girl into some terrible blasphemy? She would listen, she would not condemn him unheard, so, turning to Opis, she at once replied kindly, "We shall be very grateful if you will give us the pleasure of hearing you sing, since we are not permitted to hear Asahel."

"The hymn I shall sing is the one which I first heard my father and brother sing when we were leaving Sparta. I asked my father to teach me that one first, and you shall judge for yourselves whether I ought not to love it." Speaking thus, Opis raised her sweet and carefully trained voice to the Eastern melody taught her by Asahel, and when her listeners heard the words they no longer wondered at the change which Asahel had wrought. A sacred peace, born of a pure faith, rested upon every feature of the orphan while she sang:

"When my father and my mother forsake me, the Lord taketh me up. . . .

"I should utterly have fainted, but that I believe verily to see the goodness of the Lord in the land of the living.

"Oh, tarry thou the Lord's leisure; be strong, and He shall comfort thine heart, and put thou thy trust in the Lord."

"It is very, very beautiful, and very devout," said Androclea, kissing her young guest when she finished singing. "But now, dear child, let me show you to your chamber. You must take a long sleep in preparation for to-morrow's journey. Remember, I do not wish you to be too over-tired to enjoy your first sight of our beloved Athens."

Thus Androclea, with true motherly skill, avoided any further question concerning Asahel's faith. She had no wish that the minds of her daughters should be unsettled, and thus it was with a sense of an averted danger that she saw Opis safely embowered in the dainty little chamber assigned to her. Then, returning to her own chamber, misgivings floated through the mind of the anxious mother, who felt that even in Attica there must be some limit upon freedom. She would pity and help the orphaned stranger, but she would do it with her own hands; there must be no further peril for the faith of her Thetis, who was already too fond of novelty and too easily impressed. The Deity adored by Asahel might be, and most probably was, very powerful in His own country, and certainly that hymn was very reverent and beautiful. But if Athena were to be degraded in the eyes of her daughters, why, yes, perhaps it would have been better if Asahel had not accepted her invitation, and if Hyllus had not claimed her protection for his foundling. Thus, then, in pursuance of her resolution, when day dawned Androclea herself appeared in the chamber of Opis, half blaming herself for her inhospitable feelings, and yet supported by a consciousness that she was but performing her duty to her national deities and her beloved daughters. These contending feelings made the gentle-hearted lady more than usually careful to omit no outward duty of hospitality, while her heart was inwardly rejoicing over the departure of her guest. One of Penelope's unused walking-dresses was brought into the chamber of Opis, and Androclea herself assisted the nurse in robing her young mistress. The soft long locks of the young girl were now confined in a net of silver thread, which was fastened to her head by a jewelled sphendone. This was in shape something like a large old-fashioned ornamental comb, and was placed upon the top instead of the back of the head. From this sphendone was suspended a long flowing veil of fine gauze. The cloak which Androclea clasped round the neck of Opis was woven of the very finest goatshair, and was one which could scarcely be produced in these days, so soft and lustrous was the material, so graceful were its folds. This dress at once transformed Opis from a wild-looking Arcadian beauty into an Athenian lady of rank; and when she was at length seated upon her mule, and turned once more to bid farewell to her generous entertainer, her young heart swelled with sincere grateful love. The anxious motherly care of Androclea was as soothing to her wounded heart as she had already found the fatherly thoughtful love of Asahel. Thetis and Penelope, who knew nothing of their mother's anxiety, were profuse in their expressions of regret at her departure, and joyful anticipations of a speedy reunion in Athens; while Androclea blamed herself, that even while bestowing an affectionate motherly kiss upon the young orphan, she had been conscious of a secret joy in her departure, and a hope that something might occur which would prevent the intimacy she had promised to her daughters last night.

The autumn of the year 403 B.C. was a most eventful one for Athens. The victory of Arginusæ had not restored the failing spirit of her people, as it should have done, and had but served to stimulate Sparta to more vigorous measures. Lysander, who had been recently re-appointed to the practical command of the Spartan allies, was well known as one of Sparta's sternest and most determined sons. Poor, but of noble birth (he himself claimed descent from the Heracleidæ), he had raised himself to his present high position by his personal bravery and daring strategic qualities. This appointment, while it had raised the spirits of the Lacedæmonians and their allies, had proportionately depressed the hopes of the Athenians, who had in the last levy sent out every available fighting man in Attica to assist their own admiral Conon in his resistance to the relentless Lysander.

When Asahel and his party passed through the villages of Attica, he could not but be heart-grieved over the tokens of misery he witnessed. In many places the large, plentiful harvest was beaten down and rotting upon the ground, for want of men to reap and garner it; figs and olives were falling upon the ground uncared for; while empty houses, with deserted homesteads, told too plainly the history of the many invasions of Attica, by her warlike neighbours, during the long war, which had now lasted, with but short intermissions, for twenty-seven years. Opis, who did not perceive the decay which grieved Asahel, was overpowered by the beauty of all she saw. The tiny towns, each with its Agora and temples clustering round—each temple a gem of Attic art, and glistening in all the purity of Pentelic marble — the carefully cultivated vales and tiny plains, the vine and myrtle crowned hills, were then very different from the bare ruggedness of Attica in these days; for irrigation was understood and practised then, as it never has been since, and forests were then standing, which are now felled.

Evening was drawing her veil over the landscape, when at last Athens, the glory of Greece, appeared fully in sight; her tower-guarded walls enclosing a circumference of some twenty-five miles. From the midst of those walls rose a high hill, upon which the Acropolis was visible, glistening in majestic beauty, and irradiated by the last rays of declining daylight. Above the Acropolis rose the marvellous figure of the brazen statue of Athena, whose colossal grandeur, towering high above all other objects, was lighted up by the glowing sunlight, which had faded away from the lower earth, yet seemed to be sinking to its rest, with its last gaze fixed upon the presiding genius of the fairest city upon earth.

No two cities could be more unlike than were Sparta and Athens; they were as diverse as the genius of the people and their laws. The last view of Sparta, which Opis remembered, had shown her the stern heart of Greece, girded by her tiny rivers, and sheltered by her rugged mountain heights, nestling in her security—a city without any walls but those which sheltered her valley. Athens, on the contrary, sat erect, crowned by the blue sky; she looked down upon the wide spreading sea, which lay in rippling beauty outspread beneath her feet. Adorned by her children with a profuse magnificence, which they gloried in devoting to their beloved city, she sat thus between earth and heaven, ever seeming to be looking upward, and drawing the hearts of her children away from earth and earthly cares, to the beauty and repose of that heaven upon which she gazed unshadowed by any intervening barrier.

It was with a sense of ecstatic awe, that Opis entered Athens in the short twilight. She had seen enough to impress a far less vivid imagination than hers; and when at last she found herself in bed, in the small chamber to which she was conducted by Asahel, upon entering his house, it was long before she could even close her eyes. When at last Opis slept, her dreams were filled with visions of colossal statues, gigantic brazen horses, which seemed starting into life, and it was long before gentler visions of Androclea and her daughters brought dreamless, resting sleep to the wearied frame of the young wanderer.

When Asahel had seen his guests refreshed after their long journey, and had himself conducted Opis to the best chamber in his small house, he sent Gershom, with news of their arrival, to his friend, the well-known physician, Menares; then retiring to his own chamber, he penned the following epistle:

"To David, the son of Eleazer, the son of Barak, the son of Caleb the recorder, Asahel, the son of Barak, sends greeting. My well-beloved brother, my heart longs to hear news from thee—news of our people, and news of our holy city. Write to me, my brother, swiftly, and send it by the messenger who will deliver this epistle into your own hands. Tell me of your own health, and of the health of your beloved wife, Rachel. Tell me news of all those, from whom, as you know, I long to hear, that they are in good health, and filled with the blessing of peace. Tell me news also of Shimei, my enemy, and let me know whether I am yet avenged upon him and his. Can I return in peace to my own home, upon the slopes near Bethlehem? or must I wait still longer, ere the villainy of my slanderer be exposed? Write to me with full particulars, concerning all those matters which, you know, lie so near to my heart. And now, my brother, prepare yourself for a surprise, which will be a pleasant one, I am thankful to know. Whether I return to my own home or not, I fully intend to eat our holy Passover with you. I will be with you in full time for preparation, but you must not be surprised if you see me sooner. I am most anxious that Gershom should once more be united with our own people, in the observances of our holy law; and I also long for the blessing of the sacred feast once more. My brother, I need thy help. I too often forget my birth, and its sacred obligations; my small tincture of heathen blood stirs within me, when I see the glory of the carved images and molten idols by which I am surrounded; and I often find myself excusing or consenting to idolatry, even when I do not share it. Thus I have given you the reasons which have determined me to visit you. I have still another reason. The air of Greece is full of strife and bitterness, and I feel well assured that the end of the long struggle is at hand. The messenger who delivers this, will give you full particulars concerning the movements of the contending parties.

"Again, my brother, my chief item of news comes last. I have been in Sparta visiting our old friend Hyllus. I found him well in health, with his daughter, a loving and goodly maiden, modest, and all that I could wish to see her; but Hyllus is sadly changed; he has become hard and bitter towards Athens, although he was the same to me that he had ever been. In the house of Hyllus I met with a young maiden, an orphan, or at least a foundling, upon whom Hyllus, unlike the rest of his people, had taken pity. He has brought her up with his daughter for more than fourteen years, but during this last year an evil spirit has taken possession of the maiden, and made her life wretched, and driven Hyllus and all his household to despair. I will explain the matter to you more fully when we meet and you see her, for I brought her away from Sparta at my own request, to the great relief of Hyllus. My beloved brother, give thanks with me, and for me, to the God of our fathers, whose hand has been upon me for good in this matter. I firmly believe that the spirit has left my Opis, and it will, I believe, never return to her. Prayer for her, and with her, to our holy and loving Father has driven out the evil one; and when first I heard my child pray in humility, 'Create in me a clean heart, and renew a right spirit within me,' I felt assured that her prayer would be heard. I took her with me and Gershom into Arcadia, where the pure air and repose from strife healed her worn body, as the Holy Spirit for which we prayed was healing her soul. My brother, I love the maiden as though she were in truth my own child; and I have hopes that she may yet be so, for Gershom and she love each other already; thus, on her account, I have determined to visit you. If your Rachel will take charge of my child for a short time, I shall have time to see whether the affection which my children already feel for each other will be such as will justify them in entering into the sacred relationship of man and wife. I have no fear of your Rachel refusing my request or repenting it afterwards, for to know my Opis well is to love her. Farewell, my brother. May the blessing of peace rest upon you and all yours, now and for evermore."

CHAPTER V.

> "To sage philosophy next lend thine ear,
> From heaven descended to the low-roofed house
> Of Socrates: see there his tenement,
> Whom well inspired, the oracle pronounced
> Wisest of men."
> —*Milton's Paradise Regained.*

WHEN Opis awakened upon the next morning, she realised fully for the first time the great change which had fallen over her life. The small chamber in which she had slept was almost bare of furniture, although it was scrupulously clean. Doris, who was already dressed, and engaged in arranging the contents of their saddle-bags, seemed in no very contented mood with the arrangements of the house.

"Well, child," she said, in answer to the cheerful salutation of Opis, "well, if this foreign physician can cure you, we will not grudge enduring some hardships; but it seems to me that we shall have less than Helot comforts here. I wonder what Nausicaa would say if she saw the bed upon which you slept last night."

"Slept, Doris! yes, indeed I did sleep; slept all

night without awakening once, and my head is as cool, my side as free from pain this morning as—as—what shall I say?" cried the young girl, springing from her bed and advancing towards Doris; but as Opis passed the small window, she suddenly stopped, her arms dropped by her side, and, advancing to the window, she gazed upwards upon one of the most exquisite panoramas of true art which earth has yet witnessed. The sun was rising and lighting up with radiant glory the pure white Parthenon which rose from the rock of the Acropolis. Six hundred feet above the level of Asahel's low-roofed house, this marvel of Grecian art rose in its first bloom of youth. More than two thousand winters have beaten their storms upon the Parthenon since Opis saw it, and yet, defaced, polluted, ruined though it be, it still kindles every heart which looks upon its beauty. When Opis looked out that morning, the pure white marble shone like alabaster. The votive golden shields which were suspended around it glistened in the beams of the rising sun, and the ruddy colouring which glowed from the graven entablatures seemed to invest it with a living glow of beauty.

A true lover of Hellas (Mr A. J. St John) has said: "At Sparta, a spirit of calculating economy entered into the very worship of the gods; they seemed, in the manner they lodged and entertained them, to have always had an eye to their common tables and their black broth. Between the temples of Athens and Sparta there was, in fact, the same contrast that

'More than two thousand winters have beaten their storms upon the Parthenon: . . . defaced, polluted, ruined though it be, it still kindles every heart that looks upon its beauty.'—HEROES OF ANCIENT GREECE, p. 90.

now exists between St Peter's at Rome, and a Calvinist conventicle."

This may seem a hard judgment upon Sparta, and may be partly untrue as to motives, since Sparta possessed no rich quarries of that pure, rare marble, which rewarded every effort of the Athenian artist by adding a glory of its own. But if unjust to Sparta, the fact was a fact nevertheless. Opis had never even dreamed of such a vision as that upon which she gazed. The whole summit of the Acropolis was crowned with the sublime majesty of sacred architecture and true artistic representation of departed heroes. The sunbeams were just lighting up into glory the radiant statue of Apollo, which had been placed by Phidias to greet the first dawn of day, as the colossal Athena received his parting rays. There were the magnificent temples of Zeus, of Poseidon, of Erectheus, and others; while the brazen horses of the chariots, in which departed heroes were grouped around the citadel, seemed to be leaping down from the rocky height upon the city below.

Opis gazed long and wistfully upon every object, but at last her eyes found a resting-place, for the martial maid, the goddess of wisdom, the defender of Athens, could not be hidden; her full face was turned from Opis, but none the less was her calm serene beauty visible; and all the efforts of Doris to attract the attention of her mistress were useless. Those calm, grand, restful features, so full of thought, and free from earthly passion, seemed to exercise a fascination over every heart and head. While Opis gazed, the lessons of Asahel during the last few weeks were entirely obliterated; and looking upward, her lips moved in devout prayer to the guardian goddess of all true maidens. Nor was it her lips alone which moved, the whole soul of Opis bowed down in reverent homage and devout affection, to the image itself, whose sublime presence seemed to shadow forth a visible protection to her orphaned life, her outraged heart.

The enraptured strain was at length released; and turning to Doris, Opis at length suffered her to speak of dressing, and continue her complaints concerning the lack of accommodation in Asahel's house.

"There is neither thalamos nor peristyle here, Opis; it is but a sort of poor Helot's house—one common room, in which you will have to eat your meals with all comers; a few bare chambers for sleeping in—this is the best in the house—and one room for the freewoman, Ismene, who serves Asahel. I slept with her last night."

"Poor Doris, I am sorry for you; but as to myself, I promise you to be well and happy. I shall not be troubled by the want of a thalamos, since it will always be a happiness to me to be with Asahel; and as to fine furniture, it is far better to have that glorious Acropolis within sight, than to have all the luxurious couches in the house of Hyllus to rest upon."

"I am glad to find that you take it so cheerfully, child; as to me, of course, in some respects, I am much better off. Ismene is a freewoman; and yet she treated me last night, as no poor Spartan ever did; and for you also, there is a small court and garden, full of flowers and rare herbs, and in beautiful order."

"Oh! we shall be happy, Doris, you will see; and you shall be a freewoman, like Ismene, soon, if I can manage it."

"May the blessing of Heracles the Deliverer be upon you, Opis; you have ever had a tender heart for the Helot; but I hope that when the Ladies Androclea and Penelope come, they will see to your being better lodged, for I know well that Nausicaa would grieve if she saw you now."

"Both Nausicaa and Hyllus would rejoice if they saw me so ruddy and so brown. I saw my face in a steel mirror yesterday, and I scarcely knew it. Do not murmur over blessings, my Doris; but now I must go to Asahel."

When Opis descended, she found the eating-room empty. Asahel had, however, left a message saying, that he would return in a short time. The elderly woman, who acted as housekeeper for him, had, however, received orders, which she had faithfully fulfilled. The meal which was spread before Opis was perfect in its cleanly cooking and dainty serving. There was nothing which served to remind her that she was not eating from the well attended table of Hyllus. Pure white linen, of the finest quality, was spread upon the table, each dish was daintily garnished with fresh flowers and leaves, while the perfectly cooked fresh fish was such a rare treat to Opis, that she needed no other inducement to make and enjoy a hearty meal. She had scarcely finished eating when Asahel arrived, and, after a few close inquiries concerning her health, and repeated assurances from Opis that she never intended giving any further trouble about the matter, he told her that he intended to devote the whole day to showing her some of the beauties of Athens.

"You will take me first to the Parthenon, that I may offer my sacrifice to Athena, will you not?" As Opis spoke, she looked up to Asahel with kindling eyes. "Oh! how glorious she is, and what a palace, what a celestial temple the Athenians have built for her! I love my little chamber already, for through my window I can see the guardian goddess."

If Opis had presented a dagger to the heart of Asahel, she could scarcely have produced a greater effect; the calm bronzed features of the strong man worked as though they were convulsed, while a deadly pallor overspread his countenance. It was impossible to see him, and not notice the change; all absorbed in her own enthusiasm as Opis was, she was arrested by the sight.

"Oh! forgive me; I have grieved you. I had forgotten you will not like to go with me to the temple. I can wait quite well until to-morrow, when Doris can take me to pay my sacrifice and adoration."

Asahel seemed relieved. "Yes, dear child, that

will be the best. I cannot go with you into your temples, as you know; but your nurse will be sufficient protection for you there—even in Athens. I have already made arrangements for giving up the whole of the day to you, so that it will be best to follow my first arrangement, while Ismene and Doris can take you to the temples to-morrow. When the Lady Androclea arrives she will take you to those to which you could not well go with Doris alone; and, if you are advised by me, you will not attempt to visit the Parthenon without Androclea or some lády of rank."

"I will do just as you think right, my dear father. I have such a glorious view from my window that I ought to be contented. What would not Nausicaa give to have one glimpse of that which I can see every day!"

When Opis had left the room, Asahel leaned his head upon his hands, and bowed it in deep thought. "Is it ever to be so? Am I always to find that I can do nothing to extricate any human being from their troubles. Fool that I was to undertake this charge! These heathens speak of escaping from Scylla but to fall a captive to Charybdis. Thus has it been with me. I have freed this child from her misery in Sparta but to drive her frantic by Attic exclusiveness. How can I dare to tell her in her present frame of mind that, unless I can prove her to be of pure Attic blood, she may not enter within the precincts of the Parthenon; and yet, how can I prevent her finding this out? Fool that I have been!" Rising from his seat, Asahel passed to the open doorway, which looked into the garden court, and, raising his eyes reverently to the blue sky which shone pure and unclouded above him, he raised his hands and prayed fervently—" O Thou Holy One, Thou Lord God of my fathers, Thou hast shown me my own littleness so often ; help me now, I beseech Thee. If this child had but kept in the same mind in which she passed through Thy mountain-paths, I had not feared for her; but, now! the glamour of that great brazen idol has bewitched her, and nothing will serve her but that, which, alas! she cannot have."

It was well for Opis that Asahel spoke these words in his native Hebrew, for his speech was interrupted by a light tap upon his shoulder, and, turning round, he saw the bright face of his young charge looking up expectantly into his, without one foreboding of the pain which he foresaw for her. It was impossible to look upon that fair young face without feeling its influence. Asahel took it between his hands, and imprinting a father's kiss upon her forehead, led her out to the entrance-gate, where the mule stood ready saddled. "We will visit the Agora first," said Asahel. "I am not quite satisfied with your bridle; and as I intend taking you to Piræus, we must have no unsafe harness. The Agora is the centre of Athenian daily life: 'the pupil of the eye of Greece,' it has been called; and I feel sure you will like to see it."

A very few short narrow streets separated Asahel's house from the Agora, that market-place of Athens whose fame is so intimately connected with her historic life. In the city over which Pericles, the friend of Phidias, had ruled, the market-place was certain to bear traces of that love of beauty which adorns even the most homely details of daily life; thus the Athenian Agora, traversed by avenues of plane and olive trees, was surrounded by some of the noblest buildings in the city. In the centre of the vast circumference stood a sacred group—twelve altars dedicated to the twelve chief deities of Greece. There was the altar erected to Pity, and there the memorable altar of Vesta, upon which, some three or four years later, Theramenes leaped, fruitlessly invoking protection from the murderous majority, and from which he uttered these mournful words, so suggestive of a decaying religion, a decaying national life: "By the gods, I am not ignorant that this altar will be no protection to me."

Passing the altars, at the extremity of the Agora tents were pitched, in which vendors from a distance displayed their wares. In another place a group of citizens might be seen discussing the merits of some Thessalian coursers. There stood poor Attic freemen waiting to be hired in their respective trades, and again there was the spot where slaves were sold. Passing about from group to group were flower-girls, not only carrying the tiny bouquet or the larger nosegay, but bearing chaplets and garlands, those essential festive adornments to both men and women. Near the steps of one of the temples a group of musicians was waiting to be hired, and the air resounded with the melodies by which they endeavoured to attract notice. Near one of the marble colonnades, under which sophists were discussing the latest novelty, a group of dancers awaited the arrival of some rich citizen who might need their services for his evening's entertainment, and while thus awaiting remunerative employment, exhibited their skill and grace for the benefit of the passers-by.

Asahel, who knew Sparta well, and knew that her citizens employed hired dancers far less than did the luxurious Athenians, stayed the course of the mule that Opis might see the singular Thracian dance which these performers were now exhibiting. One portion of the dancers played upon flutes, while others seemed to be engaged in following the plough, every movement of the ploughmen being timed in unison with the music, and, although no plough was used, it seemed impossible to mistake the meaning of the motions, so skilfully were they performed. Suddenly, a warlike blast was heard, and a band entered, who attempted to seize the ploughmen, every movement being timed to the sound of the fife, and every movement being most singularly graceful. Finally, by the superior skill of the ploughmen, the marauders were bound and fettered, not hastily, but still as moving under some musical impulse, then the captives were carried in triumphal procession to the steps of an adjacent temple, when the victors immediately concluded the exhibition by a brilliant choric dance, in which they united their voices with the melody of the flutes and other instruments.

The dance was most singularly fascinating to Opis, and she was not surprised to see two citizens advance from the crowd as soon as the exhibition was over, and compete with each other for the services of the dancers upon the coming evening.

Leaving the crowd which had assembled round the dancers, Asahel led the mule to the other side of the Agora, where the most fashionable shops were situated —perfumers, tailors, and mercers, around whose open doors the exquisites of Athens lounged and retailed the latest gossip. There were the embroiderers' shops, and retailers of those delicate articles of ladies' dress, which drew ladies of Athens to the spot, and here Opis looked out through her veil with curious wonder upon the luxury to which she was so unaccustomed. Noble matrons, with their daughters, attended by obsequious slaves, filled the street with a splendour and magnificence unknown to Sparta. All around was the hum of a busy, thoughtless life. The idler was sure to meet with some acquaintance there if he only rested long enough upon one of the benches which were placed outside the principal shops for the convenience of loungers, where the spacious panorama of the Agora was spread out before them.

Guiding the mule gently through the crowd, Asahel at length reached the shop of which he was in search. Upon a bench outside a young gentleman was seated, scarcely lounging, but looking out with watchful eyes upon the busy crowd before him. He took no notice when Asahel summoned the owner of the shop, who presently made his appearance.

"The bridle of this mule does not seem to me quite trustworthy, and I have come to ask you to do what you can for us."

"Trustworthy!" said the craftsman after a moment's examination, "it must be mended with a new one. Such leather was never curried in Attica. Poor, worthless stuff. Where did you buy it?"

"Pr'ythee, content thyself with providing a new one, and do not abuse worn-out friends," said Asahel, quickly; "but if the operation will take long, suffer this young lady to find shelter under your roof. It is scarcely fitting that she should be exposed to the public gaze while her bridle is under repair."

"True," said the man, courteously. "Suffer me to lead you within, young lady. We will be no longer than we can help. But your bridle is worn out, and Asahel has done well in bringing you to me."

Opis was soon sheltered from the busy outward world in a small chamber, which opened upon the workshop; here she sat alone, looking out upon the quiet inner courtyard of the house, where an olive-tree, a few evergreens, and a fountain, gave a sense of repose from the excited stir of the world on the other side of the house. In the meanwhile, Asahel was undergoing a sharp cross-examination from the bridle-maker, who, although closely superintending his workman, was nevertheless fully determined to satisfy his Attic curiosity concerning Asahel's charge.

"An invalid under your medical care, eh? Surely not from the East. The glimpse I caught of her face through her veil told me a story of pure Greek descent."

"I travelled with my young charge yesterday from the villa of the Lady Androclea."

"The Lady Androclea! that explains all. Ah! now I understand the matter. She is half crazed by Hygeia, they say, and is for evermore trying experiments upon her poor pensioners. I wonder how many she kills, for one whom she cures?—but, hush, we must guard our tongues; that is Euthydemus, a great friend of her son's!"

"Aye," said Asahel, thankful for any change in the conversation; "he seems intelligent."

"Intelligent! my good friend, he ought to be; he has more and rarer copies of the works of the poets and philosophers than any man in Athens, young though he is. Euthydemus is not yet of age to speak in our public assemblies, but when he does make his first oration, he will astonish some people, I assure you."

"He ought to be worth something, since study is the best preparation for government," replied Asahel.

"Ah, my friend, you have spoken wisely: and yet even Euthydemus might be improved. He relies too much upon himself and his books. Thus Socrates is not half pleased with him, for he declares that book learning is but one half of knowledge."

"In a man-governed country like yours, perhaps so."

"Precisely, precisely," replied the craftsman, courteously. "To rule men, you should know something about men. You must know something of their passions and their sympathies."

"And, like Pericles and Phidias, find out that there are evil passions against which no rectitude can shield you; like Aristides, find out that the very name of justice is odious to the unjust majority which governs."

"Tut, tut, my friend, you are talking nonsense; Pericles would never have fallen if he had not risen to such an overtowering height; and as to Phidias and Aristides, why—why, all that was long ago; and I really am surprised that you should pity Phidias. I thought you looked upon him as a 'blasphemer, a carver of false gods.'"

For one moment Asahel was silenced by this truly Athenian method of excuse, but he would not be stayed altogether.

"I pitied Phidias, the honest workman, who knew his countrymen so well that he was compelled to put their gold where they might test it, and yet not even thus could his honesty shield him from their envy. And although it may be long since Aristides suffered, it is not long since the son of Pericles, with his five fellow generals, suffered death from the ingratitude of the Athenians."

"My good Asahel, you know we have already repented their death. My own belief is, that the people were seized with frenzy from Athena, because Neptune had captured the corpses of some of her children."

Asahel smiled. "Where the gods are jealous of each other, it is hardly to be expected that their worshippers should be free from envy—but here comes Socrates."

The wrath which was fast rising on the face of the craftsman sank at once as he advanced to meet the old man who was approaching, surrounded by a group of his friends. Socrates was then about sixty-seven years of age. He was dressed in a coarse, plain robe, of dark cloth; his feet were bare, and his head uncovered. He had never been either handsome or prepossessing in appearance, but age had dealt with him more kindly in this respect than it does with some others. One feature alone redeemed the face of Socrates from being an ignoble countenance. His eyes, lighted up with the fire of truth, beamed out from their pent house in attestation of the spirit within.

Returning the respectful greeting of the craftsman with a kindly word, Socrates seated himself upon the bench by the side of Euthydemus, who bowed to him respectfully, and acknowledged the greeting of his friends among the followers of Socrates, but all his movements were constrained, as though he were afraid that passers-by might include him among the pupils of the sage. At length he rose and prepared to leave. Plato, Crito, and young Xenophon were standing by their master, but looking out upon the Agora, when they were aroused by hearing Socrates speaking in one of his most cutting tones, and, in a sarcastic manner, picturing the first oration which Euthydemus would make, in order to assure Athens that his wisdom was all self-taught, and exclusively his own.

"He will make his opening thus: 'I, O men of Athens, have never learned anything from any person, nor, though I heard of some that were skilled in speaking and acting, have I sought to converse with them; nor have I been anxious that any one of the learned should become my master; but I have done the exact contrary, for I have constantly avoided not only learning anything from any one, but even the appearance of learning. Nevertheless, I will offer you such advice as may occur to me without any premeditation.' So it might be proper for a person to commence a speech who desired to obtain a medical appointment from the government: 'I, O men of Athens, have never learned the medical art from any one, nor have I been desirous that any physician should be my instructor, for I have constantly been on my guard, not only against learning anything of the art from any one, but even against appearing to have learned anything; nevertheless, confer on me this medical appointment, for I will then endeavour to learn by making experiments upon you.'" *

* From the translation of Xenophon by the Rev. J. S. Wat-

Even the grave, thoughtful face of Plato relaxed at this sally, and there was a general burst of laughter, in which Asahel joined heartily. Even Euthydemus looked more amused than hurt as he walked away.

"He will learn to value our Socrates some day, for there is good stuff in him, better than there was in that rotten old bridle of yours," said the craftsman; "and now I will go to your patient and tell her that she may safely take her airing, for my leather at least——"

"Is better than Cleon's," interrupted Asahel, who seemed to be infected with the freedom of speech which Socrates had brought with him; but the bridle-maker did not seem to hear him; he assisted Opis to mount her mule, and bade good-day to her guardian very hastily, for he was unwilling to lose one word which might fall from the lips of the sage, who was now quietly conversing with his friends as he rested upon his way to the Academy.

Opis spent a long happy day. It was one of those lovely late October days which seem to linger lovingly over earth and sea, breathing the fragrance of every fleeting flower, and rekindling in the memory every glory of the summer which has departed. When Opis passed through the Piræan gate of the city and entered upon the glorious terrace which surmounted the massive long walls which led to the sea, a new picture was presented to her view. Far away, five

son, to whom, with the Rev. W. Smith and others, I am indebted for translation of Thucydides.

miles from Athens, and yet distinctly visible as she descended the slope, lay the blue sparkling sea. Opis, nurtured among the mountains, had never seen the sea, and this first glimpse was a revelation of a new life.

"Great Neptune, how lovely is thy dwelling-place!" she cried instinctively, to the sad discomfiture of Asahel, who was gradually beginning to perceive that it takes a long time to eradicate heathen customs and ideas. He took no notice of the aspiration, however, but drew the attention of his charge to the walls of Themistocles, upon one of which they were now passing with such ease beneath the shadow of the trees which had been planted upon them. These walls were the wonder of Greece, and Opis looked reverently upon the massive work of those men who had first driven out the Persian from their homesteads and then fortified their city with such firm, enduring workmanship. The mere masonry of the walls was marvellous, but they possessed another beauty now in the numerous equestrian statues and busts of heroes with which they were adorned. Opis was too young to be much interested in the fortifications of the city, and when Asahel pointed out to her notice the wonderful harbours enclosed by walls which formed a secure breakwater, the docks in which unused galleys might be kept in preparation for war, the graving-docks, the regular docks used by merchant vessels and filled with curious ships from all the seaports of the known world—these, together with the large shipbuilding yards, drew no interest or enthusiasm from the young girl, who scanned them with wondering eyes as though they were but a part of some confusion in which she had no part, and from which she longed to escape. Noticing the abstraction of his charge, Asahel led the mule to one of the inns, and then, to the infinite delight of Opis, led her to the strand, where some boats were moored awaiting the arrival of passengers to Salamis or Ægina. Opis thought she had never seen such a lovely sight as she saw upon that shore, where she stood like some child of five years old watching the water ripple in tiny wavelets over the clear sand, advancing and retreating in ever tremulous life. She gathered the lovely shells which had been thrown up by a late storm, and was in a state of ecstasy when she discovered a purple-spined sea-urchin perfect in form and fresh in vivid beauty.

"Would you like to sail with me in one of those boats?" asked Asahel, who was delighted to see the happiness she felt.

"Not to-day, surely; I am half afraid of the sea, although it is far lovelier than I had expected." Then looking up into his face, with strange forgetfulness she said, reverently, "I ought not to go upon the water until I have sacrificed to Neptune—ought I?"

"Listen to me, my dear child," said Asahel, at last roused to speech. "You are in my charge; you rejoiced in the prospect of coming with me, and yet, although I have assured you that there is but one loving and merciful God, the Creator of the heavens, and of the earth, the sea, and all that in them is, you will persist in bringing up all your old terrors of unseen powers to darken and pollute your own soul, and utterly destroy my happiness. Have you forgotten the faith I taught you in Arcadia, the lessons you learned there, Opis? 'The Lord is my light and my salvation; whom shall I fear?'"

"The Lord is the strength of my life, of whom shall I be afraid," responded Opis. Then looking up, she said simply, "Forgive me, dear father; you must forgive me. I said that I would trust you, and I do."

Half-an-hour later Opis was out at sea looking up at Athens and the Athenian rocky citadel above her, and Opis was happy—yes, most truly happy, for, strange to say, Asahel's outspoken words had struck a new chord in the heart of the young girl. It is in truth woman's nature to love the strong voice of command when she feels that command has the sanction of Divine authority; thus the strength of feeling shown for his faith by Asahel infused a new principle into the heart of Opis; that first day in Athens was one upon which she ever afterwards looked back as one of the brightest in her life. Most thoroughly did she enjoy the undulating movement of the boat, and Asahel found an earnest sympathetic listener when he pointed out to her the spot where Aristides sought out the ship of Themistocles on the eve of the eventful battle of Salamis. Up the Saronic Gulf they sailed under a clear blue sky upon a placid sea, the shores on both sides of the gulf presenting a panorama of marvellous beauty. There was the temple-crowned island of Ægina, and there the groves of the Academy, which inspired more peaceful and sacred thoughts than any connected with Salamis or Ægina. Late in the afternoon the boatmen touched the quay at Piræus. While Asahel was preparing to follow Opis from the boat, she heard the boatman ask, "Have you seen the Portent?"

"I thought I saw the meteor last night," replied Asahel.

"I have seen it for these two or three nights brighter and brighter each night. It is an awful Portent, surely!"

"Remember the words of Holy Writ by the prophet: 'Be not dismayed at the signs of the heavens, for the heathen are dismayed at them.' And again: 'Whoso putteth his trust in the Lord, shall abide under the shadow of the Almighty,'" replied Asahel, cheerfully.

"Yes! I am too apt to forget it has been a rare happiness to have seen you to-day, Asahel; it has reminded me of old times: and I, alas! forget my faith too easily."

"Nothing like daily remembrance, Simeon; but come up to my house some evening soon, I have news for you."

"Is that man a Hebrew also?" asked Opis, when Asahel joined her.

"Yes. His grandfather and mine were exiles and slaves together. I have longed to free him, but have never been able hitherto; now, however, I have the means of doing so, and I trust he will be free in a few days."

Opis looked up with an emotion too deep for words into Asahel's face; his was a character she had not been accustomed to contemplate, and it was with a reverence almost religious that she now regarded her adopted father; she said some few words to him, expressive of her feelings, after a while. But he answered very simply—"To relieve my countrymen from slavery is one of the simplest duties of my religion: there is no merit in it."

The ride home in the cool evening was very pleasant; and when supper was over, Asahel led Opis to the roof of the house, and directing her gaze eastward, asked her what she saw?

Far away in the horizon a luminous cloud floated, something globular in shape; it seemed like a restless globe of condensed fire, moving with uncertain movements, and apparently tossed hither and thither, without any wind. While Opis gazed, with half-terrified wonder, sparks were emitted. "Preserve us, O celestial Jupiter, surely thy thunders are about to strike!" she cried earnestly.

"Forgotten again, my child," said Asahel, gently. "Did you not hear me remind Simeon to-day—'Be not dismayed at the signs of the heavens though the heathen be dismayed at them.' That may be a portent of the advent of Him, who has promised to visit us; but, if so, it can be no portent of evil, but a messenger of love to those who love the Lord and wait for His appearing. That may be the lamp which shall precede those, of whom we shall sing—' How beautiful upon the mountains are the feet of those who bring glad tidings;' when 'the glory of the Lord shall be revealed;' when 'He shall feed His flock like a shepherd;' when 'the Lord God shall come with a strong hand, and His arm shall rule for Him;' and 'behold His reward is with Him, and His work before Him.'" Then gently putting his arm round Opis, Asahel turned her towards the west, where Arcturus was setting, and shedding a brilliant light, calm and soft, over the distant waves, while the northern crown glistened in placid beauty above. "No, Lord! we are not dismayed, for Thou only art King. The earth is Thine, and the heavens are the works of Thine hands. No evil can come near us without Thy permission, and even in the valley of the shadow of death I will fear no evil, for Thy rod and Thy staff they comfort me."

That night when Opis retired to rest she did not look through her window, to win the protection of the guardian goddess of Athens. But before she lay down upon her pillow, she commended herself, and all whom she loved, to the care of that Heavenly Father, towards whose holy household Asahel was gently and gradually guiding her lonely soul.

CHAPTER VI.

"Vengeance will sit above our faults; but till
She there do sit,
We see her not, nor them."
—*Dr Donne.*

OPIS was soon very, very happy; her sense of beauty was fully satisfied, and her affectionate heart, although longing at times for news of Nausicaa, was still fully occupied by the new relation which Asahel had assumed towards her. Upon that evening by the sea-side, he seemed at once to have assumed that authority, which was in reality the one great need in the life of poor Opis. From that day her intense longing to enter the Parthenon passed away. At first she assured Doris that when the Lady Androclea came to Athens, they would together offer their sacrifices; but Doris, who had already discovered for herself that no Spartan might enter the sacred precincts, and had been forewarned by Asahel also, now used every effort to divert the mind of her charge from the forbidden subject. And in good truth Athens was filled with subjects and objects quite sufficient to distract the thoughts of even a confirmed monomaniac. The Agora alone was a never failing source of amusement and interest, then there were the delightful walks in the environs of the city —those delightful environs whose beauty still awakens the enthusiasm of every beholder. The flower-perfumed earth; the sea, whose every movement was full of interest to the unaccustomed eyes of Opis; the Attic air, which, we are told, is still unlike all meaner air, and to approach more nearly to the properties of celestial ether than any elsewhere; the groves of the Academy; the slopes of Hymettus—all these sources of enjoyment were free to Opis. The southern suburbs of the city were absolutely free from danger, as far as Sunium; but northward the Spartan lines were now so closely approaching the suburbs, that Attic guards were mounted day and night, and all ingress and egress carefully watched.

In the early days of November Athens was stirred by the news that Darius, the Persian king, was ill— sick unto death, many people said—and speculation was soon busy as to his successor. Cyrus, his younger son, was well known to be favourable to Sparta; the feelings of his brother, Artaxerxes, were not so well known, but all reports agreed in asserting him to be a man of quiet, unambitious temper—one far more likely to leave Grecian affairs to Greek settlement, than any of his predecessors had been. Closely following this report, news arrived that young Cyrus had been summoned to his father's death-bed,

H

and that, before leaving his government at Sardis, he had had a long interview with Lysander, and had not only supplied him with large sums of money, but had also bestowed upon him the tribute of certain cities, to support the Spartan cause—only warning him not to engage the Athenians, unless he was in much stronger force, since a defeat would not only be fatal to Lacedæmon, but to Persian supremacy in Asia also.

This news stirred the heart of Athens to the core, and when once more the Athenian generals sent home for fresh subsidies, fresh recruits, their demands were complied with at once. The war was life or death to Athens now, for all her sons were engaged in the deadly struggle. One day the whole city was aroused by the news that Lysander's fleet was sailing to Decelea to form a junction with King Agis. The walls of the city were manned night and day by excited, restless crowds, but the alarm was short, for almost immediately their own fleet was reported to be in sight, and presently the Spartan armada was seen in full flight, with the fleet of Athens in pursuit.

This event, which had at first created so terrible an alarm, was soon converted by the light-hearted Athenians into a jest; there were plenty of eye-witnesses to the flight of Lysander, as it was called, and but few who knew that he had obtained all he wanted in his interview with King Agis at Decelea. November days dragged heavily on at Athens; the Lady Androclea had arrived, and Asahel, faithful to his promise, took

Opis to visit her. Whose is the fault in such cases?
Is it the fault of the noble countess, who receives the
daughters of some poor gentlemen with such winning
courtesy in the country, that in town she can scarcely
be called her own mistress; and an invitation to some
second-class evening party, some mixed reception, is all
she can be permitted to bestow? The ogre Society has
her in his chains, wife of an English earl though she
may be. No, it is hardly her fault. In the country
she is the central sun of her system, and thus gladly
receives all whom she attracts to move in her own
orbit for good or for evil. In town she is but a
satellite, and is herself drawn in compulsory obedience
round the orbit of her luminary, and woe be to her and
them if she introduces any wandering comets into that
which is her own sphere but by permission. There are
those who say that the poor comets have also orbits,
larger and wider, sometimes, than even central suns.
Nay, some are even daring enough to suppose that
the comet is no wanderer, but a celestial messenger
at home in every sphere, in every orbit of his Divine
Governor.

Thus was it with Asahel; he found himself as
welcome to Androclea in the town as he had been in
the country; and, upon leaving his young charge with
her hostess when she went to spend the day, he perceived nothing of that which froze the enthusiasm of
Opis, and made her unwilling to accept another invitation. Something of this feeling was due of course
to the entire change of thought in the mind of Opis

herself, something to the changed circumstances in which she was now living. Those who return home from their sea-side lodgings must well remember how large and lofty the old familiar rooms look, how difficult it is at first to move easily in them, though you may have inhabited them all your life. It was thus with Opis. She had been brought up in more than the usual comfort and luxury of a Spartan noble's house, her taste had been cultivated from babyhood, and yet no such home as that of Androclea had ever been opened to her, for none such existed in Sparta. The walls painted by the artists of Sicyon, the halls adorned with Phidian statuary, the thalamos carpeted with soft Persian carpets, and furnished with rare taste, where carved ivory couches, embroidered velvet hangings, amber and embossed steel ornaments, met the eye upon all sides. Such luxury alone would have deterred Opis from a wish to spend much time in scenes so apart from her present peasant home, for such in truth Asahel's house appeared. Nor were these the only reasons. In spite of every effort Penelope and Thetis made to renew their first happy intimacy with Opis, a great gulf now lay between them. Do what they would, no efforts of theirs could separate the heart of Opis from Nausicaa, her Spartan fostersister; and now, when the struggle of the long war was so evidently deepening to its last death-grapple, when Athens, when all Attic hearts felt outraged beyond endurance, how could a friend of Spartans expect to find a congenial home in an Athenian household? Lysippus, the bright boy whose adventure with Asahel had led to his introduction to Androclea—Lysippus was now among those who were battling for the honour of Athens against Sparta. He was too young to have served in ordinary times, but had answered the last appeal from Conon, and his services had been accepted; thus Androclea's husband and both her sons were now among those who had taken their lives in their hands, counting death for the freedom of Athens better than an inglorious life of subjection to Sparta and her Persian ally.

For these reasons, the arrival of Androclea and her daughters made little difference in the daily life of Opis. Asahel had induced her to interest herself in his studies; he was an enthusiastic student, and soon communicated some of his interest to Opis. She assisted him to dry and prepare the herbs which she had helped him to gather in Arcadia. Occasionally she went with him to visit some poor patient, and was then enabled to verify for herself the curative effect of the herbs she had prepared. These visits to the poverty-stricken homes of Athens did Opis far more good than did the change of air, or of the scenery around her. Gradually there arose within her heart the Divinely implanted impulse of love, not that selfish love which loves because it is beloved, or hopes to be so—that love so human in its jealousies and ambitions to be first in the affections of its beloved —but the Divine love, which pities, which relieves, which suffers and sacrifices its own enjoyment for the good of the object of its care.

The store which the generosity of Hyllus had placed at her disposal enabled Opis to relieve the necessities of many of the poor around her, and as Doris found amusement in the labours of the loom and the needle, Opis united with her in manufacturing warm clothing for many of the poor wives and children of the men who were on sea or land engaged in the final struggle for the supremacy, the existence of Athenian freedom.

Gershom was so constantly engaged by his master, the physician, that Opis saw little of him during those dark winter months, saving only upon the Sabbaths, when his return made the day the brightest in the week to all, and for him the new delight of receiving a sister's welcome from one so engaging as Opis, the new pleasure of helping his father to render her familiar with their holy law, the happiness of hearing her sweet voice uniting with theirs in Sabbath prayer and praise, was a sustaining happiness through the rest of the week.

Peace reigned supreme in the house of Asahel; but if Opis was thus happy, how was it with Penelope and Thetis? Their time also was fully occupied, for, in addition to their usual fashionable engagements, there were daily sacrifices to be offered for the protection of their beloved ones exposed to such deadly peril. Aristarchus, their father, was at Samos, superintending the supplies needed by Conon for his fleet. Letters passed between the husband and wife with great regularity; for since the battle of Arginusæ Athens had regained her command of the sea, and was thus enabled to protect her communication with the islands. December brought really bitter weather; cold winds blew piteously upon both land and sea. The numerous Leschæ, those public refuges for the houseless, were crowded by day and night with throngs of hungry poor, who had many of them obtained their day's sustenance from the offerings of the wealthy, left upon the outer porch of some temple; now they gathered round the Leschæ fires, supplied by the city, and there talked and gossiped as loungers ever have done, and ever will do.

In the third week of December, a group of men had gathered round one of these Leschæ fires, the cold winds had driven in many who were not houseless, but who were tempted by the bright light and the motley company, who were engaged in settling the affairs of all men and all estates. Now they speculated upon the never-failing subject of conversation, the wonderful meteor, which had shone in the eastern sky—a luminous horror—for seventy-five days. Again the wounded soldiers retailed their experiences of service under Nicias or Alcibiades. The Persian king was dead, and, to the delight of the Athenians, had nominated his son Artaxerxes as his successor. This arrangement was freely canvassed by the frequenters of the Leschæ, for every Athenian felt himself fully qualified to decide upon all public matters. There seemed to be a general opinion among the speakers that the ambition of the younger brother, Cyrus, would never permit him to take the second place.

"One of the two must give way," said a wounded veteran. "In Athens, if one of our members becomes too vigorous and aspiring for the general health, we cramp its energies by the application of a bath of oyster shells. In Persia, they have but one method, and it certainly is more effective; for an Aristides or an Alcibiades may recover from the effects of a few thousand oyster shells, but I never heard of any one emerging from the hands of the chamberlain of the great king."

"True," replied another; "but the question in this case seems to be, Who is the too aspiring member? Must the eldest or the youngest son make the acquaintance of the great chamberlain?"

"No question about the matter at all," replied another, "for Artaxerxes aspires but to rule his own dominions, while Cyrus aspires to add Greece and all her colonies to his empire."

"Then, by Jupiter the Preserver, I pray that his Mithra may lead him swiftly and surely into the domains of the royal chamberlain. Greece, or Athens at least, has suffered enough from Persian ambition already, I should say."

"And I should say," replied another, "that she has suffered enough from her own ambition. Hearken, my friends! if we had not been so anxious for the pre-eminence over Sparta, she would not now have been leagued with Persia to humble us."

"How I loathe to hear you youngsters talking of Spartan ambition and Spartan presumption," growled the veteran. "If you had but been true to Hellas, true to Sparta, as she was to us at Thermopylæ and Platæa, we need have feared no Persian; but Athens has grown into a city of talkers and of boasters; and it is little wonder we are all trembling for the next news from Conon."

"You remind me of something I heard Socrates say," replied the first speaker.

"Aye, and what did he say? He is one of the best of these new-fangled talkers."

"Nay, nay, my master; no words against Socrates in my presence, if you please. Socrates knows how to act, as well as talk. He has fought for Athens as well as you in his day."

"Well, well, let it pass. What did Socrates say?"

"Young Pericles and he were talking one day about the old times and the new, and Pericles said, 'You intimate that honour and virtue are far away from our city, for when will the Athenians reverence their elders as the Spartans do, when they begin even by their own fathers to show disrespect to elder men?'"

"A pretty piece of impertinence from young Pericles," retorted the veteran, "when I remember well how he almost broke his own father's heart by ridiculing him openly, and even affirming in the court that his father, the great statesman, the world-renowned Pericles, spent a whole day with the sophist Protagoras in arguing the question, 'Whether a horse which had been accidentally killed at the public games had been killed by the javelin, or by the man who threw the javelin, or by the judge of the games, who did not prevent the man from throwing the javelin which struck the horse."

"Your memory fails you, my revered friend," said the first speaker haughtily; "that was not young Pericles, but his brother."

"True, true, my friend; I had forgotten, and your story would account for the feelings of Pericles, since he knew how the last days of his father had been embittered by the irreverence of his eldest son."

"It was not only the irreverence of our young Athenians, but their neglect of manly exercises, he deplored, as well as the derision bestowed upon all those who cultivate them. Our want of obedience to the magistrates also he deplored; nay, he said that now we make it our pride to set the magistrates at naught. 'When shall we be of one mind, like the Spartans,' said he."

"Aye, even their kings, sons of Hercules though they be, yet set the people an example of obedience by their own submission to the Ephori."

"Then Pericles said that we are the most envious of each other of all nations under the sun, and that we delight more in lawsuits than any other people. 'The Athenians conduct their affairs as if they were the affairs of some foreign country,' he said. They contest about the management of them, and rejoice, above all things, in having the power to engage in such contests."

"True enough," said several voices.

"And what said Socrates?"

"I do not think I can easily forget his answer to the question of Pericles, which had been, 'By what means could we recover our former dignity?' Socrates said: 'If, then, we wished them to claim property, of which others were in possession, we should most effectively urge them to lay claim to it if we proved that it belonged to their fathers, and was their rightful inheritance; and since we wish that they should strive for pre-eminence in valour, etc., we must show them that such pre-eminence was indisputably theirs of old, and that, if they now exert themselves to recover it, they will be the most powerful of all people.' And again he gave as a reason for our degeneracy that we had grown indolent with excessive exaltation and power; and after attaining great pre-eminence, grew neglectful of themselves, and consequently became degenerate."

"True enough," said a sailor, who had not yet spoken. "If you wish your vessel to anchor safely in haven, you must keep as good a watch at the ending as the beginning of your voyage, nay, rather better, for on the open sea there are but the storms of heaven to battle against, but when you think your toil is over, then there is the hidden rock and the rising shoal."

"But few horses gain the prize more than once. Athens grows old. She has had her prizes. Whose turn will it be next?"

"Athens is no older than Sparta, and not nearly the age of Persia or Egypt; and yet no one talks of their declining power."

"Men and nations are only great when they have faith in noble aims," said the sailor. "Set the light clearly before you to shine upon your chart, and be sure that your light is a true one; and then, though one crew after another may be swept from the deck, so long as there is a man on deck capable of seeing the light on the shore and the light on the chart, your ship is safe. It is only when a man steers by the lights of the Syrens that he is wrecked."

There was a young boy listening eagerly to the conversation of these men. The heavy rain beating pitilessly without, had driven him under cover; and gradually drawing nearer and nearer to the fire, he had escaped notice crouching among his elders, and eagerly drinking in every word. As soon as the sailor had finished speaking, however, he was discovered, and at once seized upon in the true spirit of loungers for torment.

"You presumptuous young ape, how came you in here among your elders and betters? Pay your ransom money. What can you do? Dance, or sing, or leap through the hoops?"

The child raised himself to his full height; and looking haughtily into the eyes of his questioner, replied, with kindling eyes, "Talkers and boasters you are, and ever will be; your fathers, and your sons, and brothers, are battling on the waves for you and yours, and yet you can do nothing better than ask me to dance or to sing for you?"

"You little rebel, are you one of those who are learning irreverence for your elders. Dance or sing, I said; and dance or sing you shall."

"Leave me alone. Touch me at your peril," shrieked the child. "Is Athens to be disgraced by such as you?" and he stamped his foot angrily.

The man, thoroughly aroused, now pursued the child from the Leschæ into the street, the boy, overwrought by the conversation he had heard, calling loudly upon Athena to protect her children, when suddenly the clouds seemed to part. There was a rush of flame through the eastern sky; lower and lower it descended, and then sank behind the Acropolis, as though it were sinking into the sea. The meteor, which had been visible for seventy-five days, had fallen at Ægospotami, near to the Bosphorus.

A few days after the fall of the meteor, Thetis was unrobing herself. She had sent her attendant to bed, since she had wished to be alone, to finish the long letter she was writing to Lysippus. The letter had been long finished; but a strange restless feeling seemed to drive away all wish to retire to rest. At length, instead of disrobing entirely, she threw a loose gown over her shoulders, and ascended to the

as
cla
and
which was t......
pressed in the tightly clasped hands —
ing beads of the sisters, who reclined ......
......bler and more disciplined ......
In a few moments the ......

as still attired in the peculiar
ed those who served the sacred
us sanction assisted Androclea
with more courage than she
one. The boy advanced very
h upon which the ladies were
ating a ring to Androclea, said
your son, Glaucon, to bring
s assurance that, in life or
forget your teachings or your

psed before Androclea could
e she held her son's ring; but

see, you know, that we thank
ot leave us yet. Tell us how it
first if Lysippus lives."
tell," replied the youth. "Of
nothing; but Glaucon might have
w, if he had chosen. We were to-
aralus' when he saw his friend Alexius
ree Spartans. Glaucon at once took
ve me the message I have delivered,
overboard, swam to the assistance of his
commander was resolute in his obedi-
e orders of Conon, and therefore sailed
was ordered to my post, and saw no more
n. As to Lysippus, I am not sure that he
nos. I know that Conon commanded his
Aristarchus, to stay there until his return; Sure
mmar

roof of the houses, and endeavoured to regain some of that calm serenity which belongs of right to the hour of nature's rest. The December sky was brilliant with pure starry light, and the heavens seemed full of an unusual peace and beauty, as though they were rejoicing in the absence of that fiery neighbour which had troubled the repose of Athens for so long a time. Far above Thetis rose the snowy columns of the Parthenon, while the starlight just glinted and glistened upon the spear and crested helmet of Athena. Below lay the long walls; and Thetis, looking on through the faint light, could almost fancy that she saw the sea; but there was no moon, the air was still and quiet. Yes! all was quiet externally; but why was it that the heart of Thetis throbbed with such a strange foreboding terror? She could not overcome it, and at last became sensible that there was in reality some external reason for her horror. Suddenly she became aware of a strange wailing sound, which seemed to proceed from the Piræus. Nearer and nearer it approached. A faint horror scarcely rising above the breath of the moving air, and yet quite apart from it—a certain and a terrible wail of human misery.

Scarcely able to stand, Thetis crouched upon the parapet of the roof, and listened eagerly. She soon became conscious of the approach of men up the long walls, not as though they were aroused to repel invasion, but as though they were repeating some awful tidings to fresh listeners at every step;

and at every nearer approach that awful wail of horror was swelled in depth of intensity and of agony.

Unable to endure her misery any longer, Thetis rushed to her mother's chamber, but she met her and Penelope on the stairs. No words were spoken, together they descended to the street, and there stood in the portico of the house, trembling, yet finding support in attempting to support each other.

At last the wailing, sobbing crowd approached, passing on towards the house of the Archon Alexius. Penelope rushed out, leaving Thetis to support their mother. "What is it?" were the only words she could utter. She was not recognised in the darkness, so the answer was clear and full:

"All is lost at Ægospotami. Lysander has taken all our galleys but eight, and will massacre every man he has taken."

CHAPTER VII.

> " Thrice is he armed that hath his quarrel just,
> And he but naked, though locked up in steel,
> Whose conscience with injustice is corrupted."
> —*Shakespeare.*

PENELOPE sank senseless upon the ground, so soon as those terrible words were spoken; while her mother and sister, who ran to her assistance, heard the woeful tidings from others. But no one of the large crowd stayed to wail for their sorrow; they were supported into the house by their servants, who were now eagerly thronging through every passage. The whole city was soon aroused, and in truth there was a great cry from Athens— weeping and lamentation sounded on every side— until at last the streets were deserted, and each family mourned apart until morning dawned. There was, indeed, scarcely one house in Athens which had not at least one member in that doomed army; and the women and children gathered together in almost speechless agony, or endeavoured to alleviate the sufferings of some more especially bereaved member.

Women's tears were not the only ones shed that night. Lamentation for the dead was not the only sorrow. No! the shadow of Nemesis brooded, with heavy wings, over each Athenian heart, for the forerunners of national retribution seemed already to have entered into the city.

Long before day-dawn the chief men of the city were assembling in each other's houses, and although they spoke only of the measures to be proposed in council for securing the city from the victorious Lysander, yet vividly present to every heart was the memory of the insults and the injuries inflicted upon her weaker neighbours by Athens in her hour of sovereign supremacy.

Ægina and her expelled inhabitants, the Thebans, the Scionæans, the Andrians, and the Corinthians—all rose up before awakened conscience to add to the terror of the night. Thebes was inveterate in her hatred, Megara in hers, for each state had been grievously oppressed by Athens, while she had the power to do so. And now, to whom must they turn for help? Argos alone could be relied upon, and Argos could not defend herself.

In the hour of adversity men naturally turn to the consolation of faith in the Divine power; but to the heathen mind defeat, disaster, or an inauspicious omen, was a sign of Divine displeasure. And the messengers, who brought the news of the defeat, affirmed that they had seen the twin-gods, the guardian deities of Sparta, alight upon Lysander's vessel, when he advanced to the assault. Two bright stars of light had clearly proclaimed the presence of the immortal twins, and proved that the Spartans were fighting under celestial protection. Thus even the consolations of Heaven seemed to be taken away from the citizens of the most superstitious city in Greece; and it was with beating hearts they asked each other the question—"What will Sparta exact in the hour of her triumph? Will she expel the citizens from their beloved city, as they had so frequently expelled others; or would she avenge the defeat at Arginusæ, by the decimation of Attic nobility, the destruction of Attic freedom?" There was no more sleep that night at Athens.

The cocks were just beginning to announce the late day-dawn, when a servant entered Androclea's chamber, and informed her that a young sailor, from the "Paralus" (the sacred galley which had brought the news to Athens), was waiting below, and wished to know whether she was able to receive his message.

Both mother and daughters at once started to their feet, and all trace of weakness seemed to disappear, as they walked towards the reception-room. Androclea seated herself upon a couch between Penelope and Thetis, and the only trace of the deep emotion which was trembling through every vein, was expressed in the tightly clasped hands, and the drooping heads of the sisters, who reclined against their nobler and more disciplined mother.

In a few moments the stranger entered; he was

a mere youth, and was still attired in the peculiar garb which distinguished those who served the sacred galley; and this religious sanction assisted Androclea perhaps to receive him with more courage than she otherwise could have done. The boy advanced very slowly towards the couch upon which the ladies were seated, and then presenting a ring to Androclea, said simply: "I promised your son, Glaucon, to bring this to you, with his assurance that, in life or death, he would never forget your teachings or your love."

Some moments elapsed before Androclea could muster her voice, while she held her son's ring; but at length she spoke:

"Be seated. You see, you know, that we thank you, but you must not leave us yet. Tell us how it happened. Tell me first if Lysippus lives."

"That I cannot tell," replied the youth. "Of Lysippus I know nothing; but Glaucon might have been with me now, if he had chosen. We were together on the 'Paralus' when he saw his friend Alexius engaged with three Spartans. Glaucon at once took off this ring, gave me the message I have delivered, and leaping overboard, swam to the assistance of his friend. Our commander was resolute in his obedience to the orders of Conon, and therefore sailed away. I was ordered to my post, and saw no more of Glaucon. As to Lysippus, I am not sure that he left Samos. I know that Conon commanded his father, Aristarchus, to stay there until his return; and as Lysippus had been assisting his father on shore, I believe—I dare not say certainly—but I never once saw him in the fleet after we left Samos; so I believe that he was not with us."

"Then we have been deceiving ourselves, and, after all, our beloved ones may still be safe," said Thetis joyfully. The youth was silent.

"Now tell us how it happened, for our beloved Athens has suffered, if we have been spared. We must not forget the certain dead in the renewed hope for ourselves," said Androclea.

"I can tell you but of our own movements, lady," replied the youth. "After Lysander had taken Cedræ, and sold its inhabitants into slavery, Conon steered for Samos, where three fresh generals were chosen— Tydeus, Menander, and Cephisodotus. At length we heard that Lysander, after pillaging all our merchant vessels and the cities of our allies, had taken Lampsacus by storm, plundered the place, and found a rich store of provisions for his fleet. When our generals heard of this, they at once put to sea, following him; and at length we cast anchor at Ægospotami. We had a hundred and eighty ships, all well manned, but not well provisioned. Lysander was anchored just opposite to us, on the other side of the Hellespont. On the day after our arrival, at sunrise, our generals gave the signal, and we were drawn up, ready for action, opposite Lysander. The straits being but about two miles across, we waited, and we waited, but Lysander would not engage, his maxim being, it seems, that 'where the lion's skin fails, it must be eked out with that of the fox.' After waiting all day, and finding that the enemy would not fight, our generals gave the order to retire; and we, hungry and weary with repressed excitement, had to forage for our suppers, Sestos, the nearest city where we could buy food, being fully two miles away from the ships. This scene happened every day for four days, but upon the second or third day Alcibiades, who is living in his splendid castle near Sestos, during his exile, came down to our camp, and in his interview with our generals, assured them that in spite of Athenian ingratitude, his heart was still in Athens; her disgrace or suffering would be his also; and for the sake of their common country and kindred blood, he implored them to remove the fleet to Sestos, where it would be sheltered in harbour, and the crews be within easy reach of provisions, thus avoiding the risk of leaving the vessels unmanned before such a perfidious enemy as Lysander. However, it is written, that 'Whom the gods wish to destroy, they first deprive of reason.' It is said that Conon would have taken his advice, but Philocles, Menander, and Tydeus refused to listen to his counsel, assuring him that the fleet was under their orders now, not under his. I saw Alcibiades as he left the camp, and his magnificent face was all clouded over, his head bowed down upon his shoulders, so that he seemed a full cubit less than when he entered the camp; but bent down and sorrowful as he looked, we youngsters were rejoicing in having seen that 'the darling of Athens' looked worthy of his name."

"O Athena, preserve us from thy tongue, boy. Do we sit here to listen to your praises of Alcibiades?" said Thetis, passionately.

"Forgive me," said the startled youth. "And yet, young lady, if you had so sorrowful a history to tell, you would be in no hurry to tell it yourself."

"You do but tell us what has been; the evil is past, we cannot now avert it," said Penelope, aroused at last to speak.

"Our beloved Glaucon is not the only one for whose fate we are still anxious," said Androclea, gravely. "We thank you more than I can tell, but although I can well understand your dislike to narrating the history of our defeat, yet if you can do so briefly, we shall be under a deeper obligation."

"Upon the fifth day, at sunrise, lady, we once more put up our parapets, and drew up in battle array, the Lacedæmonians doing the same; and gibes and taunts flew pretty sharply about. Now some of us had noticed that every day after we returned to our station we were watched by the crews of some small pinnaces sent out by the fox. Upon that fifth day, Glaucon was upon the 'Paralus' with me; Conon, our beloved admiral, was upon his galley, close to ours. The crew of the admiral's ship had not fully dispersed, for he had been very careful in provisioning his men; Glaucon and I were looking over the side of the galley, watching the pinnace returning as usual to give Lysander notice that we had disembarked, when suddenly we saw a bright brazen shield hoisted to the masthead of every pinnace, which, instead of returning as usual to the fleet, stayed midway in the strait. Glaucon instantly suspected something unusual, and reported what he had seen to our superior officer, who at once sent him off to report what he had seen to Conon. I was sent with him. Conon at once sounded the alarm, and summoned his men, but before we had returned to the 'Paralus,' we saw the Lacedæmonian fleet in full sail, bearing down upon us. O lady, if you had but seen that terrible sight! if you had but felt that hour of anguish and despair! Most of our men were out of the ships—some at Sestos, some asleep, some cooking their supper, but not half a quarter upon their ships. By the efforts of Conon, some seven or eight ships were at last got into working order—that was all! Eight and the 'Paralus' out of one hundred and eighty!

"Lysander's large fleet was well manned by soldiers who were well paid, well fed, flushed with their late victory over Lampsacus, and fired by the certain and easy prey which lay before them upon the beach of Ægospotami. There was no fight, strictly speaking; it was a mere massacre of unarmed men, and a capture of unmanned vessels. Conon gathered his eight consorts round him, and led us to Lampsacus, where he helped himself to some of Lysander's sailing tackle, of which our ships stood in sore need, then he sailed off with his war-ships to Cyprus, where he trusts to find shelter for his crews from King Evagoras, but he sent the 'Paralus' home at once to bring the news." Here the youth bowed his head, as though overcome with agony, and cried out bitterly, "Oh, woe is me, woe is me that I should have to bring such tidings back from my first voyage."

Androclea rose, and placing her hand gently upon his head said, tenderly, "You have brought me good tidings, dear boy. Is it nothing that you and my Glaucon were kept free from those sins of negligence and recklessness which have brought about this catastrophe? Is it nothing to have lightened a mother's heart by assuring her that living or dead, her son has been true to his trust? Sparta is not alone in having mothers who refuse to shed tears over the grave of a faithful warrior. I shall shed no more tears for my Glaucon, and you, I hope, have still a long life before you in which you must help to redeem Athens from the sins which have destroyed her." Androclea stood for a few moments in thought, looking down upon the ring of her beloved son, then suddenly taking the hand of the youth, she said, "There, we have all many and precious memorials of our Glaucon; his memory and his message can never die out of his mother's heart; but you, who knew him for so short a time, must have some token which shall incite you to his nobility and fidelity in the future. Take this, and with it a mother's thanks, a mother's blessing."

The youth looked up with joyful eyes, half wet with tears, "Ah, lady, but it is robbing you."

"You cannot rob me of the memory of my son, but you can strive to resemble him; and now you must tell me your name, for I shall want to see my boy's ring sometimes, and you must bring it here to show me, and tell me of your own welfare."

"My name is Codrus, my mother is the daughter of Nicias, and my father Theron of Sunium."

"Then you must introduce me to them if they permit you, for I shall be honoured by their acquaintance. It was very kind of you to come here before you went to your own home."

Penelope had been listening eagerly to every word, but seemed unable to speak, or even to move from her drooping posture; but as her mother turned to resume her seat, a thought seemed to strike Penelope, the colour flushed once more into her lips and pallid cheeks, and, advancing to Codrus, who was leaving the room, she said, "Did you not say that eight ships escaped? Do you know—can you tell me who escaped in these ships?"

"Let me see," said the youth, brightening up with the thought that he might relieve the anxiety of others, "There was Nicodemus of Samos and young Polycrates, then there was Euthydemus, son of Menares, and Lysicrates of Thoricus, and Cimon of Anaphlystus."

"O Athena, best beloved, thou faithful protectress of all true votaries, I thank thee."

The youth looked up, but understood at once, and simply saying, "I am thankful that I have brought some good news to your home, lady," he turned once more to the door, but Androclea stayed him.

"You must not leave us without taking refreshment."

"Without any further loss of time, lady, I promised to return at once, and must obey orders."

"Then, remember my mother's bidding concerning the ring," said Thetis. "We shall all wish to see it often."

"I believe she grudges me her mother's gift," said the youth, as he strode swiftly back to Piræus; "but, O Glaucon, brave heart, I will be true to your memory, and Sparta shall yet rue the day when she set a fox in a lion's skin over her fleet."

When the late cold winter's sun shone brightly over the city, it shone upon a thronging multitude, all surging towards the Pnyx. Already the heralds had summoned a council, and thousands of citizens, young and old, were hurrying to bear their part in it, or to gain the first news of its decision. Asahel had heard the terrible news almost as soon as it had arrived, and had, after some hesitation, determined to tell all to Opis at once. She shed abundance of tears, but these he had rejoiced to see, for he had feared some return of her old painful frenzy. There was, however, now no contest in the heart of Opis; she had surrendered herself fully to the Divine Spirit for which she had prayed, and in her case it had been the contest between life and death, love and hatred, which had convulsed her weak frame—now love had fully taken possession of her soul, and she was at rest. After the first shock of sorrow for the lost, the first thought of Opis had been of Nausicaa, and a thrill of joy passed through her heart when she felt that Nausicaa would suffer no pain from the event; her next thought, however, was one of sorrow for those around her, those poor pensioners of hers in the city, who were so anxiously awaiting the return of some father, son, husband, or brother, from the doomed fleet.

"I grieve for the Lady Androclea," said Asahel; "she must be in sore anguish of heart, not only for her husband and eldest son, but for that Lysippus, whom you saw; such a bright promising youth as he seemed to be—a sunbeam in his mother's house, and a well-spring of gladness to her heart, I could well perceive that he was."

"I will go to her at once, if I may, Asahel."

"Most assuredly, my child; I will take you there myself."

Thus, while the women of the city were receiving visits of condolence and sympathy, the men were debating anxiously the best measures to be adopted for the general preservation. It was at last determined to block up all the harbours but one. Lysander's fleet should gain no entrance, if it were possible to prevent it, and steps were instantly taken to fulfil this duty. The walls, which Themistocles had built in defiance of Spartan jealousy, were still strong, and in perfect repair; but these must be more efficiently guarded, both by day and by night, since the Spartan army, under King Agis, was sure to follow up the advantage gained at sea.

All was now anxious, busy life and stir in the bereaved city. A siege was certainly foreseen, and every precaution taken to enable the inhabitants to endure it. The news had spread swiftly through the night, and from all the surrounding villages families now arrived, seeking protection within the walls. In the course of a few days, and before the harbours were fully blocked up, there were fresh arrivals by sea, and the council would gladly have refused these new arrivals shelter, but knew not how to do so, since they were refugees from the islands and the Ionian colonies, who had been driven out by the Spartans, and their lives but spared, on condition that they went to Athens, and nowhere else. Thus it was evident that Lysander's subtle plan was, by overcrowding the doomed city, to render a prolonged resistance impossible; he had enlisted famine as a certain ally. These fresh arrivals brought news of the fate of the three thousand Athenian prisoners taken by Lysander at Ægospotami.

After that fatal engagement, which had lasted but one hour, Lysander plundered the Athenian camp, erected trophies, then fastening the captured ships to his own, he sailed for Lampsacus, his fleet resounding with the music of flutes and triumphal songs. Upon arriving at Lampsacus, a tribunal was erected, and a council of the allies held, to decide the fate of the prisoners. At this council, Sparta was not the chief accuser; the allies had each some mortal crime committed by Athens against them, to object against her in her hour of trial. The Corinthians and Andrians, in addition to other crimes of the fallen enemy, declared that, but a short time ago, Philocles the Athenian general had captured two galleys—one from Andros, and one from Corinth—and that, contrary to all usage among polished Greeks, he had thrown the crews down a precipice. Every state had some sin to object against the enemy; but the latest order of the united Athenian admirals seemed to be the one which decided the fate of the prisoners, since it was not aimed at Corinth, or at Sparta, at Thebes, or Megara, but at all. It was proved that, at Lampsacus, all the admirals they had captured (excepting Adimantus, who had opposed the decree) had decreed that every prisoner taken in the next engagement should have the thumb of his right hand cut off, to prevent his ever being able to handle an oar or draw a sword. The half-drowned, who return to life, assure us that, in the final moment of consciousness, every event, every sin of their lives, flashed in vivid flame before the judgment-seat of conscience.

It was thus with the Athenian generals and their fellow-prisoners; they had to listen to the recital of their sins against the opposing states, and then to find that the resolution to put them to death was unanimous, Adimantus, the general who had opposed the horrible decree for the mutilation of the prisoners, being the only exception made. Mercy was shown to him, as he had pleaded for mercy for others. Lysander asked Philocles, what he thought he deserved, who could propose such a barbarous decree.

"Do not start a question when there is no judge to decide it," was the haughty reply; "but proceed at once, as you would have been proceeded against, had you been conquered."

Speaking thus, and arrayed in his most magnificent dress, Philocles led the van of the long procession, which, bending before the axe of the executioner of the allied states of Greece, did in reality close the long contest of the Peloponnesian war.

About a week after the arrival of the "Paralus," Androclea received the following letter:

"MY OWN DEAR MOTHER,—How can I bear to write to you? I do not know, yet my father has commanded me to do so, and I must; he is unable to write, as he is occupied night and day. There are two parties in the island—one wishing to give it up to the Lacedæmonians, without any contest; the other, determined to oppose them to the death. My father will stay so long as there is the least prospect of our preserving it for Athens, but desires me to assure you that he will not rashly risk your happiness. If he finds it impossible to keep Samos for Athens, he will return to you at once, or go to Cyprus. For me, my father has permitted me to place myself under the orders of Conon at once. I sail for Cyprus to-morrow, and will not leave Conon until I have, under him, effaced some of the shame and misery of Ægospotami from off the banners of our fleet. I cannot yet bear to speak of our Glaucon, or even to write of him to you, my dear mother, who know well what he was to me, his careless younger brother. O my mother, I will strive to resemble him; but some years will have to pass before I can speak of him.

"Tell Penelope that Cimon is safe; he is constantly engaged with my father; and tell Thetis that she must look well after my dogs and hawks now, for it will be long, long before I see them again. And for you, my mother, what message can I send you? Only one, that I will strive, in life or in death, to prove myself worthy of your love and your teaching.—Written from Samos, by your son, LYSIPPUS."

A short time after Androclea had received this letter, Athens was stirred by the certain news that Lysander was bearing down upon the city, with his fleet of two hundred galleys.

CHAPTER VIII.

> "The trumpet's voice hath roused the land,
>   Light up the beacon pyre;
> A hundred hills have seen the brand,
>   And waved the sign of fire.
> A hundred banners to the breeze
>   Their gorgeous folds have cast;
> And hark! was that the sound of seas?
>   A king to war went past."
>
> —*Felicia Hemans.*

WHILE Opis was thus gaining strength of mind and body, amid the expiring throes of Athenian supremacy and the troubled hearts of Athens, Nausicaa was pursuing her usual avocations in her mountain-girded home, all sense of loneliness, which she might otherwise have felt in the absence of Opis, being overpowered by the sense of relief from the terrible anxiety which her malady had occasioned during the past year. Hyllus was more than usually occupied. He was absorbed in some new studies, for his friend Nicodemus of Chios had sent him a book upon the subject of the heavenly bodies, and the cause of their luminous appearance.

This book he had written with the purpose of debating the theory of Anaxagoras the philosopher, who proposed that the stars were created of a stony substance, that they were heavy, and in themselves had no light, but simply reflected the light of the ether by which they were surrounded. He also taught that the stars were not stationary, but were carried and kept in their orbits by the rapid motions of the heavens. This theory Nicodemus wished Hyllus to consider. Also, to consider the opinion of Socrates the Athenian, who did not exactly affirm but suggested that the earth upon which we live is but a sediment from the ether; that we live in a hollow of the true earth, but imagine we live upon its surface, just as the inhabitants of the sea might suppose themselves to be living upon the surface. The real earth being pure, is situated in the pure heavens (Socrates supposes), in which are the stars.

Now, the question Nicodemus wished Hyllus to consider was this: "What is this pure ether (so called)? From whence does it derive the light which Anaxagoras supposes the brilliant stars to reflect? and what does he mean by the rapid motions of the heavens? Does he mean that the ether has a motion of its own, which impels the stars in their courses? For Socrates says, 'For the earth itself being pure is situated in the pure heavens, in which are the stars, and which most persons, who are accustomed to speak about such things, call ether.'"

"What is this ether, my friend?" wrote Nicodemus,

"and from whence does it derive its luminosity and motion?"

These speculations of Anaxagoras and Socrates had served to stimulate the active mind of Hyllus to many experiments; and he was taking notes of these experiments upon air and its properties, light and its effect upon non-luminous bodies, in order that he might aid in verifying the speculations of his friend. In fact, it is just possible that if the lives of some of the philosophers of those days had been prolonged, some of the most recent discoveries of these days might have been forestalled.

These studies of Hyllus were lightened by his fatherly care for Nausicaa. He never suffered a day to pass without spending some hours in her company, either instructing her in some one of the many languages he had mastered, imparting some elementary scientific knowledge, or taking her long walks through the woods or up the mountain paths.

One afternoon late in December, Hyllus proposed a walk through the forest to the temple of Diana. This was a small temple which had been erected by the piety of one of his ancestors before the death of his father. Hyllus had, upon the anniversary of its dedication, joined in the hunting party and sacrifices with which the day was honoured; but during his Eastern travels, this custom was broken through, and he had never resumed it. Upon the dedication feast, his steward presided over the hunt, and offered the sacrifice on his behalf, distributing also the supply of food and wine, with which the guests who attended the feast were regaled; but for many years Hyllus had never been present at these festivals, nor had he yet taken his daughter to witness the ceremonies.

Although Nausicaa had never seen the temple upon its festal day, she loved it as a second home, and was always welcomed by the attendant priestess with a mother's welcome. The father and daughter frequently walked to this lovely spot, and either in the flush of summer or the gloom of winter it was always a favourite walk. Upon this December afternoon the wild-flowers, which Nausicaa delighted to gather, that she might question Leda the priestess concerning their names and properties, were now withered or dead, but the pines were in full perfection, clothed in their warm and richly-perfumed dress. Where the denser forest opened upon some sheltered glade, herds of deer appeared grazing in perfect security, and delighting Nausicaa by their graceful movements. Once or twice her father summoned the attendant Helot, and taking a javelin hurled it towards some unguarded stag; but upon that afternoon his aim was not true, and no booty rewarded his exertions from among the deer, although a hare and some partridges prevented his feeling that his walk had been without some fruit. The temple itself was but small, yet it was perfect in its simplicity. The enclosure in which it stood was cultivated with the greatest care. Fruit trees were planted in the sacred enclosure, and there, in its proper season, might be seen every fruit indigenous or cultivated in Greece. Flowers bloomed even in December round this lovely shrine of the huntress goddess, so carefully were they tended by the loving fingers of her priestess. Before the entrance of the sacred enclosure stood a white marble pillar, upon which was engraven in coloured letters an inscription somewhat similar to that which Xenophon inscribed upon the entrance to his votive temple: "This ground is sacred to Diana. He that possesses and reaps the fruits of it is to offer every year a tenth of its produce, and to keep the temple in repair from the residue. If any one fail to perform these conditions, the goddess will take notice of his neglect." Passing through the dark pine forest, this white marble pillar was the first sacred object seen through the living vista. After a short time the temple itself appeared, a bright and lovely spot amid the darkness by which it was surrounded.

"Do you perceive—have you ever noticed, my Nausicaa, that at the distance we now are from the temple, it appears no larger than the mausoleum of Iphicrates?"

"Often, dear father; and I questioned Leda as to the cause, and she said that distance always lessens objects."

"True, my child. Then ask yourself what must be the size of those celestial luminaries which seem no larger upon the loftiest summit of the loftiest mountain-range than in the lowliest valley. If I am distant from Mount Olympus or Mount Æta but two parasangs, they seem to be tiny elevations, but when I approach more nearly, they cover a third of the horizon. It is not thus with the heavenly bodies; they are the same—ever the same—upon the mountain height, or in the deepest depths. Ever the same, never revealing their nature to man, but ever tempting him to fruitless speculation."

Poor Nausicaa was sorely puzzled sometimes by these flights of her father.

Speculation destroyed the pleasure, the consolation of her faith in the histories of Leda, for one of the chief interests Nausicaa found in her visits to Leda was the listening to her recitals of the histories of the heroes. Surely it was far pleasanter to believe that the lovely Hyades which shone so brightly in the winter sky were the seven loving sisters of Hyas, who, having wept themselves to death with sorrowing over their lost brother, were translated by Jupiter to the home of the immortals, a bright diadem upon the forehead of the celestial Taurus. Andromeda, and Cassiopea, with the mighty hunter Orion, — were these living immortals to be dethroned, and even the celestial twins to be degraded into stony matter, not luminous, but reflecting the light of the ether?

Nausicaa frequently sighed over these illusions, and felt an instinctive dislike to the false friends of her father, who could thus tempt him to turn to dull earth and cold matter the heroes and heroines of her early faith. Nausicaa was, however, a Spartan, and that one word implied true reverence for age and all

150 *A STORY OF ANCIENT GREECE.*

parental care, so she made no reply to her father's remarks, not daring to say how repulsive she felt them, but simply saying, "I will warn Leda of your approach, dear father," ran forward.

The door of the temple was open, but the young girl did not venture to enter until she had uttered a devout invocation to the divine huntress; she then proceeded to the interior, from whence a woman in the prime of life soon issued, in answer to her summons, and received her with a warm embrace.

"Dear Leda, my father is with me; come out and bid him welcome."

The patron, for whose welfare Leda offered daily sacrifice, was received with all honour by the priestess, but in a few minutes she left them, saying to Nausicaa, "I have something of rare value to present to you, dear Nausicaa, from my protecting guardian at Athens."

"A letter from Opis," cried Nausicaa, eagerly, and in a few minutes her supposition was confirmed, for Leda entered, bearing a packet for Nausicaa, with an enclosure from Asahel to Hyllus. Nausicaa tore open her letter, and was soon eagerly and delightedly reading the vivid description Opis gave of her journey, and her happy home in Athens. Hyllus, however, could not resist a slight temptation before breaking his seal, and looking up with a strange smile, he said, "I suppose I must look upon these letters as lawful plunder from Athens, nd not imagine that my old friend Leda is in correspondence with the enemy."

"Diana knows how to bestow favours upon such

'A letter from Opis,' cried Nausicaa, eagerly; and in a few minutes her supposition was confirmed, for Leda entered, bearing a packet for Nausicaa.—HEROES OF ANCIENT GREECE, p. 150.

true votaries as Hyllus and his daughter; and they must not inquire too closely into the means she employs, lest she resent the insult," said the priestess, gravely. Then turning to Nausicaa, she said, "I also have had a letter from the dear child. Is it not a happiness that she is recovering?"

Very soon Leda and Nausicaa had exchanged their letters, and were comparing notes and rejoicing together over the evident improvement in the health of Opis. While Hyllus sat apart rejoicing in Asahel's letter, in which, although there was no political news, yet there was much of interest, both in his account of the kindness of the Lady Androclea and of the happy effects of the Arcadian journey upon the health of Opis, with some reference to the scientific questions which were causing so much speculation among the sages of Greece.

"You spoke just now, Leda, of the power of your goddess. If Diana would but reveal some of her celestial secrets, she should have no more devoted worshipper than Hyllus of Sparta."

"The gods ever reveal themselves to those who seek them faithfully," replied the priestess.

"Well said, my honoured Leda. Diana has in you, at least, a faithful seeker and devout worshipper. Tell me what she says to the doctrine of Anaxagoras. Is the home over which she presides in the waxing and waning influence of the crescent moon, but of a stony substance, receiving light from the ever-present ever-moving ether? or is it not? Tell me what answer the goddess gives when next I visit you."

"I can answer you from my own judgment now," said Leda, "and if I am favoured with deeper knowledge, you, Hyllus, have the right to claim it. Living here as I live, alone amid the deepening forest, with no constant companion but the goddess, no friends for weeks together but the Nymphs and the Dryads, I have, as in duty bound, made the changing phases of the home of my deity my constant study; and I should say that Anaxagoras must be wrong undoubtedly, since that which grows, which increases or diminishes at certain and stated times, must have life. That there is a world or store-house of stony matter in the celestial ether no one can doubt, for have not fragments been repeatedly cast upon this earth? but these are dark, not luminous. Now, the celestial illuminations, we have been taught—and I see no reason to doubt the truth—are simply due to the presence of the deities or the immortals. Thus, when Diana is in her full glory, the whole of her house is irradiated with light, then the sea rises as in adoration of her glory, flowers bloom and fruits ripen. These things I have seen; they are not speculations like those of Anaxagoras."

Nausicaa looked at her father. Would he not now be convinced of the folly, not to say wickedness, of his new friends? But Hyllus folded up his letter very calmly, simply saying, "I wish that I could see Asahel again. He has a way of looking at these things with clearer eyes and a higher light than we can ever attain to. Nausicaa, my child, we must be returning home. I wish that I could take you to Athens to see Opis; but we must ask Leda to sacrifice unceasingly for the victory of Lysander, then peace will come, and we shall be happy once more."

It was late when Hyllus and Nausicaa returned home. Their house was so situated that they did not need to pass through the city to regain it, but as they neared the road which led to the Skias, they were astonished to hear the sound of glad acclamations. Already a triumphal festival had commenced, for the messages sent by Lysander with news of his victory had spread so swiftly, that although but three days had elapsed since the engagement, the welcome news was now speeding from lip to lip, and the air was filled with gladness and rejoicing. In Athens there was weeping and wailing among the women, and despairing obstinate resistance in the hearts of the men; but in Sparta the lyre and the flute sounded through the streets, the citizens were adorning themselves with chaplets, and all were preparing to unite in the sacred triumphal solemnities.

The assembly at which the glad news of the victory was officially announced was crowded with an exultant throng, each one of whom considered himself personally a victor in the victory of Lysander. Then King Pausanias led the way, followed by a long train of flower-garlanded sacrifices and chaplet-crowned people, to return thanks and thank-offerings to the twin gods, whose aid had crowned the Spartan arms with triumph.

Almost immediately following the news of the victory, messengers arrived from King Agis, announcing his intention of blockading Athens by land, while Lysander commanded the sea, and summoning the Lacedæmonians and allies to join him at once before the walls of Athens. A levy was instantly made. Every man capable of bearing arms in Lacedæmonia or the allied states at once prepared to complete the work which Lysander had commenced, and Hyllus prepared to take his place in the army with a joyful, hopeful heart.

The first flush of gratified national feeling soon passed from the heart of Nausicaa, and her affectionate imagination was vividly engaged in picturing the miseries which awaited the people of Athens, and possibly even Opis herself. "Promise me, dear father," she said, on the evening before his departure, "that your voice shall always be raised on the side of mercy for Athens. To-day Gogo, the daughter of Eumolpus, said that her father intends to vote not only for the demolition of the walls of Athens, but for selling the inhabitants into slavery and razing the whole city to the ground. You, my father, will not forget Salamis, and our once happy united Greece; you will not blot out Athens from the lists at the Olympic."

Hyllus kissed his daughter tenderly. "Do not fear for your father, my child. I have not forgotten, and am not likely to forget our ancestors, our common

Hellas. Athens is in truth the eye of Greece still, but she has become diseased by selfishness and pride for so long a time that she has looked not for the well-being of Greece but for her own selfish aggrandisement. If you knew a little more of medicine, my Nausicaa, you would know that there is a disease which covers the eye with a scale or skin; the suffering patient can no more look abroad upon others and their welfare when thus diseased, but if the scale be removed, the eye sees clearly, and is useful to its owner and to others. Have faith, my Nausicaa, that I at least go to Athens but to remove this scale from the eye of our beloved Hellas, and you must pray the gods that the operation may be performed without endangering the patient."

These words of her father reassured Nausicaa, and she was ready to take her place joyfully among the noble maidens and matrons, who assembled to witness the departure of King Pausanias and the army upon the following day. At day-dawn King Pausanias had sacrificed, with august solemnity, to Jupiter and the gods with him. The omens being propitious, fire from the altar had been placed in the cresset of the fire-bearer, who preceded the king upon the march; this fire would never be extinguished, but used for kindling all future sacrifices, until the army returned home. At this solemnity two of the Ephori and the principal officers were alone present. When the sacrifice was concluded, each officer was presented to the king, who personally gave him his orders for the day. These duties fulfilled, the troops, who were waiting with expectant hearts round the temple, were rejoiced by the doors being thrown open, and the appearance of the fire-bearer; he was closely followed by the heralds, and then, arrayed in his royal robes, King Pausanias approached, followed by his officers. A shout of triumphant welcome pealed through the morning air; and thus, amid songs and prayers for success from the immense crowd which lined the way, the army passed on to invest Athens. Nausicaa was not the only one who thought the march of that army a most splendid sight. Every soldier was dressed in a bright purple robe, for war was the Spartan's festival, and thus he assumed his festal robes, when entering upon its duties. Every soldier bore a shield of polished brass, and the rising sunlight shining upon these gave them the appearance of golden shields, while the brightly burnished spears flashed in the sunlight, like the purest silver. The long hair of every warrior was combed and adorned with a chaplet, and as they marched on with the peculiarly easy march of perfect discipline, singing the pæan as they passed, the wives and mothers, whom they were leaving, sped them on their way without one tear of regret.

And thus the allied forces of Greece at last invested Athens. Before the arrival of Lysander's fleet there were daily arrivals of immigrants from the colonies and islands. Aristarchus arrived among those from Samos, having been summoned by the Archon; he brought a letter from Cimon for Penelope; and this letter closed all doors against the hope to which Thetis had clung: "Codrus but saw Glaucon spring into the sea, he saw no more; now who can say what happened afterwards? Glaucon may still be living; possibly picked up by one of Conon's galleys, and Lysippus may meet him at Cyprus; or he may be still in Thrace. Alcibiades was sure to assist all of our people whom he could find needing his help. We do not know that Glaucon ever engaged with the Spartans; or, if he did, we do not know that he was killed." Thus Thetis had reasoned, but Cimon's letter dashed all her hopes of seeing Glaucon to the ground. Cimon had seen the adventurous plunge into the sea, and watched with horror the combat which ensued. He assured Penelope that he had attempted to join and assist her brother, but was forcibly withheld by his commander, and when he last saw Glaucon he was sinking upon the earth by the side of his prostrate friend. Thetis had resisted all mourning garments, until that letter arrived; but she made no more resistance after that, and for many, many long days, all the old bright light seemed to have passed from her life.

In the course of a few weeks the appearance of the whole city was changed. Great numbers of the new arrivals, as well as many of the old citizens, fled to the Piræus, as being within easy reach of some hope of escape, some prospect of procuring food from the sea. The forces of the united Spartan kings were posted in and around the lovely walks of the Academy, and each of the allies had its own camp and duties round the circle of the city walls. In due time Lysander arrived, as he had promised, making a triumphant progress to the Piræus, with his two hundred ships; but as he found that there was the most determined spirit of resistance within the city, and that no precaution had been neglected by the investing army, he left a few ships to prevent supplies entering by the port, and then sailed up the gulf to Ægina, where he restored the exiled Æginetans to their home, from which they had been driven by Athens in her hour of supremacy.

Well watched and well guarded as the splendid walls of Athens were, there was one enemy which so largely populated a city could not bar out. Famine brooded over Athens and the Piræus, and was preparing to stalk through the streets with no slow or uncertain step. Every citizen found that his house must now be made a refuge for those friends, who had received him with generous hospitality in happier times at their villas in Anaphlystus, Sunium, or Besa, while, even with the most hospitable intentions, many found themselves unable to receive one-half of their claimants. Tents and booths were erected in the waste places of the city, to accommodate the vast influx of homeless exiles; and during that cold January weather it would be a hard matter to estimate the depth of suffering to which the inhabitants were reduced.

Aristarchus and Androclea kept open house to its

full extent, and never was mother more ably seconded in every plan for the welfare of her household, than was Androclea by Penelope and Thetis. Foreseeing the inevitable famine from the first, every edible, whether a simple necessary of life or an imported luxury, was at once taken from the care of servants, and locked up in a store-room, of which Androclea kept the key. While it was still possible to do so, Aristarchus added to this store, by purchases of grain, oil, and wine; nor were these precautions selfish, since every room in his large house was filled by houseless friends, who had been unable to carry away any store of provisions from their own homes. Every morning Androclea and her daughters entered the store-room, and there carefully weighed out a well considered allowance for each person; while Penelope and Thetis, laying aside all dainty fastidiousness, in order to spare their beloved mother some anxiety, watched the food during the process of cooking, in order to ensure its safe arrival at its destination. This precaution was absolutely necessary, since the long residence of the family in the country had permitted a lax discipline to prevail among the slaves in the town mansion.

Before the arrival of Lysander's fleet, and while the port was still open, Asahel received the following letter:

"DEAREST ASAHEL,—Brother, best beloved one in our holy faith, and one in the unity of our common brotherhood, fulfil your desire, and return at once. You have now nothing to fear from the enmity of

Shimei, for he has passed to the judgment prepared for the wicked, and your old home is now, and ever will be, untroubled by his neighbourhood. Come to your own home, my brother, and bring with you the poor Gentile maiden of whom you spoke. She will receive a mother's welcome from my Rachel, and may He who commanded us to 'love the stranger and protect the fatherless,' bless her, and reward us as we entreat her well or evil. Bring Gershom with you if possible; but, if not, let him follow at his leisure. There is ample time for youth to fulfil the desires of its heart, but the time grows short when our sun has passed its meridian, and we long to see you, my brother, ere the shadows darken and the night closes round us. My brother, there is a sound of strife in the air; we hear it even here under the shadow of Mount Zion. We have no longer riches or power to tempt the oppressor, yet the struggles of the wicked reach us in our quiet home. Young Cyrus is conspiring against his brother Artaxerxes already, and the heathen around us are eagerly discussing the merits of the two brothers and their prospects. But we are bound to keep clear of all conspiracies. We pay our tribute to the lawful officers, and strive to live apart from Persian jealousy and Grecian discord. And for you, my brother, I had feared, lest your mind should be so occupied with the affairs of the heathen, that your love for your brethren would pass away from your heart. I had feared that you would be content to rest your bones among the Gentiles, forgetting the promise we inherit. Therefore I rejoiced over your epistle, and to my Rachel it was as some sweet incense, perfuming every sense of the body and the mind with holy peace and gladness of heart. Come to us quickly, my brother, and rejoice the heart of your kinsman, DAVID."

When Asahel read this letter he hesitated no longer; he summoned Gershom to a conference, and it was soon decided that Gershom must remain with Menares for some time longer, in fact until the good physician was able to replace the valuable help which he had received from both father and son. Asahel had no fears for the personal safety of Gershom, since he had many friends, not only in Athens, but in the Spartan army, which was then advancing through Attica towards the doomed city.

Gershom was only anxious that Opis should be safely out of the reach of the besieging army, and of the miseries attendant upon a siege. The Athenians had grown accustomed to the presence of an invading force in their neighbourhood since King Agis had returned to Decelea, but they knew well that a far sterner trial was awaiting them, one which their forefathers (nay, some were still living, who remembered the awful sufferings) endured during the administration of Pericles, when the terrible plague was added to the horrors of the inevitable miseries from famine and over-crowding.

Asahel would have preferred remaining in the city, and he told his old friend Menares that nothing but the necessity of placing Opis in safety could have induced him to leave.

L

"My dear Asahel," was the reply, "I am only afraid that if you had determined to stay, you might very soon have been compelled to leave, for I fancy that, in a very short time, every alien mouth will be expelled by the populace, who will not feel inclined to see strangers eating the bread for which Athenians are famishing. Now, Gershom will come into my house, and shall share my last crust; but you, as a householder would be exposed to envy."

"I believe that you are right," replied Asahel, "and that reason alone ought to decide our going. I must however ask you to take charge of my store of provisions—some figs, olives, and oil, a store of sesame and wheat, and some old wine. There will be sufficient for Gershom and yourself for a twelvemonth, so I hope you will not scruple to use it as your own for your household, or relieving the necessities of the poor."

"You always remind me, Asahel, of your great ancestor. You will never receive any favour from 'the children of Heth,' without full payment as from a prince to a prince. It must be with you."

"Believe me, Menares, both my forefathers and I have always known how to receive a blessing or a gift. He has but a poor spirit who will never permit others to feel the pleasure of being able to give, but in this instance it is a duty. I owe much to Athens, and her generous treatment of sojourners; and even upon selfish grounds," he added lightly, "I shall find it much more convenient to leave my useless stores with you, than pay for their shipment to Cyprus or Egypt."

"Or receive their weight in silver from the vendors in our own Agora?" answered Menares, who parted from his old friend with sincere sorrow.

Opis paid a farewell visit to Androclea—a very painful one to all parties. It is true that she had but received one night's hospitality on her way to Athens, yet her reception had been so affectionate, even while her hostess knew that she came from Sparta, that it was with an intense feeling of shame, as though she were personally concerned in the horrors of Lysander's cruel victory, that she approached the house; and when the three ladies entered the reception-room into which she had been shown, their mourning robes struck a thrill of painful horror through the heart of Opis. She stood rooted to one spot unable to move, unable to express the sorrow and shame she felt; but the noble, delicate-minded Androclea understood the meaning of the pale face and averted eyes—the trembling hesitation, which forbade poor Opis advancing to receive her proffered embrace.

"Do not fear to look up, my child. You are no Spartan, and we can never forget that your loving heart had rebelled against their barbarity even before you knew us."

The visit passed much more tranquilly than Androclea had ventured to hope. Thetis had suffered too much in the certainty of her brother's death to permit any of those outbursts which, under other circumstances, she most certainly would not have restrained. Androclea questioned her guest concerning Asahel's home, and Opis explained that it was a small portion of the territories of the great king, east of Sidon and Phœnicia. Then Opis delivered a message from Asahel, with a sincere hope that if the Lady Androclea and her family should ever find it necessary to leave Attica, they would remember that there was some one well able to offer them a comfortable refuge in Syria, one who would feel honoured by being permitted to prove his gratitude for the many kind offices he had received. With this message, Opis delivered a scroll from Asahel, upon which he had written clear directions by which his home in Judæa could be found; and Androclea half smiled for a moment when she saw that at the bottom of the scroll Asahel had appended a few lines, assuring her that she would find many rare herbs and much ancient wisdom in Judæa to repay her for the voyage. The smile soon passed from the face of the lady, however, and was succeeded by an expression of deep pain.

"Divided Greece alone has reduced us to such a possibility. Yet, dear child, there is no use in denying that it is a possibility. We all know that Lysander's answer to those who contest about boundaries is an unsheathed sword with the words: 'Whoso is master of that is master of boundaries;' and to a certain extent he is right. Sparta is now the master of our boundaries. We may be cast homeless upon the world, outcast, if not sold into slavery." The voice of the lady faltered; but recovering herself, she looked down upon Opis kindly, and continued: "It is a consolation to have received this letter. Tell Asahel from me that I thank him with all my heart, and we will most assuredly never forget his kindness."

Until that moment Opis had never realised the thought that her friends might be really cast out from their home. She stood for a few moments in awe-stricken silence. Tears relieved her at last; and falling down by Androclea, she faltered words of mourning and deprecation. At last she murmured more connectedly: "Ah, lady, you will not send such a message to my father. You do not know him. He loves to help all who suffer, and he reverences you, lady, more than any lady in all Hellas; and indeed he is not what he seems to be. He is rich in his own land, and can receive you there as you ought to be received. Send him a more kindly message than that, or he will blame me; and I, what can I do? I, who have been nursed by that Sparta which is devouring you. Promise me, dear lady, that you will come to us, and nowhere else, if you are exiled."

"I am a wife; my husband still lives, dear child; he must decide this matter, but we will ever remember Asahel's offer; and you may tell him from me, that as far as my influence goes, we will accept it, if—if ——alas, child! you do not know, you cannot dream what you ask, when you ask an Athenian matron to leave the protection of Athena; therefore you must not even wish to see us, since you cannot see us without our losing Athens."

In that moment of farewell, Opis and her Athenian friends were once more united, as in the lonely country villa. Those tears of the noble lady had washed away all the glamour from Persian carpets, Syrian embroideries, and Attic art. Four women, with women's hearts, kissed each other, and took a speechless farewell, then parted—the three Athenian ladies to brace their minds for the privations of the coming siege—Opis to pass to a tearful couch, where for some time her new-born faith in her Heavenly Father seemed to be overshadowed by the dark cloud which was impending over her friends.

The next day Asahel found a Phœnician galley ready to sail from Piræus in a few hours; so leaving Gershom to make arrangements concerning the disposal of his furniture and stores, he set sail ere midnight with Opis and Doris, leaving Gershom to gaze after the receding ship with a new sensation in his heart—a sensation that he was losing something which had unconsciously entwined itself very closely into his existence.

CHAPTER IX.

"The things true valour's exercised about
Are poverty, restraint, captivity,
Banishment, loss of children, long disease;
The least is death. Here valour is beheld,
Properly seen."
—*Ben Jonson.*

A MONTH had now elapsed since the battle of Ægospotami; the days had already begun to lengthen, and the air was fragrant with the perfume of sweet violets. Scillas and hyacinths were blooming in sheltered places; the beautiful arbutus and rose barberries were in full blossom in sunny nooks, while the Athenians, the most flower-loving of all people, were enclosed within the walls of their city, pent up from their fair country villas, and already surrounded by the low moaning cries of their famishing fellow-citizens. There were, of course, a few who, like Aristarchus and Androclea, had from the first foreseen this necessity, and who had, by limiting their own supplies, been enabled to minister to the needs of their poorer friends; but what the few rich could do among the numerous poor, was but as one handful of grass thrown among a herd of cattle in the pen which is carrying them to their slaughter.

Dying of starvation after a siege of but one month! Yes, it was even so; for the cruel policy of Lysander, which had filled the city with exiles from her conquered dependencies, had already aided the despondence of the populace, who had laid up no stores against the day which they believed to be an impossibility—the day of political retribution for Athens.

Outside the city walls the forces of the allied Greeks were in perfect ease and full enjoyment. The Spartans were too proud, too conscious of their certain superiority, to show many outward signs of triumph, but their allies were under no such restraint. The Thebans were exultant, and the most embittered against the prostrate foe, since they were the original cause of the protracted war which was now awaiting its final death-pang. The Corinthians, the people of Megara, every state which had been alternately caressed or trampled upon by Athens in her prosperous days, was now loud in denunciation, and eager for a full revenge, a more complete degradation of the city, which they had agreed to regard as their common enemy.

Towards the end of January the pride of the Athenians was so far humbled, as to permit them to send ambassadors for peace. It was but a few weeks previously that Archestratus had been thrown into prison, for suggesting submission; but Athens was still governed by a democracy, and although the most patriotic popular leader may vote for the imprisonment of another who votes for submission to the enemy, while there is still bare bread to support life, yet the same patriot, looking upon the agonised forms of wife and children who are tortured by the pangs of hunger, may at length feel compelled to submit to the will of his enemy.

Thus the heart of King Agis was at length rejoiced by the appearance of the suppliant ambassadors, who offered to submit to Lacedæmon and become her faithful allies, if they were permitted to keep possession of the Piræus and of the city walls. There has, perhaps, never been any government in the world where the onus of responsibility was so artfully evaded as it was in Sparta. Thus, when the ambassadors presented themselves to King Agis, he informed them that he had no power to treat of peace; they must proceed to Sparta. When this answer was reported in Athens there was mourning and wailing in the streets; for an embassy to Sparta meant a longer siege; yet must it at once be undertaken. The ambassadors proceeded upon their journey, but no sooner had they reached Sellasia than they were met by messengers from the Ephori, who demanded their business.

The answer to the embassy was stern but decisive; for, "when the Ephors heard what they proposed, which was the same as they had done to Agis, they bade them return from that very spot, and if they had any wish at all for peace, to come back after taking better advice."

Bitter words were these to bear back to Athens; and they were received with some lamentation by the weaker minds, while they aroused once more the spirit of resistance in the hearts of the sterner citizens, who declared that it was better, far better, to die free, under the shadow of their sacred Athenà, enclosed by the revered walls which their fathers had erected for the common safety of Greece, than to endure the ungrateful insolence of those who exulted over their misfortunes; far better to die free where Aristides, Themistocles, and Pericles had worked for the common welfare of Hellas, than submit to the cruel mercies of a Lysander, who could massacre three thousand fellow Greeks in cold blood.

And thus, for a short time longer, Athens refused "to take better advice," and resisted quietly—quietly enduring the pangs of hunger, and, far worse than hunger, the agony of seeing best-beloved ones drooping, failing, and falling away into the arms of relentless death.

Hyllus was sorely puzzled; he had not expected so long a resistance, and could not help feeling a sore heart for the suffering which it was now well known that the Athenians were so patiently enduring. The fierce passions of those by whom he was surrounded seemed but to lighten up the horror of their aims— even as the flames which leap from the burning coal do but exhaust its polished beauty, and leave it a loathsome mass of useless cinders. Hyllus was anxious about Opis for some time; but during the truce for the passage of the embassy, Gershom had contrived to send a letter to the Spartan lines, feeling sure that Hyllus would be there, and thus all anxiety concerning her was at an end; but in the letter which Leda had received, Opis had spoken in such glowing terms of the kindness of Androclea and her daughters, that this, in addition to his own knowledge of the noble lady, had roused every sentiment of anxiety and sorrow for the suffering, in which he could but feel sure that they were included. Nor was Hyllus the only one who was touched by the sufferings of the Athenians. There were many who felt as he did. And it was well known that King Pausanias was far more favourably disposed towards Athens than was his fellow-king, Agis, who felt that he was avenging personal injuries upon the countrymen of Alcibiades.

Thus there were two distinct parties, even in the Spartan camp, and at every friendly gathering, after watches were set, these feelings broke out in hot words and bitter speeches.

January, February, March, had passed away, and still Athens had not "taken better advice." It is true that Theramenes had been sent, or rather permitted by his fellow-citizens, to go to Lysander, with whom he declared that he had some influence, and whom he hoped to influence towards some more favourable and definite terms of peace. But Theramenes stayed away three months; since knowing the temper of his fellow-citizens so well, he did not venture to return to them, until he thought they were likely to listen to the only terms he could obtain.

One evening in April Hyllus went to the Corinthian camp, upon the invitation of an old friend who was receiving a larger party to supper than usual. There were two or three Spartan officers besides Hyllus, some distinguished Thebans, a few members of the Arcadian contingent, as well as several Corinthians of high rank. The party was a large one, and the feast was one which would have seemed luxurious even beyond the boundaries of Laconia. Not only was the table served with the choice food and wine for which Corinthian taste was already notorious, but the usual accompaniment of the hired musician had not been omitted. A wandering minstrel had exhibited his powers, while his son had displayed some wonderful feats of the gymnast, and his daughter accompanied the performance with sweet melodies from her lyre.

"It is absolutely necessary to have these people upon such an occasion," whispered Dion, the host, to Hyllus.

"Yes; I suppose that if you fear free speech, you must introduce the paid speaker and actor."

"I do not fear free speech, but I do fear broken heads at my banquet; and there is quite enough hot blood here to-night to justify my fears of an eruption."

While this aside was carried on, the guests at the other end of the table had already commenced a debate, upon the exciting subject of "the terms of surrender;" and Dion, hearing a few hot words, interposed—"What! has our minstrel departed? Slave! you promised me a song from your daughter, before leaving for the banquet of Leon."

The minstrel was close to the door of the tent, but the young girl, when thus appealed to, advanced at once with the lyre in her hand, and placing herself near Dion, sung in a light, half-jesting manner the following song; the words were evidently improvised, simple, and inartistic; they seemed to aim at avoiding any connection with the strife and tumult of the camp, yet, by a few plaintive chords, a remembrance of a well-known Attic dirge, for the dead at Salamis, was introduced, and a thrill of the old Hellenic bond seemed to touch most hearts with a gentle vibration while she sung:

> " A lily rose from out the earth,
>   Fair, whiter far than Æta's snow;
>   Pure Athena smiled on the birth,
>   Diana crowned with mystic glow.
>   Dark Earth rejoiced to see her child,
>   Demeter named her Undefiled;
>   But the envious wind and the sea
>   Have blasted my lily so bright,
>   They have sullied its incense so free,
>   And blackened its petals so white.
> Must I weep for the lily which blossoms again,
> Or weep o'er the wind and the bare barren main?
> Shed no tears for the lily so pure and so bright,
> But weep for the envy which blackens her night.
> Earth guards the fair lily for the heroes' delight,
> But the envy which spoils her shall darken in night."

There was universal acclamation when the young girl bowed, as she concluded her song; and Hyllus dropped his purse into her hand, as she passed him, saying, as he did so: "Take this, child, for your song; and sing it, and many like it, as often as thou canst in this stormy camp."

It is a remarkable fact that the coarsest natures, those which are the most prone to inflict material revenge upon their enemies, are seldom capable of perceiving the meaning of many words which are spoken in their presence; thus many Thebans applauded the song, and were delighted with the sweet voice of the young singer and her skilful usage of the lyre, and it never occurred to them that those sweet lips were denouncing heartfelt imprecations upon their envy and ingratitude. Some glimmering of the meaning of the maiden seemed at length to reach the mind of a few, when Hyllus spoke; and as the singer passed them she was caught and rudely detained.

"Dion, are you sure you have no Athenian spy in your tent? If that lily had been an olive I fancy we should have understood your meaning sooner, my young girl."

The singer made no resistance herself, but her father and brother at once approached to release her, and Hyllus, rising from his seat, advanced also; he took the young girl by the hand, and spoke gently, but firmly: "She is no spy, you may depend upon that; and surely, if she were so, no Athenian spy can now save Athens from her fate."

The eyes of the girl flashed. She looked up indignantly into the face of Hyllus, and that look saved her life. The Thebans supposed her to be indignant with the interference of Hyllus, and at once released her, but instead of escaping, she at once raised her lyre, and after a short prelude in a very different key from her last song, she sang, looking full at Hyllus while she did so:

> "The bladder may be dipt, but not be drowned;
> The faithless wrestler never shall be crowned.
> Light may be hidden, but can never die;
> And earth-born oxen feed, but never fly.
> The odd can never even be, nor square be round;
> The bladder may be dipt, but not be drowned."

Dion rose from his seat at once. "Polydorus, these people were engaged by me for the entertainment of my guests. I pray you, let the girl depart. I will be answerable for the safety of our camp as far as they are concerned."

The Thebans made no further resistance, and Dion, followed by Hyllus, at once escorted the minstrels to the door of the tent. "You have escaped this time, my friends, but beware in future," said Dion, sternly, as he dismissed them.

"And I pray that the oracle may be fulfilled yet," said Hyllus to the maiden; "but if the bladder will thrust itself among the rocks, it will burst rather sooner than you expect, depend upon it."

"Was there ever such a bold, daring young sibyl seen before," said Dion, as they returned to their seats.

"Would any one have fancied her capable of singing that old Athenian oracle in the very faces of the enemies of Athens."

"There was a dangerous sparkle in her eyes as she sang," replied Hyllus; "but I am afraid that I am convicted—since there can be no doubt but they are spies."

"Most assuredly; but they can do no harm now. It is far too late to save Athens by stratagem or otherwise."

The banquet proceeded after the departure of the minstrels in rather a different fashion. The lyre was now handed round to the guests, and free play was given to the expression of their varied feelings. The songs were not all martial. Some pastoral songs were sung with very good effect; and the Arcadians gained great applause by their national hymns. The feeling of indignation in the heart of Hyllus was, however, once more aroused, for one of the Thebans, taking the lyre, sang a song which had been composed by the Spartan poet Cherilus, in which Lysander was lauded with the most servile adulation, and invoked as one of the Greek demi-gods. Now Hyllus was a Spartan, and a descendant of Hercules, but this slavish adulation of the successful general was as loathsome to him as it already was to King Pausanias; and it was, as yet, an unknown form of flattery among the Greeks to erect altars for supplication to living men; moreover, he could see that it was as distasteful to his host as to himself. Thus when the lyre was passed to him, he put no restraint upon his feelings, but sang to a sharp martial air:

> "Bend Attic pride, I fear it soars too high,
> Aspiring still to boundless sovereignty.
> My pride, more lowly, claims no higher prize
> Than a wide course for free Bœotian eyes;
> Those walls impede the light, but lay them low,
> And Attic owls to Theban nests shall flow."

When Hyllus ceased singing, the two young Theban officers opposite eyed him with questioning looks, in which audacity was strangely mingled with incredulity as to the possibility of any insult being intended by this reference to the owl, which was impressed upon all the Athenian coinage; but an elderly friend of theirs, who sat upon the other side of Dion, spoke out cheerfully: "I am glad to find that you are of our opinion, Hyllus, concerning the walls of Athens. Those walls must be razed; they are a standing menace, not only to Thebes, her nearest neighbour, but to all Greece; and as to the owls," he added, with a comfortable chuckle, "I fancy that Lysander will provide some warm nests for them at Sparta; nevertheless, we shall not object to find house-room for some of them in Thebes, you may depend upon it."

"O blessed Bœotians!" murmured Hyllus, "can it indeed be true that your oxen are your models, and that it is as impossible for you to soar with the bird of Jove as it would be for an Athenian to graze upon your fodder."

The lyre was now taken by Dion himself, who once more changed the unwelcome subject by singing—

The Song of the Egotist.

"Whom do I love? why, I love myself
    Better than all the world beside;
For myself I gather the golden pelf,
    And adorn myself as a dainty bride.

"My own sweet self! you shall never know
    The toils of labour or distant seas;
If I serve others, I rob myself—
    Myself! whom I live to serve and please.

"Let others pine, or roam, or fret
    For a love they can never win nor see,
I love but one, and his love I get,
    For my love is centred all in me."

This song seemed at once to diffuse a better feeling among his guests than Dion had dared to hope for; and as his lead was followed at once by Hyllus, who told an amusing story which he had heard in his Syrian travels, the "terms of surrender" were finally banished from the festal board, and each one of the guests seemed intent upon displaying his powers of amusement; and the party separated at a late hour, mutually pleased with each other. When Hyllus reached his tent, he found a friend awaiting him.

"There need be no more discussion concerning the terms of surrender; they are fixed, and Theramenes the Athenian has carried the decree of the Ephori into the city this very day."

TERMS OF SURRENDER.

"And they are?"

"The demolition of the walls, the surrender of all their ships but twelve, payment of expenses, etc., etc."

"Oh, bitter, bitter terms; but will they be accepted?"

"Needs must where Nemesis drives."

"Well, I suppose it is best, if it is to be, that it be done quickly, and so most likely we shall enter the city at once."

"Yes, immediately, you may depend upon it. The peoply are starving, and on their return the ambassadors were met by crowds, imploring them to urge consent to any terms rather than continue the resistance."

When his friend left him, Hyllus soliloquised: "I wonder whether Aristarchus and Androclea will receive me. I must send for Nausicaa. She must be my peace-bearer, but in good truth I know not how I dare venture to appear before them."

Within the city, upon the following day, a stormy meeting of the citizens was held, to consider the terms finally submitted for their consideration by Sparta. The decree of the Ephori ran thus: "You shall pull down the Piræus and the long walls, quit all the cities (or colonies) you are possessed of, and keep within the bounds of Attica. On these conditions you shall have peace, provided you pay what is reasonable, and restore the exiles. As to the numbers of ships you may keep, you must comply with the orders we give you."

There was dead silence when this insulting message was read, yet Theramenes, who had been the most active negotiator for peace, implored his countrymen not to throw away this proposal, since the next would most assuredly be no gentler, and since all were agreed that it was impossible to oppose the allies in the field, there was but one course open to them as reasonable men."

"What!" cried Cleomenes, a young orator, who now started to his feet; "do you dare to propose our delivering up those walls to the Lacedæmonians, and thus oppose yourself to Themistocles, who built them for the protection of Athens in defiance of these perfidious Spartans and their allies."

"Young man," replied Theramenes, "I do not in the least counteract the intentions of Themistocles. He built these walls for the preservation of Athens, and for the same purpose we propose to demolish them. If walls alone could make a city happy and secure, Sparta, which has none, would be the most unhappy and defenceless city in the world."

No further opposition was offered. The bitter degradation was at length accepted as inevitable, and once more the gates of Athens were thrown open for the entrance of friends or foes—for the entrance of the most earnestly prayed for and longed for, vendors of food, who hurried to the wounded and fainting eye of Greece, with the same alacrity, and for the same purpose, as the vulture which hovers over the prostrate Arabian in the desert. Yet there was still sufficient vitality in the descendants of the heroes of Marathon and Salamis to compel the very vultures, who came to prey upon their vitals, to feed the reawakening energies of those whom they sought to devour. Hyllus entered the city alone as soon as he could gain an entrance after the opening of the gate. He took with him some rare fruit, which he had purchased for its weight in gold from a Carthaginian ship, which had arrived to make merchandise out of the necessities of the allied army, but was unexpectedly finding a richer harvest in supplying the needs of the citizens of Athens. Hyllus purchased the most exquisitely delicate basket which he could procure, and carried the fruit in it with his own hands, not daring to trust even his most trusted Helot under the circumstances.

When Hyllus reached the house of Aristarchus, he was shocked by the gaunt appearance of the porter who opened the door.

"Is Aristarchus within?" questioned Hyllus.

"He is not."

"Is the Lady Androclea at home?"

"She is confined to her chamber."

"Will you carry this basket to her, and say that, if she permits him, Hyllus, who had the honour of her acquaintance in Italy, Hyllus, the foster father of Opis, will call at any hour she may name, to pay his respects."

The porter hesitated before taking the basket, and when he did at last receive it, it was as though he were touching burning coal, then, slamming the door in the face of Hyllus, he left him outside as though he were the slave of some obnoxious master. Hyllus bit his lip, but he remembered the misery the man must have endured during the past three months, and blamed himself for not covering the peculiarities of his Spartan dress, which had at once aroused the indignation of the man. Some minutes passed before the door was opened, and when at last the porter reappeared, it was with the basket in his hand.

"My lady is too weak to see any stranger to-day, and she desires me to say that she can receive no gifts in the absence of her husband."

Once more the door was slammed in his face, and Hyllus was left standing in the street. He was a philosopher; he was nearly forty years of age, and yet, as he turned away from the house, tears, bitter tears, started to his eyes. Sparta must have fallen very low in all honour and true nobility when one of her sons could thus be spurned by one so gentle and noble as Androclea.

A few steps further on in the street Hyllus met with the minstrels who had sung at Dion's supper. The young girl was toiling behind her father, looking very weary, and in the clear daylight Hyllus saw that her features were pinched and sharpened, and the whole face pallid, as from extreme hunger. He at once stepped up to her and offered the basket. "Take it, poor child; you seem to need food sorely." The girl looked up, and at once caught sight of the dress which Hyllus wore.

"Better starve than eat the food of Spartan wolves," she said, quickly.

Hyllus was more surprised than hurt now. "You did not think so the other evening when you received my purse at Dion's."

"Oh, is it you?" she cried, looking up in his face. "No, I did not, for you were not as the others; but here is your purse. I do not need it. Nevertheless, for the sake of your championship that night, I will accept your basket. I did not recognise you at first, and only looked upon you as one of our enemies."

While the girl spoke, and while she was busily engaged in removing the leaves upon the fruit, Hyllus watched her closely. The tone of her voice and every movement proved that she was no professional dancer, no mere wandering minstrel. Then the hand which was so busily moving among the fresh vine leaves, how small and white and soft it was. And again, the features; surely he had seen them, or some which resembled them very closely, before — but where? While Hyllus was thus pondering, a cry of delight broke forth from the lips of the girl: "Citrons, oranges, bananas, and salad; oh, my beloved mother, my Penelope, my father, you shall not weary for fresh fruit now."

"And you, Thetis, will not you eat some?"

The girl looked up fearfully, as though wounded by an arrow. "Nay, my child, go swiftly to your mother.

I see now whose features you bear, and you must thank Opis and Asahel for telling me your name; but go to your mother, tell her what passed at Dion's, and win her forgiveness for Hyllus if you can." There was no need for acknowledgment on the part of Thetis. She rushed from his side, and in another moment Hyllus saw her enter her house by a side entrance. "So you have lost your adopted daughter at last," said Hyllus to the minstrel.

"She was no daughter of mine. She paid me handsomely for taking her out through the walls more than a week ago. She said that she must go out of the city, and see for herself what was doing, and hear for herself what was said outside, and, if possible, find some means of conveying food to her mother and sister, who were pining, and had at last given way. She intended coming back the next day, but we found it far easier to get out than to get into the city again. People of my trade are always welcome, but somehow it leaked out that we were spies, and so we were taken into custody the very next day after we saw you, and were only released this morning. Thetis always was wilful; anyway she always got her own way somehow, and my wife was her nurse, so when she begged me to take her out of the city, I was over-persuaded."

"I wonder you were not afraid to take the young daughter of your master to such a place as our camp."

"If it had been any one but Thetis I might have been, but she is a true daughter of Athena; not but what I am right glad to get her home, for she has eaten nothing, although we have been at feasts almost every night. A crust of the loaf which she bought from some of the camp followers is all she would eat. This morning we spent hours in the crowd, trying to buy some fresh fruit for her mother, but no one would listen to us, and at last she said she felt sure she should have done her mother better service if she had stayed at home."

Hyllus paused before he answered: "Young people seldom believe that old people are wiser than they, yet she has done me some good service, I hope; and, as I suppose you will be going to the house, I shall be glad if you will tell Aristarchus that I will call to-morrow if he will receive me."

It was with a lightened, yet still sore heart, that Hyllus reached his tent. It is so easy for the victor to see everything in a rose-coloured light, so easy for him to determine to be on good terms with his vanquished adversary—it is almost impossible for him to understand the bitter feeling of estrangement which those feel whose dearest hopes have been blasted, whose most treasured objects of affection have been destroyed, and who have been compelled by the victor's sense of righteous retribution, to submit to an abyss of degradation, not only in their own eyes, but in the eyes of all those whom they love. Hyllus was therefore most thoroughly surprised when he received upon the following day a letter from Aristarchus. It ran thus:

"My Old Friend Hyllus,—Our beloved Thetis has told us of the mild yet natural compassion for our sufferings, which you were bold enough to express among those who differed from you. She has also told us of your manly interference for her protection in scenes to which she ought never to have been exposed. My wife, Androclea, unites with me in heartfelt gratitude for your kindness; and years hence, when our wounded hearts are healed, we may be enabled to express our thanks to you personally; as it is, we do not either of us feel able to do so at present. Forgive us, and accept our gratitude for the welcome fruit which we have thankfully eaten, as a proof of our sincerity. I may mention that Androclea is very, very weak. Her tender heart would not permit her to reserve food when she knew of any who were really needing it; thus our large stores were very quickly exhausted; yet we live, and my wife prays that our lives may be preserved for aiding in the renovation of our beloved country. Thetis begs me to add her best wishes for your happiness to those of my wife, and believe me ever, Hyllus, yours sincerely, Aristarchus."

In the course of the next hour Hyllus had obtained an interview with King Pausanias, and permission to return to Sparta upon important family business; and the next day saw him well on his way towards his own home. Upon the 16th of April, 403 B.C., the triumphant Lacedæmonian army entered Athens in great state, and with every display of victorious supremacy. The long walls of Themistocles, once the pride and glory of Athens, were then destroyed by the victors, to the sound of flutes, played by the refuse of the female sex. During the progress of this degradation, Lysander made an imposing display of naval supremacy in the bay. In short, every means was adopted which would aid in forcing upon the minds of the Athenian citizens the new and startling truth that they belonged now to a subject state, and so successful was the operation that for some years afterwards the noblest Athenians did not shrink from writing in their annals, "For the Lacedæmonians, being now the masters of Greece."

King Agis was rejoicing in the demolition of the long walls, when a noble Spartan in attendance upon him spoke: "We have been reminding each other that this is the hundredth anniversary of the battle of Salamis. One hundred years ago the united army of Greece defeated the invading Persian in the bay below."

"We conquer enemies far more deadly than the Persian," was the reply of the king. "Profligacy and self-seeking, pride and insubordination, are far more deadly enemies to Greece than any foreign invader."

"Pride, idleness, and fulness of bread were the sins for which Sodom was destroyed," murmured Gershom, as he gazed pitifully upon the bowed head of his master, upon the day when the walls were demolished, for Menares, like all Athenians who could do so, remained in the closest seclusion, and was overcome with painful emotion.

"There are at least ten men in this city free from the sins of Sodom, as I can testify; but idolatry—aye, it was for idolatry we were sent into captivity—idolatry and forgetfulness of our holy law; and surely if ever there was a city wholly given up to the worship of the work of men's hands, it is Athens."

CHAPTER X.

"What stranger's this whom thus Nausicaa leads?
Heavens! with what graceful majesty he treads.
Perhaps the native of some distant shore,
The future consort of her bridal hour."
— *Pope's Homer.*

THE noble walls of the Athenian seaport were soon demolished, and when the work was accomplished, the submissive Athenians under Lacedæmonian supervision chose the oligarchy, which in a short time became infamous as the Thirty Tyrants. It is unfortunately too often the case that when a misfortune overtakes either an individual or a family, too little exertion is made in attempting to discover the cause of the misfortune; we are all too prone to believe that the fault is not our own, but is connected with our circumstances. If we had but been differently surrounded by friends, servants, or relatives, the accident could not have happened. Thus the majority in Athens would not lay the blame of their degradation upon their own overweening ambition and love of pre-eminence, their reckless disregard for the feelings of others, their mental and political pride, which would brook no equal. Their own sins were entirely overlooked, and they at once consented to believe that the cause of their disaster was their unfortunately constituted government. If they had but some of the Spartan severity and aristocratic element, they would be once more able to compete with, nay, to conquer, those whose simple severity of discipline was the inheritance from a long line of ancestors. The marvellously modelled constitution of Spartan monarchy could neither be created in a day nor a century. Yet as some excited fanatic hurries off to the quack whose universal medicine has happened to suit the imaginary ailments of his friend, so did the Athenians at once fall into Lysander's trap for a sterner and more responsible government, and eventually for a Spartan garrison in the citadel to support the Thirty Tyrants in the city.

Xenophon, the historian, who witnessed the scenes he describes, affirms that in the course of eight months the Tyrants put more Athenians to death than the Lacedæmonians had done during the last ten years of the Peloponnesian war. Citizens who had retired to their country villas were summoned upon the accusation of some mercenary informer to answer for an imaginary crime, and upon their execution, their estates were immediately seized upon and divided between the Thirty and their infamous accomplices.

The colossal brazen Athena still looked down upon the city nestling round her feet, yet her children were now beginning to learn a new lesson from her wisdom; her protecting spear seemed now a warning guide, bidding her true votaries fly from the devoted city. It was thus that Aristarchus and Androclea felt it in their villa, to which they had returned as soon as it was possible to reach it.

"No, my Aristarchus; it would not be exile, as you say, for our estate in Attica is still our own; and as Eumenes has retired to Megara, and Polydorus to Argos, I do not see why we should not avail ourselves of the opportunity."

"I know of no other place to which we can safely retire," replied Aristarchus. "Either to Cyprus or to Syria we must go, for our lives are not safe here; it is not possible for us now to choose between Samos or Chios, Lesbos or Lemnos, Byzantium or Chalcedon. All these places have now Lacedæmonian harmosts, and as to Cyprus, you, my Androclea, would gain no real rest such as our good Menares prescribes. Conon is still there, urging forward every operation which may preserve for us his few ships and secure us fresh allies. If I could but see your strength restored, I would join Lysippus and aid Conon in his plans; but until you recover some strength, what can I do but remain by your side and guard our daughters."

"We will go, my husband. I have been selfish. I have not liked to desert Athens, but I see now that all my efforts are fruitless for good. We will go as soon as you like. I know that Asahel will rejoice to see us."

Thus it was settled. Menares had decided to accompany Gershom when he returned home, and had implored Aristarchus to join them in the Syrian vessel which was to sail in the following week, and was most luxuriously fitted up for the accommodation of passengers. Menares urged that the quiet voyage alone in that lovely summer month would restore the health of Androclea and her daughters, as nothing else could do, and that the change afterwards to the simple Syrian pastoral life would be a most certain cure for the overstrained anxiety and mental torture to which all had been subjected during the past year.

Androclea was now so anxious to depart from the neighbourhood of Athens on her husband's account, that she hastened every preparation for the voyage, and in less than a week Penelope and Thetis were rejoicing in the sea breezes, and in their reviving effect upon the health of their beloved mother, who seemed to have taken her physician's advice, and to have left all care as to Athens in Attic territory.

While the noble terrace-crowned walls of Athens were being demolished, and the Spartan army was rejoicing in the fruit of its long, wintry watch round the ramparts, Hyllus was slowly travelling towards his own home, mentally revolving his own past life, and seeking to discover the point where he had turned away from happiness. "Have I then, in following my own inclinations as to study, diverted the affections of those who might have been true friends? If I had been truer to Sparta, and served my country with heart and head, might I have gained a position which would have enabled me to avert this supremacy of mere brute force and arbitrary tyranny over a fellow free state of our common Hellas? Alas, alas! who can tell? If my beloved Laodamia had lived, I should have coveted active life for her sake, but when she left me desolate, I sought but to fill my empty heart with the divine secrets of nature. If it was selfish, it was surely not ignoble. And thou, divine Astræa, art thou not tolerant of a divided heart? Must it be ever so that he who sets his affection upon the Unseen, must renounce the enjoyment of earthly love? Not so, not so; there is still my Nausicaa; she is yet my own, and she must, if possible, be preserved from the pangs I suffer."

The day after his arrival, Hyllus presented a petition to the Ephori, praying for permission to travel with his daughter. Many questions were asked and answered in the fashion which unfortunately was taught to Spartan youth, as part of the practice of a good soldier upon his enemies, not as for use towards the sacred Ephori of his native city. There was, however, no punishment for the criminal whose crime was not discovered, and Hyllus took precautions that the real reason for his wish to leave home should not transpire. After some delay, permission was accorded by the Ephori—permission to travel for a year, to any place Hyllus might choose, Athens excepted. And as Athens was precisely the place which he wished to avoid, Hyllus was satisfied.

One of the reasons assigned to the Ephori was a true one. Hyllus was known to have devoted much time and wealth to the acquirement of knowledge. He was therefore easily credited when he affirmed that he was most anxious to examine for himself the meteoric stone which had fallen near Ægospotami just before the conclusive engagement between Athens and Sparta. One who knew Sparta well affirmed that, in spite of the general belief to the contrary, the Spartans did really encourage a love of science and scientific study much more than was supposed by those who knew them only as the greatest military power of the age; and in proof of this he adduces the fact that a Spartan never answered a question thoughtlessly; there was always a clear, definite answer given, with the most logical accuracy, by every Spartan who chose to answer a question at all. Be this as it may, the tastes of Hyllus were too well known to permit his statement to be doubted. Nausicaa was delighted with the prospect of a change of scene, and with the possibility of once more seeing Opis; and it was with a glad heart that she set about her preparations for travel.

One last visit was paid to Leda in the forest temple. Leda was the one link which would bind the hearts of both father and child to their old house. To Leda Hyllus spoke more openly of his reasons for wishing to travel than he could have done to any one else.

She sympathised heartily with his wounded feeling, and in the prayers of Nausicaa for a more united feeling among the states of their common country.

"Ah, Leda! it is love we need; is it not? Oh that Athens would but love us, as I have always loved Athens!"

The priestess looked forward with dreamy, thoughtful eyes, down through the long vista of trees which lay before them as they sat in the vestibule of the temple.

"Love, child! yes, love it may be; but it must be love for something higher than ourselves. The people of Sparta are united in their love for their ancient city, with its heroic memories and mountain-guarded hearths. This is love, yet it is a love which will never—which can never—unite them in such sympathy as you would wish to see with other states."

"And why not, dear Leda? why cannot we treat Athens as if she were in truth part of our own beloved Lacedæmonia?"

"Ah, child! you know nothing of love. I serve the maiden goddess, and yet I know well that love is the most selfish of all passions——"

"Forgive me, Leda, if I say that it is *because* you serve the maiden goddess you thus traduce love. If you served Hera, you would think differently, Love! Ah, while my Laodamia lived, I loved every human being, and there was no heart more open than mine. Love is the first-born child of the immortal gods; and do not you ever give up your father's creed upon this point, my Nausicaa."

Leda remained unmoved by this outburst of Hyllus, and then answered, quietly:

"I had not finished my speech when you interrupted, Hyllus. I too worship love as the first-born of the gods, but it must not be earthly love. We priests and priestesses have no earthly love; our affections aspire to the celestial object of our worship. My sisters are those who are united in the service of the virgin Diana, whether their home may be in lonely forest shade or in stately Ephesus, in distant Syria or amid the burning sands of Libya. There is no pain, no self-seeking in this love. We serve one who is generous to all her servants. It is not so with earthly loves. If Athens wishes to secure for her children stores of wealth, or to find fresh fields for their energy, she arouses the jealousy of other states, who have also children to feed, and markets to supply, or renown to gain by land or sea. Where two persons are united in striving to obtain the same object, one must fail of obtaining it. The chief command over Greece was possessed by Athens for one hundred years. Other states coveted it, and Sparta has now obtained it. No love, therefore, can exist between the rival states; the vanquished may submit; but love their conqueror, who has taken from them the possession of their forefathers? No; never! And yet there is a love in which all may unite. I do not covet the love of my goddess for myself. I adore her, and unite with all her votaries from all lands. We all agree in our love and worship to her, not in seeking her love for ourselves."

"Then, by the twins, Leda, you are but a poor priestess. If I send a sacrifice, I expect some return for my devotion. I expect the goddess to give me or my servants good success in the chase."

"Perhaps we all receive that which we desire," said Leda, simply. "I desire that the giver of all the beauty I see upon this fruitful earth may be loved and worshipped, and, at any rate, she has one sincere worshipper in Nausicaa, who loves the gifts of Diana in forest and in greenwood glade as sincerely as her poor priestess, Leda, can do."

"And who loves the sacred Diana most of all for teaching her Leda to be what she is, and ever has been—the best friend any poor, motherless girl ever had?" cried Nausicaa, passionately. "O Leda, I do wish that you could come with us! Do try."

"What! leave this sacred dwelling-place for the strife and the hatred of the world!"

Hyllus was touched by his daughter's affectionate appeal, and by the unworldly spirit of the simple priestess, yet he could not resist one parting shaft.

"Ah, Leda! earthly love is very selfish, you tell us; permit me to say that the celestial love seems very very selfish also to my poor darkened eyes. You love the quiet service of the goddess so well, and her flower-crowned temple is so congenial to your taste, that you cannot even listen to the prayer of a poor motherless girl, who would draw you away from them."

A flush, as of deep pain, passed over the face of Leda, and she spoke in an agitated, tremulous voice, when she replied:

"You have touched a sore heart, Hyllus; believe me, I have often questioned myself as to whether my lot in life is not a selfish one, yet I did not choose it, as you well know; and I think you yourself would say in a calmer mood that it is now too late in life for me to alter all my habits, if I would."

"Forgive me, forgive me, dear Leda; I am a hardened sinner, as you well know, or I never could have wounded your feelings. You have, as Nausicaa truly says, been her best friend; and it is we who are selfish in wishing to draw you away. Forgive me; and, if you can, forget all my sins, and be prepared to receive us joyfully when we return a year hence."

"You will bring Opis with you, or news from her?"

"Most assuredly. I showed you Gershom's note; we shall have to follow her to Syria, but that is one of the chief charms of our journey in the eyes of Nausicaa."

Night was closing in when Nausicaa and her father walked home through the forest; the new moon shone through the trees, and lighted up the white marble temple with an almost supernatural beauty. Nausicaa turned, and lingered to fix the last glimpse of the beloved spot in her memory.

"My father, listen," she said at last. "Listen; Leda is singing the evening hymn to the goddess."

"Nausicaa, my child; if I were to turn round, and thank Melitus every time you handed me my wine or brought me my fruit, what should you think?"

"That you did not wish me to serve you, but preferred the services of Melitus. But, my father, why do you ask?"

"Only a puzzle, my child. Asahel would say that Leda is making the same mistake, but I do not say so. I make a point of treating the very best of daughters with the gratitude and courtesy to which she is entitled whenever she gives me the opportunity of doing so; but I fear me that Melitus gains many thanks for doing that which my Nausicaa has bidden him do for me. Child, child! what shall I do when you marry?"

"My father, I do not wish to be married. You must let me live with you always."

"And when I die?"

"Then I will go to Leda, and serve the goddess with her."

"And when Leda dies? She is nearly as old as I am."

"Ah, my father! Diana never dies. I will still serve her."

"Do not think of it, my child. Did you not hear Leda say that she who did not choose her own lot in life feared that her life was a selfish one. Never seek for unseen duties. He serves the gods best who serves his fellow-creatures best; and I hope some day to see you a happy mother of children who will honour my grey hairs, and prove a comfort to my old age; but we will not even think of these things until we return. And as to Leda, she little knows how her simple, pure-minded love for the goddess of woodland haunts would be ridiculed by her sister priestesses in Ephesus or Syria. Leda was brought up by Asahel, and has unconsciously appropriated most of his lessons, for she worships the Divine Creator of the earth, whom she calls Diana."

"Oh, my father, my father! Leda is not the only one who worships the goddess in Sparta; and as to Asahel, my father, he spoke to me the night before he left us, and I was so glad to find that he worships the celestial Jupiter, just as we do. I fancied from what nurse told me that he did not worship any god at all."

"You may depend upon it, my Nausicaa, Asahel is far more devout than any Spartan, and I half fancy that all the good we retain in our religion we owe to his people, all the evil to ourselves; but these are not questions for my Nausicaa, and I cannot permit her to trouble her head with questions which belong to the sophists. Sing me the hymn you learned last from Leda. The forest is lonely, and your voice always sounds sweetly in the ears of your father."

A few days after their farewell visit to Leda, Hyllus and Nausicaa embarked in the galley which Hyllus had purchased. They sailed from the bay which we now call Navarino; and Nausicaa, to whom the sea was as new a sight as it had been to Opis, rejoiced in the beauty of every fresh sight and sound which presented itself.

Hyllus intended proceeding first to the Thracian Chersonesus and Sestus, the scene of the late eventful battle. He then intended to show Nausicaa some of the beauties of the Ionian cities. Ephesus and Halicarnassus he was determined that she should visit. Afterwards he would proceed to Syria, spending the winter with Asahel, and very possibly return home by Egypt, visiting Cyprus on the return voyage.

Such an excursion as that proposed by Hyllus would be delightful in these days; but in the prime of Grecian beauty and of Egyptian magnificence no words can express the lovely images which such a tour presented to the mind of the traveller. Not one of the islands which cluster in the Archipelago was destitute of some lovely trophy from the realms of art. Sailing tranquilly over the blue waters to the chant of the rowers, who were not impelled to any severe strain upon their energies, since Hyllus was no restless Athenian merchant, but a Spartan noble, who naturally felt inclined to a calm and full enjoyment of the scenes around him, Nausicaa enjoyed scenes of such rare beauty as no one in these degenerate days can hope to see. Nature is ever the same, and the Grecian Archipelago still summons up a vision of lovely islands, and the mystic glory of the united beauties of earth, air, and sea; but for Nausicaa was added the beauty of human art. Every verdant island was covered with a profuse beauty of carefully-tended flowers, and was adorned by temples and statues, which glistened above the rocks like the celestial dwelling-places of a more ethereal race.

When the vessel arrived at Sestus, Hyllus disembarked with Nausicaa and her nurse, and to his great joy found that the newly-appointed harmost was an old friend, who, with his wife, received the travellers so hospitably, that Nausicaa felt none of those discomforts to which lady travellers were sometimes exposed.

The day after his arrival, Hyllus set off with Nausicaa to visit the fallen meteor. He found that it was already so great an object of curiosity, that responsible guardians had been appointed to show it to the crowds of curious strangers who came to gaze, wonder, and admire with reverential awe, for the people of the Chersonesus were fully determined to vouch for the sacred character of their celestial visitant. Upon inspecting the wonder, Hyllus found it to be what he had expected—a large meteoric stone. The guardians declared that when they saw it fall, and approached to examine it, they found no inflammable matter upon or around it. When closely questioned, they would not affirm that they had seen the stone fall from the meteor, which had terrified them for the preceding seventy-five days, yet they believed that it did do so, as its fall and the explosion of the meteor occurred at the same time; yet although the stone seemed to be too large to have fallen from the air, it was much smaller than the meteor itself. Of that they said there could be no doubt.

Nausicaa looked with reverential awe upon this visitant from an unknown world. "Oh, my father, it seems as though Anaxagoras must be right after all. This stone seems to prove it. Can it be possible that those myriad stars are indeed formed of earth and rocks like our own earth? Is it, then, possible that there are other worlds like our own?" and Nausicaa looked up into the blue sky with eyes which seemed to seek for the world of which the stone before them was a fragment.

"Other worlds than our own? That is precisely the question I am ever asking myself, Nausicaa, and this stone goes far towards making me answer with certainty that there are. Yet what their size may be, what their inhabitants, who can tell? I do not say what their nature, for this stone is precisely similar to the rocks in many parts of our own world."

"Some one who came here from Thebes the other day, suggested that when the meteor in the sky exploded, it forced this rock from some mountain near, and the force of the explosion whirled it over the sea to us; but as I said to him, such a wind, or such a whirlwind, as would have carried that stone across the Hellespont, never blew upon these shores in my life—and most certainly was not blowing when that stone fell out of the heavens; but those Bœotians have no more sense than their own oxen. What do they know about the stars and the ether, that they should flout and deride a man who has seen a plain visible fact falling out of heaven, before his own eyes?"

"I believe you, my man; I believe all you say, for I have seen other meteoric stones elsewhere, some of them exactly like this, but smaller. I have never met with any one, however, before to-day, who had seen the stone fall. I am glad to have seen you and it; but it will take a far wiser head than either yours or mine to decide whether the stone fell from the stars, or was whirled by some violent force from a neighbouring mountain."

That last suggestion was a very pleasant one to Nausicaa; she clung to her early faith concerning the stars, and was thankful to perceive that her father was not yet quite convinced that they were dull earth and stony matter.

On their return from visiting the meteoric stone, the harmost took his visitors round to view the trophy erected by Lysander to commemorate the victory of Ægospotami, and expatiated at great length upon the glorious result of that memorable battle. All his attempts to excite the patriotic enthusiasm of his guests were, however, utterly useless. Hyllus and Nausicaa looked upon the trophy as upon the grave of the three thousand prisoners massacred at Lampsacus, and made no reply to the eulogies of their host upon Lysander. At supper in the evening, however, the conduct of Lysander towards his prisoners was freely discussed, and severely blamed; not, however from any merciful feeling towards the prisoners, but from the reckless want of consideration which he had shown, in thus depriving his country of her share in the large sums of money, which the rich Athenians would so gladly have paid for the ransom of their friends.

"It was most impolitic—most improvident," was the universal opinion. Hyllus ventured to suggest the possibility of Athens retaliating, and using this action as a precedent upon Spartan armies, if it should ever be in her power to avenge the injuries she had sustained; but he found that there was not the slightest fear of such an event among his auditors.

"If Athens had not introduced the practice upon a small scale, Lysander would not have dared to imitate such a practice; so that we may feel very well assured Athens will fear to arouse the Erinnyes again. She has no one but herself to blame," said the harmost.

"I only regret that Lysander did not execute every tenth man, as was at first suggested; that would have satisfied Nemesis, and yet have preserved ample ransom money to reward the toils of those who have made such efforts, as we have done, through the whole war." This was the speech of an officer of high rank, who had been present at the engagement; and Hyllus found that this was the general opinion. The ancient Spartan contempt for wealth was fast dying out, he found, among these near neighbours of the wealthy, luxurious Asiatics.

Hyllus heard that Alcibiades had left his Thracian fortress, immediately after the battle, which he had been unable to command; some people said that he had crossed the Hellespont, and taken refuge in Persian territory; others that he had set off upon a private expedition to the shores of the Euxine. No one knew anything certain concerning his movements, however, saving only that the dazzling, brilliant Athenian—the darling of the Athenian populace—was once more an outcast, reaping the fruits of his unprincipled profligacy and overweening ambition, in the solitude of the exile, whose footsteps are dogged by the relentless spirits he has called into existence, or outraged during his career of prosperity.

After a week's stay at Sestus, Hyllus determined to sail to Byzantium, and introduce Nausicaa to the wondrous beauty of the scenery around that city, before proceeding to Ephesus. All his plans were disarranged, however, upon the very day on which he had intended to set sail.

Hyllus was most anxious concerning the comfort of Nausicaa in the galley; and upon the morning of their departure, rose very early, and proceeded to the harbour for one final visit of inspection before leaving the city. He had proceeded but a few paces from the house, when he met his host, who was engaged in earnest conversation with two men, one of whom was apparently his steward; the other a slight, but tall and remarkably noble-looking young man, who was poorly clad, and, in spite of his noble carriage, seemed suffering from ill health.

"Hyllus, my friend, suffer me to finish this business, and I will go with you to the harbour. I shall be but a few minutes."

"Shall I wait for you here, or will you follow me?"

"I will come at once;" and the harmost, turning to his servant, said, hastily, "Let there be no more delay, then. I have already expended too much time and money upon the matter. Find out the labour upon which he can most usefully be employed, and set him to work at once."

Hyllus, who was lingering for his friend, saw a deep crimson flush pass up to the brow of the young man, whose lips quivered with suppressed emotion. But no time was allowed for speech. He was hurried away by his companion; and Hyllus was at once joined by his friend.

"I am afraid that I have disturbed you."

"Oh, no. I am thankful to have escaped from importunity. The fact is, I am a victim to my own credulity and generosity. You saw that young man. His story is, I suppose, a common one; but my relations to him are not quite so usual, I imagine. After the battle of Ægospotami, we sent to bury the dead. This young man was among the wounded—among the Athenian dead was at first supposed—for he was in a death swoon through loss of blood from his wound. The Thracians who found him searched the body.

They found neither ring nor jewels to reward their search; but finding life, and a rich robe, with very finely-embroidered under tunic, he was thought worthy of preservation for the sake of ransom money. When I was appointed to the Government, I heard of the matter. The young man was recovering, and of course I considered that all captives were the property of the State, of the governor, in fact, so I paid the Thracians for their care of the young man, and then questioned him myself. He affirmed that he was the son of a rich Athenian, Aristarchus, of the tribe of Acamantis, and of the ward of Cholargia, and felt certain that his father would gladly pay any reasonable ransom demanded. I at once, and very foolishly, I must confess, sent my steward with a letter from the young man himself to his parents, and instructions from me as to ransom. Last night Demetrius returned from Athens with news that the story of the young man is certainly true, but Aristarchus and his family have fled from the city. Their estates will be in the hands of their enemy, Critias, very shortly. The whole city is in such a state of anarchy that another army from Sparta is needed to restore order; and, in short, no human being knows where Aristarchus and his family have gone, or, if they do know, they do not choose to tell. Pity me, my friend, for the expense and trouble in which I have been involved."

During this speech Hyllus scarcely knew whether he stood upon the earth or the sea; his head whirled with the emotion which almost overpowered him.

He had but little time for reflection, so acted upon the impulse of the moment, and that impulse at once led him to conceal from his friend his own knowledge of the captive's friends.

"I need a secretary. Will you sell your prisoner?"

"Most willingly, for he has been but a bad bargain hitherto."

"Well, I will buy him at the market price, but as between friends. What ransom should you have demanded from his parents?"

A sum was named which seemed exorbitant to Hyllus.

"I will give you two-thirds of that, if you will give me a discharge for your prisoner at once."

The offer was gladly accepted, and by mid-day Glaucon was sailing down the Hellespont in the galley of Hyllus, and was listening with an eager yet troubled heart to his recital of the events which had passed in Athens since the battle of Ægospotami.

"Nausicaa, my child, we are not going to Byzantium. I have ordered the pilot to steer at once for Tyre, and from thence we will go to Asahel; he will be able to assist us in our search for your parents, Glaucon, better than any one else, I am very well persuaded, and he will be delighted to do it, not only on my account, but for your mother's sake also, whom he knows well, and reverences as she deserves."

"No, no!" cried Glaucon, earnestly. "Pray put me upon the first Athenian galley we may meet, since you are kind enough to permit me to return to my parents. Believe me, I shall find them."

"Forgive me if I remind you that I have paid for your ransom from a selfish motive: you are to be my peace-offering to your father and mother. I will not detain you, but I will not give you up without my reward in the restored friendship of your parents." And then Hyllus showed to the youth the letter of Aristarchus, which he had received in the camp outside Athens.

Glaucon chafed inwardly, but gratitude to his deliverer soon overpowered every other feeling, and Hyllus found much to interest him in his narrative of the adventures of Thetis.

"I am thankful she came to no worse end, for if there ever was a human being reckless concerning the proprieties of life, it is Thetis," replied her elder brother, unsympathetically.

The stately cedar-wood galley of Hyllus floated steadily over the blue waters towards Tyre, and as it floated onwards through those late summer days, strength and renewed energy of life once more revived in the frame of the young Athenian, but a new and more sacred feeling was soon aroused in his heart towards the gentle Nausicaa—a feeling which, long ere the voyage ceased, had led him to wish that it might never end, but that every day of his life might be spent within the sacred influence which surrounded him.

Hyllus, quietly happy in the society of the young people, soon saw with delight the affection which was arising between his beloved daughter and Glaucon.

'Day by day, and evening after evening, it was the same story. The young people never wearied of each other's society.'—HEROES OF ANCIENT GREECE, p. 211.

It was precisely what he would have prayed for, if he had ever thought of seeking the aid of divine care. Looking up from the book upon which he was supposed to be engaged, he saw that sight which is always so full of tender emotions to a parent's heart —the gradual union of two young souls in an entire sympathy and love.

Glaucon had constructed a simple dredge, and after sinking it into the sea, would display some of the marvels of the deep to the admiring eyes of Nausicaa, who, accustomed in her woodland walks with Leda, to study the lovely formation of the flowers of earth, was yet quite ignorant of the wonders of floral beauty hidden in the recesses of the sea. The simplest seaweed was a marvel in her eyes, and a zoophyte, or a living shell-fish, an inexhaustible source of delight to the simply nurtured child of mountain-girded Sparta; while to Glaucon, born in Athens, the sea and her treasures seemed his birthright. He would frequently spring from the side of the galley while conversing with Nausicaa, dive after a descending nautilus, then rising up, ascend upon the oars of the rowers, and return to the deck dripping like some Newfoundland dog, but bright and radiant as though the degradation of Athens, and the uncertainty regarding his parents fate were all things of the past, with which he had no concern. Day by day, and evening after evening, it was the same story. The young people never wearied of each other's society, and Hyllus, although contented to be almost forgotten in the new interest which was stirring the heart of his child, yet found himself reverting once or twice to the words of Leda, and questioning whether earthly love may not sometimes seem selfish to an onlooker. Before the voyage ended, Glaucon had won his prize. Few words were spoken, but Hyllus promised that if Aristarchus and Androclea consented, he would gladly receive Glaucon as his son. "And as to Nausicaa, she will love you better, I believe, because you are from Athens. The one strong passion of her life has been a desire to unite Athens with Sparta in affection."

"And so my Nausicaa does not wish to marry, but does wish to live with Leda alone in the forest. Shall I put Glaucon into a boat, and send him adrift for daring to disturb our dreams of solitude with his thoughts of marriage?"

"Ah, my father, if it were any one else but Glaucon, I never could wish to leave you; but he is so different from every one else. I know Leda will love him."

"And you, shall you not be jealous of Leda's love?"

"Jealous, my father; what do you mean? I hope that every one will love Glaucon. I do not know how they can help it; and, oh, if I can but win the love of his mother and sisters, I shall be happy. You know, my father, I have ever loved Athens. Surely they will not hate me."

"If they do, Glaucon shall be made prisoner again. You know I have bought him, so he shall make his own choice—come and live with us in Spartan slavery if his friends refuse to receive our offering in love."

As to Glaucon, no doubts concerning the reception which his parents would give to his young bride ever crossed his heart. Nausicaa, not aware of her own charms of heart and mind, might doubt. Hyllus, hurt and wounded, might sometimes speculate as to the effect which such disasters as his friends were now suffering from might have upon their feelings, but Glaucon knew his mother's heart, and felt so secure that he almost longed to set off upon his search at once, in order that he might the sooner receive his reward and secure his happiness.

While Hyllus and Glaucon were thus guided towards the re-union of Hellas, Aristarchus and his family were enjoying the hospitality of Asahel, and rejoicing in the simple festivities which accompanied the marriage ceremonial which united Opis and Gershom. Androclea, now thoroughly restored to health, was absorbed in her old interest in botanical study, finding fresh delight in the assistance of Asahel, to whom every nook in the neighbourhood accessible on foot, or within reach of a day's excursion upon horseback, was familiar, and who not unnaturally felt some pride in displaying to his Athenian guests some of the treasures of his national flora. Aristarchus frequently joined in these excursions, subduing his own anxiety concerning affairs at Athens for the sake of his beloved wife.

Before the departure of Aristarchus for Cyprus, a

longer journey than usual was proposed. An excursion to the Dead Sea was arranged. Servants were sent before with tents, and all comforts for the ladies, as both Menares and Aristarchus were anxious to explore the wonders which Asahel described, and he was not unnaturally desirous of showing to them real tangible proof of the historic truth of his sacred books.

The marvellous asphaltic lake was then much what it is now, but the scenery around was very different. Although not so populous as it was four hundred years later, it was still the scene of a far busier life than we can now picture. It was but in the immediate neighbourhood of the lake that the desolation was apparent. Petra, the land of the Edomites, was then no desolate wilderness, but inhabited by warlike and highly civilised nations. The country beyond Jordan was not only fertile, but was highly cultivated, and the cities and villages very numerous. Yet, amidst this glowing picture of purple vineyards, graceful palms, lemon and orange groves, fragrant incense trees, and priceless balms, there lay, just as now it lies, the desolation of the Dead Sea. The pillar of salt was then standing, and some few ancient memorials have been swept away, but the mystic sea and its blighted shores were then a desolation amid surrounding life; while now the life has departed, and the desolation extended its sway from the sea to the countries around it.

This excursion was very interesting to all, and this

entrance into the inner life of the East, a delightful change for those troubled hearts which had been driven thither by the restless waves of Athenian unrest.

Very shortly after this excursion, Aristarchus felt that he might leave his wife with an untroubled heart. He promised to send news from Cyprus so soon as he had reliable news to send; and then, with Asahel, who insisted upon accompanying him to Tyre, he at length set off upon his long-desired journey.

"Friendship formed in adversity has surely a truer germ of life in it than any other," said Aristarchus, as the two men rode quickly down the hillside. "I do not know how to thank you for your goodness to us in our troubles. We are assured by Homer that 'it is Jove who sends the stranger and the poor;' but your law seems to go further, and you love to obey the command of your sacred proverbs in feeding your enemies, and restoring the lost and the strayed to those who hate you. The simple purity of your religious life in Judea is more striking to me, Asahel, than you can well imagine. The sacred peace of your holy Sabbath is so different from the riotous feasting of our festivals to the gods."

"You see our nation just recovering from the severe chastisement of its captivity in Babylon, when every nerve is strained to keep, in its simple purity, the law of our Divine Ruler. I pray most sincerely that the peace we enjoy at present as the fruits of righteousness may not be withdrawn from us, yet I grieve to say that the whole course of our history will be reversed if it be so. We have never been faithful to our law for any long time as a nation, and have always been chastised with sword and famine or pestilence when unfaithful. You see us at our best at present, although, politically, we are not independent. You may not believe me, Aristarchus, but our prophecies, which have never yet failed, assure us that for you also, for Greece, for all the isles of the Gentiles, a Saviour shall arise, who will be 'a light to lighten the Gentiles, and salvation unto the ends of the earth.'"

"He is most sorely needed in Athens, yet I fear we should condemn Him to death if He were to initiate the simplicity and severity of your law."

Asahel was silent for a few moments, and then spoke sadly: "I dare not presume to imagine the form in which this Saviour will appear, yet I feel well assured He will not be like your Socrates, a mere teacher—a companion of the learned and the rich. He will (so I read our prophecies) be One who will pass through the dark and sorrowful places of the earth. He will heal the broken-hearted, preach to the poor and the simple; possibly—" (here Asahel looked forward with a strange look of prevision)—"possibly sweep away the whole system of sacrifice, for through Him 'the daily oblation shall cease, and His soul shall be made an offering for sin.' He would be condemned to death in Athens, you say. May He find at least ten hearts prepared to receive Him in His promised land when He shall appear."

It was at Tyre, while seeking out a passage for Aristarchus, that Asahel met with Hyllus. Happily he was alone, for Aristarchus had gone to the Agora to transact some business, and thus time was given to prepare the father for the reception of his long-lost son.

"Our children are wiser than we, or at least my Glaucon has proved himself wiser than his father. I know not how to thank you, Hyllus, for your preservation of my boy," said Aristarchus, when at last he found himself able to speak to any one but Glaucon.

"There are to be no thanks in the case, Aristarchus. I have gained a son after my own heart, and I trust that in the union of our children we may receive a pledge for the unity of our common Hellas."

Aristarchus did not proceed any further on his journey, but returned at once to prepare Androclea for the joyful tidings, and then lingered on, rejoicing in the tide of new-born happiness which surged through every heart.

Nausicaa soon became even more to Androclea than were her own daughters. The simple yet reverent manners of the young Spartan maiden, her love of nature, kindled by her intercourse with Leda, and her grateful appreciation of that wondrous gift—a mother's love—these qualities endeared her to the noble Athenian matron as no others could have done.

The autumn and the winter months passed away, and the lovely Eastern spring still found the so strangely united families beneath Asahel's roof. One evening in the late spring, the elders of the party were sitting upon the slope of a hill, awaiting the return of the young people from a day's excursion into the woods. The sun had set, and the western sky was flooded with a rich, mellow crimson, which was fast deepening into the short twilight. Aristarchus had just announced his intention to proceed to Cyprus upon the first day of the following week, and was reproaching himself for his long delay from duty.

"Duty! what is duty, my dear friend?" questioned Hyllus. "I should say it was your duty to remain here, and provide for the welfare of your wife and children."

"And live upon the bounty of my friends? You must be aware, Hyllus, that I scarcely know whether I am not already a beggar. Critias has coveted my estates for many a long year, and I feel well assured that by this time he, or some of his creatures, are in possession of them. I ought, at least, to know whether I am to hire myself out as a day-labourer to Asahel or not."

Hyllus would not even now add to the anxiety of his friend by repeating the conversation he had held with the Spartan harmost of Sestus, and he was just pondering what answer to return when Aristarchus spoke again.

"Asahel, what is that commotion upon the high

road? Look, there are lights, torches, and a crowd. Is it some rural festival?"

"I know nothing of it," replied Asahel, rising in surprise to watch the gleaming lights among the trees.

The friends waited expectantly, and as the torches drew near, a glad triumphal chorus was heard. Sweet voices were uniting in song. As they drew nearer, they were recognised.

"It is my Nausicaa!"

"And surely that is Penelope!"

In another moment Thetis came in sight. She sprang towards her parents with a wild cry of joy.

"Io! Io! Io! the Tyrants have fallen, and Athens is freed!"

CHAPTER XI.

"Would my good lady love me best,
    And work after my will,
I should a garment goodliest,
    Gar make her body till.
Of high honour should be her hood,
    Upon her head to wear,
Garnished with governance so good,
    No deeming should her deier.
. . . . .
Her kirtle should be of clean constance,
    Lacit with lesum love;
The mailles of continuance,
    For never to remove.
. . . . .
Her belt should be of benignity,
    About her middle meet;
Her mantle of humility,
    To thole both wind and weit.
. . . . .
Would she put on this garment gay,
    I durst swear by my seil,
That she wore never green nor grey
    That set her half so weel."
                        —*Henryson.*

THE news which Thetis had hastened to carry to her parents was indeed true; and in a few minutes the joyful tidings were confirmed by the appearance of Diodorus, an old friend of Aristarchus, who had undertaken this journey for the sole purpose of bringing his friends back to Athens. In the evening the whole party assembled in the large common room used for meals, and there listened with intense interest to the history of the affairs of Athens during the past few months.

Theramenes, who had negotiated the terms of surrender, was one of the first public men of any influence who dared to oppose the Thirty; and his execution marked an era in the history of the Tyrants. From that time the daily life of the Athenians gradually assumed an appearance of horror which can scarcely be understood in these days. It was, however, in those dark days that the foundation of the alliance of Athens with Thebes was laid, which eventually led to the revival of Athenian freedom. The Thebans pitied and sheltered the fugitives who fled to them as their nearest neighbours,, and eventually Thrasybulus, one of the noblest of these fugitives, marched from Thebes with a band of determined men, his fellow-exiles—men whose hearts were nerved with horror and a stern purpose of retribution. The Thirty prepared a determined resistance, and in this they were aided by the Spartan governor in the citadel. Diodorus described with circumstantial accuracy every event of that eventful time, when, finding themselves unable to resist their outraged fellow-citizens, the Thirty sent to Sparta for help against those whom they called rebels. Lysander, ever ready to humble Attic independence, at once answered the appeal; and if he had been left to follow his own will, the Tyrants would have succeeded in their object, but again the subtly-constituted Spartan government, which seemed purposely formed for the purpose of preventing the ascendancy of one too powerful will, was of service to her prostrate Athenian sister.

King Pausanias was already weary of Lysander's overbearing influence. The Ephori shared his feeling to a certain extent; thus when Lysander was busy with the arrangements for another siege of Athens, King Pausanias, with a large army, and the two Ephors who always accompanied the sovereign to battle, suddenly appeared upon the scene, ostensibly to assist Lysander in his operations, but in reality to overrule them for the welfare of the Athenians. In a very short time Thrasybulus and his patriotic band were in communication with the Spartan king; and soon afterwards the Thirty were driven from the city, at first to Eleusis, but finally, upon their once more attempting to produce dissension and seize upon the authority, the whole population of the city marched out against them in one united body. The Thirty were annihilated, but all their adherents were forgiven upon full submission.

"And now," said Diodorus, in conclusion, "I think I may venture to say that even the Lady Androclea will find no cause for anxiety in her native city, but plenty of room for those gentle ministries to suffering citizens for which her name has repeatedly been invoked of late. I need not say that all estates wrongfully appropriated during the rule of the Tyrants, will now revert to their owners, so that you, Aristarchus, will once more be master in your own house, and we have all taken an oath to forget all injuries, and govern according to our ancient laws."

Three months after the arrival of Diodorus, Aristarchus and his family were once more settled in Athens, Androclea looking even more lovely in her renewed health than she had done when Asahel and Gershom first saw her.

The marriage ceremonies which had united Gershom and Opis, had seemed very simple and reverent to Nausicaa, and she was half tempted to wish that some of the necessary ceremonial might be shortened in her own case, when, shortly after her return home, she was busily engaged in the delightful responsibilities of preparing for her own marriage. True Hellene more than true Spartan though Hyllus was, he yet scarcely liked to permit the marriage of his daughter apart from her old home, yet upon many accounts it was felt to be better for her to have the support and counsel of Androclea, since Athens was to be her future home. The first nuptial ceremony was performed at Sparta, however, for, attended by a few young lady friends, Nausicaa went in reverent procession and with costly sacrifices to the forest temple of Diana. The sacrifices were offered, and happily for the peace of mind of all present, the omens were declared to be propitious, and most favourable to the happiness of the young maiden who offered them.

This service concluded, Nausicaa advanced alone to a smaller altar, where Leda was awaiting her, and when Nausicaa bowed her head over the altar, the priestess cut off a long shining tress from the fair young head; this she put into Nausicaa's hands, who laid it with tremulous fingers upon the altar of the virgin goddess, singing while she did so, a simple invocation:

> "O Diana, best beloved,
> Thy votary's gift receive;
> By thy chaste smile approved,
> Part of myself receive.
> Pure guardian of my maiden love,
> My nuptial vows approve;
> Send thy propitious aid and bless
> My Glaucon's love with steadfastness."

The last words were scarcely uttered when two white doves flew from their roosting places, and settled for one moment upon Nausicaa's head; it was but for a moment, yet as they flew through the open door, Leda bent over the young girl, who was to her as a best beloved daughter—"Those who have been blest by the goddess as thou hast been, my child, need no other assurance of happiness. Never had any bride more joyful omen, than thou hast received this day from the bountiful goddess."

"And thou, my Leda?" said Nausicaa, turning her bright face, now bedewed with happy tears, up to her old friend.

"And I, my child, am happy in your happiness; you must bring your Glaucon to see me, and I hope to see you bring another Nausicaa, who will be to me some reminder of her mother, and of those happy days when the forest temple was the boundary of your childish dreams of happiness."

Immediately after this sacrifice, Hyllus took his daughter to Athens, to stay with Androclea until her marriage.

Several hours of each day were spent by Nausicaa in hard, steady work, in the preparation of the cloak which she must present to Glaucon upon their marriage. Very frequently the whole day was spent in this employment, for Nausicaa was anxious to prove to her Athenian sisters, who were so skilful in all arts, that Spartan maidens were not quite so barbarous as they were sometimes represented to be.

During those weeks of preparation Hyllus made the most of the time still left to him, for the enjoyment of his daughter's society. He it was who introduced her to the beauties of the Acropolis, and although the noble walls, the pride of the Athenian citizens, were now destroyed, yet the Agora was still the same, Hymettus and Sunium were within reach; and Glaucon, when he was permitted to join the party, never failed to find some new object of interest with which to cheer his future bride and father-in-law. Aristarchus was now fully occupied in civic affairs, and in restoring order to the villa, which had been ravaged by the invading army and desecrated by the presence of Critias.

Menares returned to Athens with his friends, and was congratulated heartily, by those who had survived the horrors of the tyranny, upon having escaped so soon from the clutches of the Tyrants. He found that no one had escaped loss of some kind. If life had been spared, money and lands had been wrested from all those citizens who still retained any love of virtue. Socrates had been singled out for annoyance since his poverty prevented any other retaliation; and specially to silence his teaching, a law had been enacted during the tyranny which forbade any one to teach the art of disputation. The son of Sophroniscos was not so easily silenced, however, when he felt that duty compelled him to speak, and conversed among his friends as usual. The paid informers, who were ever on the watch, at length found cause for summoning him before the council; for in a conversation with some friends he had declared that "it seemed surprising to him, if a man becoming herdsman of a number of cattle, and rendering the cattle fewer in number and in worse condition, should not confess that he was a bad herdsman; and still more surprising, if a man, becoming governor of a city, and rendering the people fewer and in worse condition, should not feel ashamed, and be conscious of being a bad governor of the city."

When this remark was repeated to the Thirty, and Socrates, having been summoned, appeared before them, the newly made law against disputation was shown to him, and he was forbidden to hold converse with youth. After a few preliminary questions, the old man at length inquired:

"That it may not be doubtful whether I am doing

anything contrary to what is enjoined, define for me till what age I must consider men to be young?"

"As long," replied Charicles, "as they are not allowed to fill the office of senator, as not yet being come to maturity of understanding. Therefore, do not discourse with any one under thirty years of age."

"And if I wish to buy anything," said Socrates, "and a person under thirty years of age has it for sale, may I not ask him at what price he sells it?"

"You may ask such questions," said Charicles.

"But," interrupted Critias, the once fervent friend of the prisoner—"but it will be necessary for you to abstain from speaking of those shoemakers, and carpenters, and smiths; indeed I think that they must now be worn out, from being so often in your mouth."

"I must therefore," said Socrates, "abstain from the illustrations that I attach to the mention of those people—illustrations on justice, piety, and other such subjects."

"Yes, by Jupiter!" retorted Charicles, "and you must abstain from illustrations taken from herdsmen, for if you do not, take care lest you yourself do not make the cattle fewer."

Menares went to pay his respects to his old friend, and to congratulate him upon his escape from the Tyrants, and the restoration of order to the city. He could, however, do little more than grasp the hand of the sage, and receive a few warm kindly words in reply, for the time of Socrates was fully taken up. In his own small home he was sought out by numerous friends who needed his advice, and when Menares paid his visit, the old man was engaged in giving counsel to Xenophon, who had sought his advice concerning the letter which he had received from his friend Proxenus, who urged him to accompany young Cyrus, the Persian prince, in his expedition to the interior of the country.

Socrates seemed to fear that if Xenophon engaged in the enterprise, it would lead to his banishment from his native country, since Cyrus was well known to have assisted Lysander against Athens. But Xenophon seemed intent upon the only present opportunity of entering upon a life of adventure; and being unable to dissuade his friend, Socrates advised him to proceed to Delphi, and there take counsel from Apollo. Menares lived to see the forebodings of Socrates realised, in the banishment of Xenophon, but the aspirations of the noble-hearted young Athenian fulfilled in his immortal generalship of the ten thousand Greeks. Menares and Hyllus had long conversations during this time upon the subject of religion; for to both of them that visit to Palestine had been an epoch in their lives.

They had there gained some glimmering of light, to enlighten the subjects which had for so long a time perplexed their minds, and the good physician was now one of those who worshipped " The Unknown God"—unknown to him no longer, since in reverent faith he had accepted the revelation of His law and promises. Athens herself was, with her natural buoyancy, recovering new life from the events of the last year. Although feeling bitterly her degradation, she was now busily engaged in internal reformation, and steadily looking out for external alliances which would enable her to recover lost ground. The year which had endured the rule of the Tyrants was blotted out of her annals, and the Archon's name not perpetuated in the public records; but Conon was still at Cyprus, working steadily at his work of reconstructing the navy, and cautiously making every preparation to fulfil the aspiration which alone sustained him through those dark days—the restoration of the walls of Athens: a mere dream it seemed to all who heard of it, and yet before Conon died he was permitted to see his dream realised in the partial restoration of the walls; while he paid the penalty by dying in a Persian prison, a victim to the relentless hate of his enemies.

Lysippus, who was learning under Conon the discipline which afterwards stood his country in such good stead at Haliartus and elsewhere, was summoned home by his father, to assist in the joyful celebration of Glaucon's marriage; but Lysippus was sorely tried when he found that his beloved brother was about to marry a Spartan. He and young Codrus wondered and lamented over the fall of Glaucon, who, from a truehearted Athenian, seemed suddenly to have been changed into a peaceful Hellene; and yet whenever Nausicaa appeared, there seemed to be a sufficient reason for the change.

"I understand your desertion to the enemy now," said Lysippus to his brother, one day after a longer conversation than usual with his future sister-in-law; "Nausicaa is no Spartan, but a true lover of Athens. It is her misfortune, not her fault, that she was born in Sparta."

"My dear Lysippus, you may as well make up your mind to the whole truth at once," replied Glaucon, gaily; "Nausicaa's father is but second cousin, once removed, to Lysander's father."

"I do not believe that Lysander ever had either a father or a mother," was the bitter reply. "I believe that he was hatched by the Lernæan Hydra, nursed by the Gorgons, educated by Polyphemus, and most assuredly he does credit to his bringing up."

"Ah, my Lysippus, I have been among the philosophers, and have learned to see that, at any rate, Lysander's stern decision has ended our fraternal strife; and, better than all, I have been in the school of love, and find that love is not only far pleasanter, but far more powerful than hatred."

"Suppose we agree never to speak of Lysander or of Sparta for a whole year," replied Lysippus. "We shall most certainly quarrel if we do not make some such agreement."

"I agree with you at once, and very joyfully, for Nausicaa will be an Athenian as soon as she is my wife, and I do not care how soon she forgets Sparta."

Thus it came to pass that Lysippus, fresh from Conon, yet consented to act as best man to his brother upon his bridal morning, and found another sympathising friend by his side in the person of young Codrus, who still retained the ring he had received at Ægospotami, and wore it in remembrance of the bitter lessons taught by that memorable day.

A few days before the wedding-day, Nausicaa had gone with her paranymphs, Penelope and Thetis, to the temples of the Athenian Artemis, Hera, and Athena, and upon each one of the altars her sacrifice had been accepted with the most propitious omens. At length the eventful day itself arrived, and Glaucon, in a splendid chariot, drove to his father's house from the new home which he had prepared for his young bride, near Hymettus. He found Nausicaa seated by his mother awaiting his arrival, and never has bride looked lovelier than did the gentle Spartan maiden at that moment, for now the dream of her life was accomplished. The long warfare between Sparta and Athens was ended. She was seated between her father, a descendant of the Spartan Heracleidæ, and her newly found Athenian parents, who were inspired by the divine Athena herself, poor Nausicaa believed, in thus forgiving all Sparta's sins, and taking her to their hearts.

When her young husband approached, Nausicaa rose at once to greet him, and said simply: "Glaucon, I shall not be happy until we have offered sacrifice to Apollo, whose power has healed all our divisions, and united us in one divine love; I do not forget that you are receiving to your hearts a daughter of Sparta."

"And I," said Hyllus, "have one last request to make of my Nausicaa before she leaves my authority for that of her husband. There is one altar in Athens upon which I would wish to offer sacrifice for the lives spared and affection preserved during the last year. My sacrifice is prepared, but I would wish to offer it the last of all."

"Upon what altar, Hyllus?"

"The altar of the Unknown God. I think you will agree with me that, but for Asahel, his simple faith and hospitable entertainment, we should not now be celebrating this marriage. Surely the Deity whom he adores must be a mighty power, and to Him we ought to offer thanksgiving."

There was so united an assent to this proposal of Hyllus, that it seemed as though the unspoken desire of all present had found expression, and a look of intense relief passed over the face of Nausicaa. "I am so thankful," she whispered to Glaucon, who was assisting her into the chariot—"so thankful that we shall invoke the blessing of that Deity who has protected Opis."

When the nuptial chariot drove through the gates into the street, a universal acclamation of applause and blessing arose from the crowd assembled outside. Glaucon himself was a perfect model of manly Athenian beauty; and now, when his firmly-set head was crowned with its bridal chaplet, and his features were illuminated with sacred happiness, Athens might well rejoice in her son. By his side sat Nausicaa, her simple clear-eyed face shining with brilliant radiance through her transparent veil; her long hair fell in ringlets over her shoulders; her head was crowned with a garland of myrtle, while a brilliant sphendone, radiant with the rarest gems, rose above her forehead, and served as a support for the veil. Strings of orient pearls encircled her tiny neck, while her arms and wrists were clasped by bracelets and armlets, whose rare workmanship was more valuable than the gems by which they were adorned. Her robe of Tyrian purple was embroidered with gold, while the rare Indian muslin which Asahel had given her was twisted in a hundred graceful folds beneath the open robe, and fell as a girdle, confining the pure white chiton. Her sandals were of African leather, and the jewelled scarlet thongs so closely interwoven, that but the faintest view of her dainty white foot was perceptible. Costly and beautiful as was the dress in which Nausicaa was attired, the busy populace scarcely noticed it, so anxious were they to gain one glimpse of the young Spartan who was thus entering into the heart of the city. Aristarchus was highly respected by his fellow-citizens, but Androclea was beloved, and for her sake and the remembrance of her loving ministries through the siege, the whole city was stirred, and the history of Glaucon, his captivity, and rescue by Hyllus, was repeated over and over again as the procession wound up the long stately ascent to the temples. The usual paid flower-strewers were upon this occasion joined by numbers of volunteers, who brought their baskets of flowers to strew before the bride, as the only tribute which it was in their power to pay to the bounteous and noble family she was about to enter.

When the procession at length reached the temple door, the young couple were met by the officiating priest, who presented them with a branch of ivy as an emblem of close and ever green affection. They were then conducted to the altar, where the snow-white heifer, which, crowned and garlanded, had formed a conspicuous object in the procession, was now solemnly sacrificed, and the blessing of the deities presiding over marriage invoked upon the young couple. As soon as the omens were declared to be propitious, the rites proceeded. Nausicaa cut a long thick tress from her head, and twining it round a spindle, offered it upon the altar of Athena with suitable invocations. Glaucon made a similiar offering from his more closely shaven head, upon the altar of Apollo, but his offering was twined round a bundle of grass and herbs, to signify his out-door employments. Many sacrifices were also offered by the parents and friends, in order to propitiate all the deities who were supposed to preside over nuptial rites.

These sacrifices were at length concluded, and then Hyllus advanced with Glaucon and Nausicaa to the priest, and with a firm, yet somewhat pathetic voice, said, while he joined their hands: "Glaucon, son of Aristarchus and Androclea, I bestow upon thee my daughter Nausicaa, and may the immortal gods gladden your eyes with legitimate offspring."

Both bride and bridegroom having taken oaths of inviolable fidelity, the marriage was completed by fresh offerings and fresh sacrifices. So much time was thus consumed that it was already late in the day, and the party ought at once to have returned to the house of the young couple. Already the torches were lighted, and the musicians preparing their instruments, when Hyllus, appearing upon the steps of the temple, informed the spectators that the party had still another sacrifice to offer.

Again the chariots were entered, and passing now from the busy city, the party reached at last the lowly altar, simple in its unadorned severity. No presiding statue directed the thoughts of the worshipper to any known deity. Alone, beneath the clear blue sky, it bore the simple yet now world-famous inscription, " To the Unknown God." The family party united in their knowledge of the meaning of that inscription were soon encircling the altar; a reverent solemnity had settled upon every face. The temples in which they had been worshipping were all well known to them; they were dedicated to those whose attributes were clearly understood by their worshippers: men and women with human passions, human aims, and but raised above or below humanity, by their power for good or evil. But before this altar the souls of the partially enlightened party bowed down in reverent homage. Hyllus acted as priest, and truly bore upwards the devotion and aspiration of each heart when, after setting fire to the costly incense which he had brought as sacrifice, he raised his eyes to heaven, and said, in tones of deep solemnity:

"O Thou unseen, Eternal Creator of the heavens and of the earth, and of all which they contain, receive our simple offering of thanksgiving for Thy protection from the sword, from famine, and from dissevered hearts. We know not how to thank Thee as we should, yet we know well that Thou dost hear us; and we thank Thee for revealing Thy existence to us. Accept our sacrifice, we beseech Thee, and suffer us to offer up our prayers to Thee for our children united in holy marriage this day. Bless them, we beseech Thee, with Thy blessing; may their children be pleasant in Thine eyes. And when Thou shalt appear, as Thou hast promised, to visit Thine own people, be pleased to visit us with Thy salvation, we beseech Thee. Send us a Teacher, we pray Thee, O Thou most Holy One, and prepare our hearts to receive Him when He shall appear!"

Hyllus then took a goblet of wine, and after pouring a libation upon the altar, drank a portion, saying, as he did so: "Thanksgiving and worship be to the Unknown God, whom no man hath seen, nor can see."

The cup was then passed round, each member of the party pouring a libation, and repeating the adoration. And thus the long ceremonial of the day was concluded by an act of heart-felt adoration towards that Almighty, ever-living God, of whose existence the Athenian family first became conscious during their exile in Judea. Four hundred years afterwards the prayer of Hyllus was answered, when the great Apostle of the Gentiles declared to the descendants of Glaucon and Nausicaa that God whom they ignorantly served.

It was no unusual circumstance for some bridal party to pay their vows at a favourite shrine; thus the sacrifice of Hyllus excited little comment in the neighbourhood beyond admiration of his munificence, for the oblation was costly and of unusual magnificence, and the fragrant perfume filled the neighbourhood with sweet odours through the whole night.

In the meanwhile the bridal procession wended its way towards the home of Glaucon; the solemnity which had rested over the whole party was now relieved by an intense feeling of joy—joy in the thought that some portion of their debt towards Asahel had been repaid in the way which he would have wished it to be. And now the musicians raised the joyous chariot melody, the customary hymeneal song, and every heart once more arose in glad sympathy with the young couple. At last the house was reached; it was lighted up with coloured lamps, and decked with perfumed garlands. At the threshold Nausicaa stayed her steps for one moment, until Glaucon, raising her in his arms, carried her over the mystic boundary, into what was now her and his own home. As soon as she entered, the bride was presented with an earthen pitcher containing barley by the major-domo; this was given to point out her duty as bread preparer, as her husband's was that of bread provider. In the banqueting-hall she was met by a boy wreathed with acorns, who sang a fresh hymeneal lay; nor did this close the ceremonies which preceded the feast, for a group of slaves, crowned with myrtle, and wreathed with flowers, danced the mystic marriage-dance of welcome to their new mistress.

It had been a long exciting day for Nausicaa, yet she was not permitted to rest, but must preside at the feast which succeeded. Athens was a city bound and fettered by ceremony, and not one must be neglected; even Hyllus would not have wished his daughter to omit one of her accustomed duties to the ceremonial law of her adopted country. Androclea, who had been superintending and joining in every ceremony through the day, would have suffered any pain or fatigue rather than omit one invocation, or forego one accustomed rite.

It was long past midnight when the guests separated, and the young couple were left alone in their future home. Hyllus returned with Aristarchus and Androclea, and it was with a weary, sad voice he said: "Ah! I am the only selfish one among you all. I alone have a heavy heart to-night."

"Because you alone have lost a daughter. We have gained one, and have cause to rejoice," said Androclea.

"And I suppose that I ought to rejoice in having gained a son; but although I used to think that I should do so, practically I find it is Nausicaa who has gained him, not I, for I cannot ask him to come to Sparta for some years at least."

"Ah! never. I hope never! No child of mine goes to Sparta with my consent."

There was a torch-bearer preceding the party, whose lighted torch threw a full glare over the face of Hyllus when these words were spoken, and Aristarchus, who happened to look towards his friend while his wife spoke, was shocked to see the agony expressed upon every feature of the desolate father who had lost his only child.

"Unite with us in our love for the children, stay with us in Athens, and help me with your counsel. Believe me, you will be more than welcome."

"No, my friend, it is impossible. I leave for Egypt in two days."

"You little thought how deeply you wounded Hyllus to-night," said Aristarchus to his wife when they were once more alone.

"There is a poison in the very name of Sparta when it is brought before me unexpectedly, and I fear I was harsh, for Hyllus is widowed, and now childless, yet he knows better than most men how to fill up the vacancy in his lonely heart. I must give him some commissions for Egyptian plants and Æthiopian herbs, and make him promise to keep up a regular correspondence."

Three days after the marriage of Nausicaa, Hyllus set sail from the Piræus, and Nausicaa was left to wean herself gradually from every thought of Sparta in her newly-found happiness.

CHAPTER XII.

> "The soul's dark cottage, battered and decayed,
> Lets in fresh light through chinks that time has made,
> Stronger by weakness, wiser men become
> As they draw near to their eternal home.
> Leaving the old, both worlds at once they view,
> That stand upon the threshold of the new."
> —*Edmund Waller.*

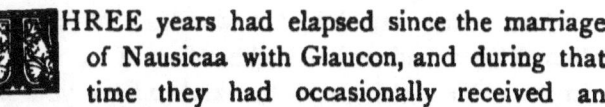THREE years had elapsed since the marriage of Nausicaa with Glaucon, and during that time they had occasionally received an epistle from Hyllus, who was still travelling in the East. Asahel had frequently visited Athens during that time, and had, upon one of these occasions, brought Opis with her eldest boy to visit Nausicaa, and make the acquaintance of her little Leda. Penelope was now married, and was with her husband travelling in Italy, and sending an occasional letter with interesting accounts of the wonders of the natural scenery by which she was surrounded, and the beauty of Rome, which had not yet suffered from the invasion of the Gauls.

And Thetis? Thetis, from some unexplained

reason, was still unwedded—a bright, radiant woman nearly twenty years of age. Several proposals had been made to her parents for the honour of her alliance, but Thetis had pleaded for a longer respite; and now her mother, half sorrowfully, half gladly, was compelled to believe that she should have Thetis with her in her old age still unmarried.

"I am selfish, my child," Androclea said one day, when Thetis had refused the offer of a wealthy Samian noble. "I am so thankful to have you still with me, that I show too plainly my pleasure when you decide to remain with us for a longer time. I know that I am selfish, and yet I will not force you to marry against your will."

"Happy Thetis, who has the very best of mothers," was the reply. "My dear mother, that terrible siege showed me the reality of life." The young voice faltered, as looking up to her mother she continued: "Mother, I never can be as others are now. I broke through the boundaries of maiden modesty when I dropped from the walls of our beleaguered city, and no man shall ever have the right to reproach me with my seeming boldness."

Tears started into the eyes of Androclea. "My own Thetis, is this really the reason?"

Thetis faltered. "I suppose not altogether, dear mother. Believe me that none of those who have asked me for their bride have seemed to me such as I could care to tell that history. Playfellows, friends, they might be, but rulers of my life, the one who must be able to shelter me from all imputation of boldness—no! Ask yourself, dear mother, if any of those who have sought me have been equal in any true nobility to my father, to our Glaucon, to say nothing of Asahel or Hyllus?"

Androclea took the bright young face between her hands and turned it upwards to her own, while she looked down into the depths of those violet eyes, half veiled and hidden by their tears. "I have been a careless mother, my Thetis. I never guessed your trouble; but, believe me, you judge yourself too harshly. We know well that it was an unselfish impulse of filial love which prompted you; and, believe me, it was the warrior maid herself who inspired you with her own courage as well as her own virtue."

A cloud passed over the face of Thetis. "My mother, you love your wilful daughter so well that you will not see her faults. Glaucon and Penelope have taught me what the world thinks of such conduct, and I found out for myself that mine was but poor wisdom. No, I have the best of fathers and of mothers, and what can I want with a husband?"

"You forget, my child, that the parents die before the children, and it is our duty to see you safely placed under the protection of a husband before we leave you."

"When I see my husband, I will say yes, if he asks me to be his wife. Until then, do not urge, my mother; and now do come, there is the chariot, and my father ready to take us to see the 'Crowning of the Poop.'"

There was a great festival that day in Athens, for the vessel sent annually by the city to Delos with grateful sacrifices for Apollo was to be crowned previous to its departure, and all Athens was astir to witness the splendid ceremonial, which had grown in magnificence year by year, but had received its latest ordered dignity from Nicias.

The vessel itself was more than four hundred years old, for it was the one in which Theseus returned victorious after releasing Athens from the annual tribute of virgins and youths to the Cretan monster; and this vessel formed a good and frequent subject for the speculations of the sophists, since it had been repaired so often that it was said no part of the original ship remained. The question to be decided then was, "Is this the vessel in which Theseus sailed or not?" In whichever way the question was decided, there could be no doubt that this vessel of thirty oars had year by year, in part at least of its framework, gone upon its annual journey of thanksgiving. The nation believed itself to have been freed from a most unholy tribute by the intervention of the Apollo of Delos, and thus year by year the children of the freed citizens returned thanks with costly offerings for their recovered freedom. There was a splendid procession from the temple, in which the sacrifices had been consecrated, down to the sacred ship in the harbour. The richly-gilded bridge, with its magnificent tapestried covers, over which the procession was to pass when it reached the sacred island, was now borne as a prominent feature of the procession. The costly sacrifices which had been consecrated were led by their attendants, wreathed and garlanded with the choicest flowers; while the sacred choir, trained with the greatest care, and selected from the noblest families in the city, now passed on through the thronged streets chanting the hymns with which they were to enter the island. Androclea and Thetis were upon the deck of a neighbouring trireme, from whence they had a clear view of the ceremonial upon the sacred ship, and heard every note of the flutes and lyres, every word of the sweet-voiced singers, and at last saw the priest of Apollo advance to the poop of the vessel and crown it with the sacred laurel and olive. As soon as this final ceremony was concluded, a glad shout of acclamation rose from the assembled multitude—a joyous sound of peaceful happiness—for from that day until the return of the vessel, no criminal could be executed in Athens. The city was purified, and must remain at peace. The great solemnity of the year had commenced. Returning in the chariot from the spectacle, and looking out upon the scattering crowd through which the trained coursers found it difficult to pass, Aristarchus at length uttered a loud exclamation of pleasure, and reined up suddenly—" Hyllus, my friend, you here?"

Thetis started hastily, and Androclea turning saw Hyllus walking leisurely up towards the city, just as though he were returning from a day's excursion to Piræus. The face, which was now turned up to them in greeting, was deeply bronzed, but otherwise unchanged by the passage of three years.

"What, my little Thetis! ever the first to welcome me to Athens. Tell me at once how Nausicaa is."

"Well, and happy in the birth of another child—a bright boy; but jump into the chariot, Hyllus, and do not block up the way any longer," cried Aristarchus.

It was a very joyful meeting, and when the chariot left Hyllus at his daughter's home, he promised Androclea and her husband to spend the evening with them, if possible.

Thetis looked somewhat sad and thoughtful as the chariot drove towards their own home. "Do you remember the letter which my father sent to Hyllus but three years ago, dear mother?"

"Ah, my child! why will you ever turn your eyes backward? Surely that letter should be forgotten now. It ought to have been burnt upon the altars of Glaucon's marriage sacrifices."

"I am compelled to remember it," said Thetis, simply, "for Hyllus seems so utterly unable to forget having met with me at that time."

Androclea turned, and saw her daughter's eyes full of tears; a thrill of pain passed through the mother's heart, for she felt that she had by her side a wounded spirit, which was open at any time to added suffering from every random shaft. "I must take counsel with my husband and Hyllus," she thought. "We will travel; that surely will do some good; but I, what a careless mother I have been, not to discover my child's pain sooner!" The meditations of Androclea and the susceptibilities of Thetis were soon diverted, however, for when they reached the Agora, Aristarchus proposed that they should alight, and walk the rest of the distance. There were busy knots of eager talkers in the Agora, and a deep stir of emotion visible upon every face they met.

"What is the news?" asked Aristarchus of some friends who stopped to salute the ladies.

"Only that the trial takes place to-morrow."

"Is that certain?"

"Absolutely certain. Melitus is to be the accuser."

"Well, a trial may mean an acquittal, but I fear the tide is too strong. Shall you go?"

"Most assuredly. Melitus is canvassing right and left, and the least I can do is to appear and vote for the old man."

"Well, be sure you call for me. We will go together." And Aristarchus, with Androclea and Thetis, passed on.

"Of what trial does he speak?"

"Only Socrates, my wife. He is old, and the young men have new lights. He is to be tried for corrupting their morals, and for teaching them irreverence for the gods."

"Socrates!"

"Even so, my Androclea; it is our Athenian

fashion. Athena bestows so much wisdom upon our young men that the old leaves of her olive tree must be pushed off, in order that the new crop may be fully developed. When the old man is dead, those who now cry out for his removal will build him a temple, and reverence him as a demi-god."

"Oh, my husband, of what avail will that be, when the falsehood which seeks to condemn him has entered already into the hearts of his accusers; and surely Apollo will avenge this insult to his wisest son."

"The gods are very patient, my wife; they have witnessed unmoved the unjust sentences passed upon our noblest citizens too often to be very deeply concerned about another."

"Not unmoved, most assuredly, for our beloved city has suffered severely enough to give some proof of celestial interference for the children of Athena."

"Then we must suppose that the few innocent of the crime are frequently permitted to shelter the guilty; but I will do all I can to-morrow to save my old—friend I can scarcely call him, for I never much fancied the company of great talkers, and have always disliked that questioning spirit of Socrates, but none the less do I reverence his love of truth and his search after virtue; and I have frequently heard Xenophon speak of him in such terms of affectionate reverence as convinced me that he was a true teacher of nobility of soul."

"I can but remember Socrates during the siege; and his hopeful endurance, his cheerful greeting, whenever he met with me in his quarter, always revived my heart. Do leave us at once, my Aristarchus, and canvass votes for him among your friends. Our city is so faction led that Melitus will gain the day simply by exciting the passions of the ignorant, unless we make some efforts to oppose him. Insist upon Glaucon's leaving Nausicaa for the day, get Menares to leave his patients to his assistant, rouse up Diodorus and every friend you have, my husband; for my sake, canvass every one who has a vote to give."

When Hyllus arrived at the house of his friends in the evening, he found Aristarchus still out in the city, and Androclea so occupied in thoughts of the impending trial that Thetis was the only one who was at liberty to entertain him; and, in truth, Hyllus himself had but little inclination to talk upon any other subject than Socrates. Thetis questioned him concerning Asahel and Opis, and listened eagerly to his brief narrative of his journey into Egypt; but whenever Androclea entered the room, Hyllus turned to her with sympathetic interest, and inquiry into the subject which was so deeply engrossing her thoughts.

"Tell me, Hyllus. What can there be in our Athenian constitution which induces these frequent instances of ingratitude to our noblest citizens? They say that strangers see our faults more clearly than we can do ourselves. Would Sparta have treated her Miltiades or Themistocles, her Aristides or her Socrates, her Phidias or her Pericles, as we have done?"

"I know not how to answer your question, dear lady, yet I can scarcely imagine a Spartan Socrates. We discuss matters very freely, and accustom our youth to do so at settled times, but our habit of respect for age and authority is so great that it is almost instinctive. It seems to me that Socrates would have been nipped in the bud, our Laconic air would have hardened his brain, and compelled it in the process to have received the impress of our ancient laws. It would perhaps be too much to say that in Sparta Socrates would not see many of the faults of which he complains in Athens."

"Possibly not," cried Thetis, warmly, "but he would surely see some greater. Opis would tell you there are many far greater."

"And Asahel would say there is but little to choose, since, judged by the purity of Asahel's law, both are alike needing a fresh Hercules to cleanse that Augean stable of national sin; and I am now very much of Asahel's way of thinking."

"Specially upon what points?" persisted Androclea.

"Most assuredly upon many points of government —points upon which we Spartans and Athenians differ, as well as many upon which we are agreed. The speculations of Socrates as to advisability could never be entertained in Judea, since their laws are all divinely originated, not framed by the authority of a Lycurgus, as in Sparta, or the gradual outgrowth of the will of the people, as in Athens. That which is a part of our religion is with them a sin. The selection of children for life or death, which is authorised here, is in Judea a crime of the highest magnitude. The statues of our deities are abomination to those who believe the Creator and Ruler of the Universe to be unapproachable by mortals, and only revealed to the pure in heart by His attributes of mercy and holiness, not by any figure. Several of the laws of their ten commands prohibit what is legal in Sparta, as well as elsewhere; and yet, if those laws were fully realised, the world would be happy, the Golden Age return."

"I feel that you are right, Hyllus. I saw enough when we visited Asahel to feel assured of this, and yet you have not answered my question. What special sin is there in our Athenian constitution which incites us to such frequent ingratitude?"

"As a Spartan, I must answer, dear lady; your suffering every question to be decided by mob law. As a servant of the True God, I must say that a city so wholly given to idolatry as Athens must be offensive in His sight, and you must expect evil angels to be sent among you when you can contentedly worship stocks and stones."

"Great Athena, avert his blasphemy and forgive his sin. Hyllus, my friend, you are sorely changed; but you must beware, or the fate of Socrates may be yours also."

"The fate of Socrates, my dear wife, is as yet undecided. I have secured ten votes already, and hope for more to-morrow. Melitus shall not have it all his own way."

The arrival of Aristarchus gave a welcome change of thought, and Hyllus was soon charming Androclea by his description of the Pyramids, and of the Egyptian Thebes; of the marvels of Æthiopia and the glories of Arabia Felix; of Petra and of Damascus; and of the lovely Ionian cities through which he had passed on his return journey. Thetis listened with charmed ears and intent eyes; there was something in the fearless spirit of Hyllus which betrayed his royal birth; his dignity of manner, combined with courteous deference, was a grace produced in those days by Sparta alone. In Athens a spirit of perfect equality led to manners of easy self-assertion. In Athens, even the slaves would push and elbow their way through a crowd regardless of all around them. While in Sparta, the sons of the nobles met their elders with bowed heads and reverent approach. In addition to this courteous dignity, Hyllus, who was but forty years of age, possessed a charm of his own in the eyes of Thetis; he alone knew of her adventure in the camp, and he alone had pleaded for Athens in her hour of extremity among his triumphant comrades. Androclea was so absorbed in thoughts of Socrates that she never noticed the rapt attention with which Thetis listened to every word Hyllus spoke; and as to Thetis herself, she never analysed the feeling which led her to feel such intense pleasure in the return of her father's friend. She was glad that he had returned, for although he did sometimes wound her heart by a reference to their first strange meeting, it was never in a spirit of blame, but rather as to a fellow-sufferer, and the daughter of his friend, whose childhood gave him a right to a more familiar confidence than he could have been entitled to claim elsewhere.

When Aristarchus went to the court the next day, Hyllus went with him, and as he was a stranger in the city, and had no vote, promised to bring to Androclea all the news he could gain from time to time through the day. Androclea and Thetis were resting upon one of the seats in the Agora, with their attendants standing near, when Hyllus approached.

"At last the trial has commenced, and I have seen and heard more of Socrates than I have yet done."*

"How? I am so glad that you have, though."

"Yes; and strangely enough he spoke upon the very subject on which we were speaking last night. When we arrived, we found him in the king's porch awaiting the summons to appear; with him were his friends, Crito, Critobulus, Plato, Apollodorus, and others; and all those who could approach within hearing were listening to him while he discoursed with a young man, Euthyphron, with whom he had accidentally met. Euthyphron had come to the court in order to bring an action against his father, who had caused the death of one of their labourers by leaving him in a ditch, bound hand and foot, as a punishment for having killed a slave in a fit of drunken passion.

---

* For the trial of Socrates I am indebted to the translation of Plato, by H. Cary, M.A., and to Xenophon, by the Rev. J. S. Watson, M.A., etc.

Socrates urged upon Euthyphron the impropriety of thus prosecuting his own father, while Euthyphron defended himself warmly, assuring Socrates that 'it is holy to prosecute any one who acts unjustly either with respect to murder or sacrilege, or who commits any similar offence, whether he is one's father or mother, or whosoever else he may be; not to prosecute him is impious: for the pollution is equal if you knowingly associate with such a one and do not purify both yourself and him by bringing him to justice.' I thought Asahel would have liked to listen to Euthyphron, but Socrates questioned him as to his knowledge of what is holy and what impious; and I feel sure we had as good a specimen of the old man's manner of sifting the grounds of his opponent's knowledge as was possible."

"Did Socrates influence the young man, do you suppose?"

"I do not know; the question was left unsettled as far as words went, but I was very forcibly struck by the strange fearless way in which Socrates spoke out his thoughts concerning the gods honoured by the people. He was in the porch of the Court of Justice, where he is to be tried for blasphemy, and yet he said that the gods quarrelled and were at variance with one another, and that there are enmities among them; warning Euthyphron that what he purposed doing might be pleasing to Jupiter, but odious to Saturn and heaven, and might be pleasing to Vulcan, but odious to Juno. All this was said openly, and I feel well assured that he must have lost many votes by his speech, even though he may have gained another admirer in Hyllus of Sparta."

Androclea looked up, and said simply: "Socrates could not have meant any irreverence, for I know that he advised every one to worship the god of his own country."

"A certain sign of his want of any certain faith himself, I am afraid, my dear lady. It is a pity he never knew Asahel; but I must leave you now, for I must try to gain some fresh news to bring you."

Once more Androclea and Thetis were alone, yet they could not rest. The Agora was thronged by an eager crowd—ladies attended by their servants, idlers anxious to know the result of the trial, strangers in the city—all were in a restless fever of anxiety. The friends of Melitus and Anytus could be easily distinguished by their offensive and aggressive airs of righteous indignation, while those of Socrates seemed like Androclea, overwhelmed with surprised and pained anxiety. At length the suspense became insupportable, and Androclea proposed a visit to Nausicaa; and there, in the simple untroubled face of the young mother, and the baby prattle of her little ones, the deeper anxiety was at length forgotten.

The sun was sinking low when once more Androclea and Thetis found themselves in the neighbourhood of the court. They had neared the king's porch before they became aware that the trial was over. There were cheers, mingled with hisses and cries of shame; and presently the road became impassable from the stream of the returning populace, wearied with their strained attention during the trial. The steward who was in attendance upon Androclea advised her to mount the steps of a temple which overlooked the road, and in a few minutes the ladies were seated in the portico looking down upon the busy crowd which had been for many hours engaged in listening to that now immortal trial. Anytus passed with his friends, his head high in the air, his whole appearance that of a man who had just performed a most virtuous action. He was soon followed by his chief, the principal accuser of Socrates—Melitus, a young man with a hook nose, lank hair, and a scrimp thin beard, who was carried in a sort of triumph by his friends, and every face seemed to say, "This is the man who is about to restore the worship of the immortal gods and true virtue to Athens."

"There is no need to ask the result of the trial. It is written in the face of Melitus," said Androclea sadly. She had scarcely spoken when there was a change in the appearance of the crowd. Grave and reverend men, nobles of Athens, passed by with bowed heads and sad grave faces. Again there was a change, and presently the officers of State appeared. Socrates was in their midst, guarded by "The Eleven." The old man looked as bright and cheerful as if he was passing out to his daily walks among the groves of the Academy, those groves which he was never to visit again. His faithful friends, Crito,

Plato, and the rest, followed him as closely as they were permitted to do. Plato, pale and indignant, was tearless, but Apollodorus could scarcely restrain his passionate emotion. One impulse moved both mother and daughter; they passed swiftly down the steps of the portico that they might gain one last glimpse of their city's noblest teacher, ere he passed through the prison gateway. Just as the prisoner passed the steps, he was putting his hand upon the head of Apollodorus, and gently chiding his tears and unrestrained emotion. "I am grieving," said Apollodorus—"grieving that I see you going to die undeservedly."

A sweet smile passed over the face of Socrates. " Would you, my dearest Apollodorus, rather see me die deservedly than undeservedly, then? How is this?" he continued, as, turning round, he saw others in tears. "Do you now weep? Do you not know that from the moment I was born death was decreed for me by nature."

These were the last words Androclea heard Socrates speak, and they were the first Thetis had heard; but the simple confidence, the bright untroubled look of the old man who was thus passing away to his death, was too much for the over-strained heart of Thetis. She bowed her head upon her mother's shoulder. " Mother, mother, it is not possible that he is condemned to death."

Before Androclea could recover herself sufficiently to answer, they were joined by Aristarchus, Glaucon,

"But by three votes, my dear wife. It has been a bitter, bitter disappointment. If we could but have mustered three more votes he would have been saved."

"I have seen him, my husband; we saw him pass."

"I am thankful for that; you have seen how he bears it. Ah me, you should have heard the last words of his defence; they ring in my ears yet. 'And now it is time to depart,' he said, 'for me to die, for you to live, but which of us is going to a better state is unknown to every one but God.'"

The supper party at the house of Aristarchus that night included many of the friends of Socrates, and there was a general feeling of relief in the remembrance that the sentence of death could not be executed until the return of the sacred galley from Delos. The poop had been crowned but yesterday, and a month at least would elapse before the vessel returned.

Aristarchus tried once or twice to divert the conversation from the subject which was uppermost in all minds, but every effort was in vain. Every heart was full of Socrates, and every tongue delighted in telling his good deeds or his wise sayings. Chærecrates was there to bear witness to the wisdom which had advised him to be the first in seeking a reconciliation with his brother, with whom he had been at variance for some time. Hermogenes, another friend, informed his auditors that, previous to the trial, he had urged Socrates to consider and prepare such a defence as was likely to touch the hearts of the impressible Athenians, but Socrates assured him that his whole life had been spent in preparing his defence, since, said he, "I have constantly lived without doing any wrong, and such conduct I consider to be the best preparation for a defence."

"What I liked best in his defence was, when he assured us that, after Apollo at Delphi had told Chærepho that 'Socrates the Athenian was the wisest of men,' he could not understand what could be meant, 'for,' said he, 'I said to myself, What is this enigma? I am not conscious to myself that I am wise, either much or little. What then does he mean by saying I am the wisest of men?'"

"How did he explain the oracle, then?"

"Simply by discovering, through the questions he asked others, that he alone knew himself to be ignorant. Every one else with whom he conversed supposed that he knew a great deal; thus Socrates declared that the real meaning of the oracle is, 'Human wisdom is worth little or nothing.'"

"And I," said Glaucon, "thought that the finest part of the apology when he said, after describing the dishonourable devices by which it was easy to escape death in battle or in trials like his own: 'It is not difficult, O Athenians, to escape death, but it is much more difficult to avoid depravity, for it runs more swiftly than death; and now I, being slow and aged, am overtaken by the slower of the two; but my accusers, being strong and active, have been overtaken by the swifter, wickedness. And now I depart condemned by you to death, but they condemned by truth as guilty of iniquity and injustice; and I abide my sentence, and so do they.'"

"And there can be no doubt what the sentence will be," said Aristarchus. "Twenty years hence he will be revered as a demi-god."

The night was already far spent when the party broke up, but before Hermogenes left he said to Androclea: "I do wish you could have heard the last words of our friend to the judges; as well as I can remember them they were: 'Punish my sons when they grow up, O judges, paining them as I have pained you, if they appear to you to care for riches, or anything else before virtue, and if they think themselves to be something when they are nothing.'"

"May the divine Athena preserve for her children loving memories of her most favoured son," was the earnest response of Androclea's heart, and in a few moments the guests had departed; and Androclea, proceeding to the thalamos to bid Thetis good-night, found her already in a sweet happy sleep.

CHAPTER XIII.

> " Be good, sweet maid, and let who will be clever,
> Do noble things, not dream them all day long,
> And thus make life, death, and the great forever
> One grand sweet song."
> —*Canon Kingsley.*

THE beautiful villa in which Opis had been entertained on her first journey to Athens was still standing; the walls had been left untouched by the invading army, but it had been despoiled of all its furniture, and every surrounding spot bore traces of the ruthless invader's occupancy. Horses had been turned loose in the garden devoted by Androclea to the cultivation of her choicest herbs, and not one vestige remained of those for which she had cared with such devoted tenderness. The lovely flower-garden was still a wreck, notwithstanding the pains which had been taken to restore it to some of its former beauty; and the lovely veiled statue of Hygeia seemed utterly out of place in the midst of the general desolation.

The great festival of crowning the poop being over, Androclea and Aristarchus were anxious to return at once to the villa, and there superintend the operations of their workmen and slaves in harvesting the fruits, and once more raising a fitting throne for Hygeia; thus upon the evening of the day after the trial of Socrates, Thetis was rejoicing in the freedom of their approaching country life.

When the chariot drove up the long avenue which led to the house, some splendid dogs rushed out to greet their master.

"Ah, Gnome! Vega! Good dogs. Are you as anxious to be off to the woods as your master?"

"Did you ever see the Anadendrades look so beautiful?" said Androclea.

"Demeter has been here herself, while we have been in dreary, dusty Athens, my dear mother. But does not this remind you of what Homer says:

" ' Tall thriving trees confessed the fruitful mould,
The reddening apple ripens here to gold;
Here the blue fig with luscious juice o'erflows,
With deeper red the full pomegranate glows;
The branch here bends beneath the weighty pear,
And verdant olives flourish round the year.' "

"Yes, my Thetis. Hellas is still in some respects what Hellas was when Homer wrote; but you might have continued the verses. If my memory serves me rightly, there is something about—

" ' Here ordered vines in equal ranks appear
With all the united labours of the year.' "

"My dear Androclea, if you and Thetis begin to recite Homer, I am afraid you will lose half the beauty before your eyes."

"No fear of that, my dear father. No one could look upon those Anadendrades unmoved."

It was indeed a beautiful sight. For some distance before them vines were carefully trained against trees specially prepared for the purpose; and they rose from terraces in the profuse beauty of verdant arches or pillars, crowned with fantastic capitals of wreathed and garlanded grapes. The noblest efforts of the architects of Athens could never exceed the natural beauty of some of those trained vines, where every variety of purple, gold, and green, with ruddy brown, was intermingled with the most graceful expression of artistic form.

"Yes, the vintage promises well; and I see that Demaratus has begun harvesting operations already. He is there on the terrace with his workers," said Aristarchus, cheerfully.

"What a happiness to be at home again, far from cold, cruel Athens!" said Androclea; and as she spoke, the baying of the dogs and the noise of the chariot wheels announced their arrival to the household. They were met at once by the housekeeper and steward, with many of the servants, and were received by all with joyful welcome.

The next few days were spent by the family in so continuous a round of busy interest, that all other thoughts were banished. The season of vintage was always a busy one. The whole of the labourers and slaves turned out together, as for a joyous festival. They crowned their brows with ivy, and under garlands of ivy the grapes were carried to be pressed in the wine-presses, or stored for winter use. In addition to the labours of the vineyard, the orchard, with its rich store of apples, quinces, pomegranates, and citrons, required the master's eye, and the supervision of the mistress.

Aristarchus spent much time in the woods and upon the hills, and in the course of the second week he was joined by Glaucon and Hyllus, while Nausicaa, with her two babies, added to the enjoyment of Androclea and Thetis. During these pleasant autumnal evenings, all ceremony was banished. Thetis, with her mother and Nausicaa, joined the party in the general sitting-room, even though sometimes neighbours who had joined in the day's hunt remained to partake of the family supper.

Those were happy evenings. The ladies, in the simple fashion of Homeric days, produced their dainty spinning-wheels or delicate embroidery, and listened while the adventures of the sportsmen were recounted —the long and exciting chase after some splendid stag, which had at last been brought to bay by the marvellous tact of Smilax or of Vega. Sometimes the eldest child of Nausicaa was allowed to toddle about among her elders before going to bed; and her baby prattle and winning ways united all hearts in sympathy.

One evening, when Aristarchus and Glaucon, thoroughly wearied out by a long day's chase, had retired earlier than usual, Androclea and Hyllus were left alone. Androclea had been carefully arranging some herbs which Thetis had collected during the day, and Hyllus, interested in the subject which engrossed her, had not felt the weariness of his tired body. The herbs were at last all safely enclosed in their unglazed earthen jars, and the stoppers had been duly sealed, when Androclea, turning to the hearth, stirred up the logs for one final blaze of warmth and cordiality before retiring to rest.

"You have no idea what a comfort Thetis is to me," said the gentle lady, simply. "Those herbs have been gathered and dried by her care alone, and I have been so busy that they must have been lost but for her dainty fingers."

"What will you do when she leaves you? I scarcely expected to find her here when I returned, and I hear that it is her own choice alone which keeps her at home."

Androclea turned to her friend with a strange expression of pain upon her face. "If you were not so closely connected with us, Hyllus, I could not speak to you so openly, and yet I cannot resist telling you the truth. For my own sake, of course, I would wish to keep Thetis by my side for ever, but this cannot be; and what do you think burdens my child's heart? You can never guess, I am sure. She feels so much shame whenever she remembers her flight from the city, that she says she will never give any man the right to reproach her with over-boldness."

"Over-boldness! Surely there never was such a case of perverted conscience. If ever I felt genuine respect for any one, I felt it for Thetis, child though she was."

"I wish you would tell her so," said Androclea, unconsciously. "If she thought that you did not look upon her conduct as a degradation, her self-respect might possibly be revived. As it is, I found her in tears the other day, because, she said, 'You seemed never able to forget her wilful conduct.'"

A strange expression settled upon the face of Hyllus, but he said little more; and soon afterwards his servant entered with a lamp to conduct him to his chamber.

Hyllus declined joining the hunting party next day; and when he had seen Aristarchus and Glaucon safely off, he turned at once into the herb-garden, expecting to find Thetis there. He was not mistaken. She was working busily among the herbs which she had collected and spread upon the altar of Hygeia. As soon as Hyllus appeared, Thetis looked up. "What! have you renounced the service of Artemis so soon? Then you must, if you please, assist me in that of Hygeia. Do you see those vervain roots, they have been safe all through the desecration. My mother feared they were lost; but I have just discovered them sheltered beneath that prickly pear, and that they have escaped from the hoofs of the horses of your countrymen."

"I am thankful that something has been saved," said Hylas, as he removed the overhanging branches of the weird cactus, which overshadowed the dainty plants. "I shall be thankful when all the evil perpetrated in those days is removed, or changed into a blessing."

"A blessing! How can that be? Can you or your kings restore to us our dead from Ægospotami?"

Just at this moment the little Leda came tottering down the walk towards the herb-garden. "I think my Nausicaa would say that in her case it has been turned into a blessing."

"Forgive me! forgive me!" cried Thetis, hastily. "You at least have restored to us our dead, and that is the reason, I suppose, that you are here to see me recover my mother's vervain," she added, archly; "but I must go and tell her I have found it."

"Not yet, Thetis. I stayed from the hunt purposely to speak to you to-day. You can turn my evil into a blessing, if you will. If any one in Athens may be said to have deserved well of her own city for faithful affection, and from Sparta for recalling us to some sense of piety, some fidelity to our common Hellas, it is you. Your song that night produced a far deeper effect than you supposed. I was not the only one who felt the shame of our hard, bitter intentions while you sang."

Thetis looked up. Her bright face was pale as death now; her arms drooped by her side, and she

'Forgive me! forgive me!' cried Thetis, hastily. 'You at least have restored to us our dead, and that is the reason, I suppose, that you are here to see me recover my mother's vervain.'—HEROES OF ANCIENT GREECE, p. 266.

seemed unconscious of all, save of some distant pain. Recovering herself at last, she said, "Do you speak thus to flatter me, Hyllus? Surely you must feel that it is cruel even to refer to that terrible time."

"And why should I flatter you, Thetis? I speak the bare truth to you as I spoke it to your mother last night. I have never respected any one as I have you; and I should have asked you to be my wife three years ago if your mother had not shown such deep hatred towards Sparta, and I—I felt that I should be wearying your young life by asking you to mate with my advancing age. I feel now that your parents would not repulse me; but I have not spoken to them. I ask you yourself, Thetis, can you trust your happiness to me? No younger husband can love you as I do, Thetis; and yet I feel that I am asking too great a sacrifice, am seeking too great a treasure; for what can I offer you in exchange?"

Thetis looked up. All her pallor had disappeared, and the old bright flush of her happier days shone forth from every feature. "I believe you, Hyllus, now, and I am very, very happy."

Not one more word was spoken, for little Leda had just reached them; and Thetis, snatching her up, rushed hastily towards the house, to the utter consternation of the nurse, who was compelled to retrace her steps.

Life and death, do they ever go hand in hand? Is death but the herald angel to a reviving life? Yes, they ever go hand in hand upon earth; and the death of one state of existence is but the birth into the life of another. Thus while the household of Aristarchus was rejoicing in the prospect of the marriage of Thetis with Hyllus, the heart of Athens was stirred to its depths by sorrow over the approaching death of Socrates.

Hyllus had been summoned to Sparta by the Ephori, who had appointed him to an important post in the city; and upon his account, the preparations for the marriage were hastened forward with unusual speed, so that in less than a month after leaving Athens, the whole family returned to celebrate the wedding rites.

The marriage of Thetis was very different in many respects from that of Nausicaa. A tender shadow of sorrow seemed to brood over the heartfelt happiness of all. The impending execution could but thus overshadow their joy. Yet nothing could really cloud the radiant happiness of Thetis, or the heartfelt gratitude of Hyllus.

Upon the day after their marriage, Hyllus and Thetis set sail for Sparta, the galley in which Nausicaa had left her own home three years ago bearing back another true womanly heart to fill her place. Aristarchus accompanied his daughter for some distance out to sea, and left Glaucon to drive his mother and Nausicaa home. Passing up the road from Piræus, they met a group of friends, who seemed to be stirred by a far deeper emotion than usual.

"Has the galley arrived yet?" asked Glaucon.

"It was seen off Sunium last night, and will be here to-day."

"Here to-day!" Yes, the news had spread through the city already, and the usual festal greeting which awaited the galley was felt to be a terrible mockery by most true Athenians.

"It is an ill-omened galley, and ever has been," said one of the idlers who awaited its arrival. "The pilot hoisted a black sail upon its first return voyage, and our king was sacrificed through the mistake. Now it comes sailing on with floating banners and the sound of flutes, four hundred years old; yet it is the herald of death to one of the noblest sons of Athena."

"A king over the spirits of men, who leaves no successor to his throne, no Theseus to supply his place."

"There are many wand-bearers, but few inspired, as the priests say at Eleusis. Young Plato promises well, but he is too reserved and proud to win many hearers."

"There is one consolation for those who love Socrates: we know that he has taught us nothing really new—virtue, temperance, and justice, are ancient deities; he has but invited us to worship them with true reverence, looking beyond the image to the virtue signified. We must keep the sacred fire alive ourselves when the favourite of Apollo has left us."

Thus spoke the outer world, but in the interior of the prison, Crito, the venerable friend and patron of Socrates, had been with him from day-dawn until the latest hour permitted by the authorities. Crito had spent large sums already, and was prepared to spend much more in perfecting a plan for the escape of the prisoner, and when he entered the prison, it was for the purpose of persuading Socrates to consent to the arrangement; but all his efforts were in vain.

"What then?" replied the sage. "Is it right to do evil, Crito, or not?"

"Surely it is not right, Socrates."

"But what then? To do evil, when one has been evil entreated; is that right or not?"

"By no means," replied Crito.

"Observe then what follows. By departing hence without the leave of the city, are we not doing evil to some, and that to those to whom we ought least of all to do it or not? Consider it thus. If, while we were preparing to run away, or by whatever name we should call it, the laws and commonwealth should come, and presenting themselves before us, should say, 'Tell me, Socrates, what do you purpose doing? Do you design anything else by this proceeding in which you are engaged than to destroy us, the laws, and the whole city, as far as you are able? Or do you think it possible for that city any longer to subsist and not be subverted, in which judgments that are passed have no force, but are set aside, and subverted by private persons?' What should we say, Crito, to these and similar remonstrances, for any one, especially an orator, would have much to say on the violation of the law which enjoins that judgments shall be enforced? Shall we say to them that the city has done us an injustice, and not passed a right sentence? Shall we say this, or what else?"

"'This, by Jupiter, Socrates?'"

"What then, if the laws should say, . . . 'Then, O Socrates, be persuaded by us who have nurtured you, and do not set a higher value on your children or on life, or on anything else than justice, that so, when you arrive in Hades, you may have all this to say in your defence before those who have dominion there. Now you depart, if you do depart, unjustly treated, not by us, the laws, but by men; but should you escape, having thus disgracefully returned injury for injury, and evil for evil, having violated your own compacts and conventions which you made with us, and having done evil to those to whom you least of all should have done it—namely, yourself, your friends, your country, and us—both we shall be indignant with you as long as you live, and there our brothers the laws in Hades will not receive you favourably, knowing that you attempted, as far as you were able, to destroy us. Let not Crito then persuade you to do what he advises rather than we.' These things, my dear friend Crito, be assured, I seem to hear as the votaries of Cybele seem to hear the flutes. And the sound of these words booms in my ear, and makes me incapable of hearing anything else."

These and other considerations upheld the sage in his resistance to all entreaties; he would neither imperil the safety of his friends nor flee from the consequences of his own teaching; and with sorrowful hearts his devoted friends were at last compelled to yield to his conviction, that as it is impossible to enjoy life with a diseased body, so for him life in his old age, polluted with cowardice or ingratitude towards the laws of his native city, or a want of faith in the verdict which he should receive from "the one who understands the just and the unjust, the one, even truth itself." Such a life was not possible for Socrates.

The assurance of a better life beyond this was, however, strong and firmly fixed in the heart of the sage; he had strengthened this faith by the conclusions of reason, and had also that unseen witness, which is perhaps the surest support of faith in the evidence for an invisible ministration between life and death. He assured his friends that he had dreamed upon that very morning that a beautiful and majestic woman had approached him. She was clad in white garments, and seemed to call to him, and say, "Socrates! three days hence you will reach fertile Phthia."

The day after the return of the sacred galley, Socrates drank the hemlock presented to him by the executioner of the city, in the midst of a large party of his devoted and weeping friends.

Androclea spent the day in the temple of Æsculapius, offering propitiatory sacrifices to the deity who was supposed to preside over the powers of life and death.

Aristarchus, returning from his voyage with Hyllus late upon the day of the execution, was listening to the song of the rowers, who were singing, in memory of Euchidas of Platæa, a simple ballad, narrating one of those heroic acts of obedience to the national oracle which had preserved the national independence, and stimulated its youth to emulation in all noble endurance. The rowers sang in unison, and their oars kept time to the music while they sang :

> " It was the eve of an autumn day
>   One hundred years ago,
>   All Attica lay dark and dim,
>   Yet no cry was heard of woe.
>
> " There were darkened hearths in Athens,
>   Darkness on Besa's height ;
>   There was darkness in the Laurium,
>   Anaphlystus showed no light.
>
> " And from the wave-washed harbour
>   Of the dim Piræan shore
>   To the mustered host on Platæa's coast
>   The south wind whispers bore,
>
> " Of the surging hymn of freedom—
>   Freedom singing through the night ;
>   Freeborn, we wait through the darkening hours
>   For the gift of our freeborn light.
>
> " And the mustered host on Platæa's coast,
>   Expectant, silent waits ;
>   With straining eyes through the gathering gloom,
>   It peers through the northern gates.
>
> " Awaiting the swift Euchidas,
>   Who had left ere dawning day,
>   To bear from the Delphian altar
>   Pure flame from the god of day.
>
> " For all Attic fire was extinguished
>   By true Athenian hands,
>   The fire which had been polluted
>   By invading Persian bands.

"No fire which a Mede had kindled
  Might blaze in an Attic home,
Better sit for years in the darkness
  Of a free-born, free-kept dome.

"And far away Euchidas,
  Young athlete, bright and brave,
Bears high the holy cresset,
  True freedom's light to save.

"He has borne it from Parnassus,
  And down the rocky steep
Of Cithæron, and past the gates
  Where Theban heroes sleep.

"On, swiftly in the sunlight,
  Never stopping by the way,
Sprinkled with lustral water,
  And crowned with sacred bay.

"Day's last red light was sinking
  Behind Ægina's height,
When the wind was stirred, and a cry was heard,
  'It comes!* The sacred light!'

"Radiant, not soiled, not panting,
  Euchidas bore his prize,
On, through applauding voices,
  On, past bright kindling eyes.

"Bore it on to the sacred Archon,
  Through our nation's pomp and pride,
Bowed in lowly salutation,
  Then drooping, fell, and died.

"O Euchidas, true light-bearer,
  While Hellas lives, thy name
Shall kindle faith and duty
  To a hero's death and fame.

---

* The distance traversed is said to have been over 90 miles, between sunrise and sunset.

> "For to every Attic city
> They bore a blazing brand;
> And the light Euchidas kindled
> Enlightened all the land."

"The light Euchidas kindled," murmured Aristarchus to himself. "Yes, that was the light of freedom from foreign invasion; but who shall enkindle for us the light of holiness, and of righteousness? That light must be carried from some other shrine, I fear me, and lighted at another altar."

Some two months later, Asahel received the following letter:

"My dear Asahel,—When are you coming to visit us? Bring Opis and Gershom, and all their little ones, with you as soon as possible. We are lonely, my friend; and why? Thetis has been carried away from our household hearth and our Neptune-guarded city. Whither, and by whom? you ask. What will Opis say when she hears that her old home under the shadow of Taygetos is now the home of my Thetis? It is even so. Hyllus has wooed and won my youngest child; and she was so happy in the prospect of her marriage with him, and so utterly unfitted to be the wife of any younger man, that we are compelled to rejoice in her happiness; but we are very lonely.

"We are deserted by other friends also, and are specially anxious about Xenophon, who, as you know, joined Clearchus in his expedition to Persia under Prince Cyrus. To me the expedition seemed madness from the first, and there are already rumours floating about that the prince is killed, and the whole Greek contingent endangered; but you possibly know more of this matter than we do here. If you do not come at once, send me reliable news by the bearer of this, if you can; but come to us, Asahel, if you can possibly do so.

"I suppose you have heard that we have lost Socrates. I feel almost ashamed to speak of the matter even to you, but already the slumbering conscience of the city has been aroused, and there is little chance of the faction which condemned him to death escaping punishment.

"Menares has, I suppose, given you particulars concerning the trial and execution. The month spent in prison was spent by Socrates in long conversations with his friends and late pupils. I wonder whether Menares told you of his singular assertion that he had dreamed several times, at intervals during his lifetime, that his warning spirit desired him to apply himself to the study of music. 'Socrates,' it said, 'apply yourself to and practise music.' This was a singular dream to be repeated; but, to my mind, the most singular part of the matter is, the interpretation which Socrates put upon the dream, for he said: 'And I formerly supposed that it exhorted and encouraged me to continue the pursuit in which I was engaged, as those who cheer on racers—namely, to apply myself to music, since philosophy is the highest music, and I was devoted to it. But now, since my trial took place, and the festival of the god retarded my death, it appeared to me that if by chance the dream so frequently enjoined me to apply myself to popular music, I ought not to disobey it, but do so, for that it would be safer for me not to depart hence before I had discharged my conscience, by making some poems in obedience to the dream.'

"Now, the plain and simple interpretation of the dream seems never to have occurred to Socrates. Music, pure and simple music, the harmonious mastership of the lyre, or any other instrument, I should have thought the meaning of the dream; yet Socrates must, even in so simple a matter, encumber the meaning (so it seems to me) with sophisms. Is it possible that, if he had acted in simple obedience, he might have been permitted to receive some such revelation as has been vouchsafed to your prophets, my Asahel? Who can tell? 'He *has* been,' as they say in Sparta, and he has done much to awaken the mind of our Hellas to those truths which you would wish us to receive. I mean specially that faith in holiness (if only he had known the true source of holiness), that faith in the immortality of the soul, which is embodied in many portions of your sacred books; specially I remember one passage: 'I know that my Redeemer liveth, and that He shall stand at the latter day upon the earth, and though after my skin worms destroy my body, yet in my flesh shall I see God.' This is the utterance of no mere speculation, but of a firm faith in immortality, and to Socrates in his last hours this faith seems to have been given. Phædo, who was with him to the last, assures me that he said, after proving in his own fashion the difference between the invisible ruling, governing principle within man, which we call soul, and the perishable body: 'Can the soul then, which is invisible, and which goes to another place like itself, excellent, pure, and invisible, and therefore truly called the invisible world, to the presence of a good and wise God (whither, if God will, my soul must also shortly go)—can this soul of ours, I ask, being such, and of such a nature, when separated from the body, be immediately dispersed and destroyed as most men assert? Far from it, my dear Cebes and Simmias.' Thus you see, my Asahel, that the faith you would have wished to see and hear sustained our Socrates at the last; not that he was capable of receiving the full and noble teaching of your faith I grant; specially I was reminded of your words by his last request to his faithful friend, Crito: 'Crito,' he said, 'we owe a cock to Æsculapius. Pay it, therefore, and do not neglect it.'

"These words were his last, spoken when the benumbing influence of the hemlock had already stiffened feet, legs, and thighs. A few moments after speaking thus, he gave one convulsive movement and expired.

"Now, your words, my Asahel, of which I was reminded by this last request of Socrates, were spoken when we were riding together down the hill-side near Bethlehem. You said that when He, the promised Universal Saviour, shall appear, He will sweep away the whole system of sacrifice. At least you said that you thus read your ancient prophecies concerning Him who is to be a light to enlighten the Gentiles, as well as to be the glory of His people in Israel. Sacrifices and augury, the whole system to be swept away! What a change does this imply, and with what will it be replaced? What propitiation can replace the sacrifices offered by all nations, barbarous or free?

"My wife longs to see you as much as I do. She has felt this disgrace to our beloved city very deeply, and now that no one thinks, speaks, or writes of any one but Socrates, every word spoken by him in life is remembered and repeated. Those words of his respecting music made a deep impression upon Androclea when they were repeated to her by Plato, and she wrote some verses to express the thoughts they suggested. I think you will like to see them, and therefore send them to you. But come to us, my Asahel, and revive our drooping hearts with some of the lessons of your higher wisdom. Do not lightly set aside the prayer of your sincere friend,

"ARISTARCHUS of Athens."

The verses enclosed by Androclea ran thus:

"What then is music? What the wondrous power,
    Which the enraptured Delphian's 'Wisest' sought to reach?
What is the mystic rapture born in that bright hour,
    When the fair morning stars sang joy too great for speech?

" Is music then a mingling of pure souls,
    In holy concord with the souls above?
The air we breathe, the air which round us rolls,
    Is it the birth and death of harmony and love?

"The mortal master rules this floating air,
　　Compels its full submission to his power.
　Now though the pealing organ bids it rise in prayer,
　　Now though the flute soothe love's soft evening hour.

"Is ether then one grand harmonious lyre,
　　Where spirits freed from dross for ever spread
　Their tremulous incense, sacrificial fire,
　　And holiest harmonies by angels led?

"I know not! All is mystery to me;
　　Yet one thing certain by my soul is known,
　God has a living harp suspended free,
　　Above earth's storms, her selfish faithless moan.

"And to this harp, attracted age by age,
　　The bards approach with earnest kindling eye,
　Each sways the lyre, and each when tempests rage,
　　Lies, vanquished and 'forgotten,' down to die.

"He says 'Forgotten,' but my soul says 'No!'
　　The strain must be immortal from a harp divine,
　The bard enkindles for his race the glow,
　　The sacred flame which burns while light shall shine.

"High soars the harp, the sacred harp of God,
　　The harp which kindles nations to true life,
　Woe worth the bard, who strings that lyre of God,
　　For faithless aims, or base ignoble strife."

A SELECTION FROM CATALOGUE
OF
Popular and Standard Books
PUBLISHED BY
WILLIAM P. NIMMO, LONDON AND EDINBURGH.

⁂ Complete Catalogue of Mr. Nimmo's Publications, choicely printed and elegantly bound, suitable for the Library, Presentation, and School Prizes, etc. etc., will be forwarded gratis, post free, on application.

'Mr. Nimmo's books are well known as marvels of cheapness, elegance, and sterling worth.'—OBSERVER.

NIMMO'S POPULAR EDITION
OF
THE WORKS OF THE POETS.

In fcap. 8vo, printed on toned paper, elegantly bound in cloth extra, with beautifully illuminated imitation ivory tablet on side, price 3s. 6d.; also kept in cloth extra, gilt edges, without tablet; in fine morocco, plain, price 7s. 6d.; also in Caledonian wood, fern pattern, with Photo. Portrait, etc., on side, morocco extra back, price 10s. Each Volume contains a Memoir, and is illustrated with a Portrait of the Author engraved on Steel, and numerous full-page Illustrations on Wood, from designs by eminent Artists; also beautiful Illuminated Title-page.

1. LONGFELLOW'S POETICAL WORKS.
2. SCOTT'S POETICAL WORKS.
3. BYRON'S POETICAL WORKS.
4. MOORE'S POETICAL WORKS.
5. WORDSWORTH'S POETICAL WORKS.

[Continued on next

Books published by William P. Nimmo,

NIMMO'S POPULAR EDITION OF THE WORKS OF THE POETS,

CONTINUED.

6. COWPER'S POETICAL WORKS.
7. MILTON'S POETICAL WORKS.
8. THOMSON'S POETICAL WORKS.
9. GOLDSMITH'S CHOICE WORKS.
10. POPE'S POETICAL WORKS.
11. BURNS' POETICAL WORKS.
12. THE CASQUET OF GEMS. Choice Selections from the Poets.
13. THE BOOK OF HUMOROUS POETRY.
14. BALLADS: Scottish and English.
15. BUNYAN'S PILGRIM'S PROGRESS AND HOLY WAR.
16. LIVES OF THE BRITISH POETS.
17. THE PROSE WORKS OF ROBERT BURNS.
18. POEMS, SONGS, AND BALLADS OF THE SEA.

*** This Series of Books, from the very superior manner in which it is produced, is at once the cheapest and handsomest edition of the Poets in the market. The volumes form elegant and appropriate Presents as School Prizes and Gift-Books, either in cloth or morocco.

'They are a marvel of cheapness, some of the volumes extending to as many as 700, and even 800, pages, printed on toned paper in a beautifully clear type. Add to this, that they are profusely illustrated with wood engravings, are elegantly and tastefully bound, and that they are published at 3s. 6d. each, and our recommendation of them is complete.'—*Scotsman.*

NIMMO'S SELECT LIBRARY.

New Series of Choice Books, beautifully printed on superfine paper, profusely Illustrated with original Engravings by the first Artists, and elegantly bound in cloth extra, plain edges, price 3s. 6d. each, or richly bound in cloth and gold, and gilt edges, price 5s. each.

THIRD EDITION.

1. **Almost Faultless: A Story of the Present Day.** By the Author of 'A Book for Governesses.'

'The author has written a capital story in a high moral tone.'—*The Court Journal.*

SECOND EDITION.

2. **Lives of Old English Worthies before the Conquest.** By W. H. DAVENPORT ADAMS.

'The author's aim is to illuminate what may be regarded as obscure, certain periods of historic England, accompanied with biographical sketches.'—*Courant.*

SECOND EDITION.

3. **Every-Day Objects; or, Picturesque Aspects of Natural History.** By W. H. DAVENPORT ADAMS.

FIFTH EDITION.

4. **My Schoolboy Friends: A Story of Whitminster Grammar School.** By ASCOTT R. HOPE, Author of 'A Book about Dominies,' 'Stories of School Life,' etc.

'This is a most interesting book. Boys, for whom it is especially written, will thoroughly enjoy it.'—*Westminster Review.*

SECOND EDITION.

5. **Drifted and Sifted: A Domestic Chronicle of the Seventeenth Century.**

'The author of this interesting, and we may add pathetic, story appears to possess the art of reproducing bygone times with much ability.'—*The Record.*

6. **Warrior, Priest, and Statesman; or, English Heroes in the Thirteenth Century.** By W. H. DAVENPORT ADAMS.

7. **Totty Testudo. The Life and Wonderful Adventures of Totty Testudo.** An Autobiography by FLORA F. WYLDE.

'The book is of engrossing interest, and the reader will be astonished, as he lays it down, to find that he has been able to get so much entertainment and instruction from the personal adventures of a tortoise.'—*Inverness Courier.*

8. **On Holy Ground; or, Scenes and Incidents in the Land of Promise.** By EDWIN HODDER, Author of 'Memories of New Zealand Life,' 'The Junior Clerk,' etc.

Books published by William P. Nimmo,

NIMMO'S CROWN GIFT BOOKS.

Crown 8vo, beautifully printed on superfine paper, profusely Illustrated by eminent Artists, in cloth extra, plain edges, price 3s. 6d. each, or richly bound in cloth and gold, and gilt edges, price 5s. each.

THIRD EDITION.

1. **Sword and Pen; or, English Worthies in the Reign of Elizabeth.** By W. H. DAVENPORT ADAMS.

'A more *wholesome* book for young readers we have seldom seen.'—*The Athenæum.*

SECOND EDITION.

2. **Norrie Seton; or, Driven to Sea.** By Mrs. George Cupples, Author of 'Unexpected Pleasures,' etc.

'Mrs. Cupples has given to the boys in this volume just the sort of sea-story with which they will be delighted.'—*The Scotsman.*

SECOND EDITION.

3. **The Circle of the Year; or, Studies of Nature and Pictures of the Seasons.** By W. H. DAVENPORT ADAMS.

'Its purpose is to tell both young and old, but especially the former, how much of interest there is in everything connected with Nature.'—*Bell's Messenger.*

SECOND EDITION.

4. **The Wealth of Nature: Our Food Supplies from the Vegetable Kingdom.** By the Rev. JOHN MONTGOMERY, A.M.

'It would be difficult to put into the hands of any boy or girl a volume which more equally combines the instructive and interesting in literature.'—*N. B. Mail.*

FIFTH EDITION.

5. **Stories of School Life.** By Ascott R. Hope.

6. **Stories of French School Life.** By Ascott R. Hope.

'We were among the many who greatly admired Mr. Hope's "Stories of School Life" and "Stories about Boys," and when we found that he had undertaken to illustrate French school life, we gladly opened the volume. The stories are interesting in the highest degree; they appeal to the best sympathies of the lads for whom they are written. They set forth the right and the true against the false, and they are full of good, hearty humour.'—*Public Opinion.*

London and Edinburgh.

NIMMO'S UNIVERSAL GIFT BOOKS.

A Series of excellent Works, profusely Illustrated with original Engravings by the first Artists, choicely printed on superfine paper, and elegantly bound in cloth and gold, and gilt edges; crown 8vo, price 3s. 6d. each.

1. Tales of Old English Life; or, Pictures of the Periods. By WILLIAM FRANCIS COLLIER, LL.D., Author of 'History of English Literature,' etc.
2. Mungo Park's Life and Travels. With a Supplementary Chapter, detailing the results of recent Discovery in Africa.
3. Benjamin Franklin: A Biography. From the celebrated 'Life' by JARED SPARKS, and the more recent and extensive 'Life and Times' by JAMES PARTON.
4. Wallace, the Hero of Scotland: A Biography. By JAMES PATERSON.
5. Men of History. By Eminent Writers.
6. Women of History. By Eminent Writers.
7. Old-World Worthies; or, Classical Biography. Selected from PLUTARCH'S LIVES.
8. Epoch Men, and the Results of their Lives. By Samuel NEIL.
9. The Mirror of Character. Selected from the Writings of OVERBURY, EARLE, and BUTLER.
10. Wisdom, Wit, and Allegory. Selected from 'The Spectator.'
11. The Spanish Inquisition: Its Heroes and Martyrs. By JANET GORDON, Author of 'Champions of the Reformation,' etc.
12. The Improvement of the Mind. By Isaac Watts, D.D.
13. The Man of Business considered in Six Aspects. A Book for Young Men.
14. The Pampas: A Story of Adventure in the Argentine Republic. By A. R. HOPE, Author of 'Stories of Whitminster,' etc. *Illustrated by Phiz, Junior.*
15. The Tower on the Tor. By Richard Rowe, Author of 'Episodes in an Obscure Life,' 'The Boys of Axleford,' 'Jack Afloat and Ashore,' etc.

*** This elegant and useful Series of Books has been specially prepared for School and College Prizes: they are, however, equally suitable for General Presentation. In selecting the works for this Series, the aim of the Publisher has been to produce books of a permanent value, interesting in manner and instructive in matter—books that youth will read eagerly and with profit, and which will be found equally attractive in after-life.

NIMMO'S ALL THE YEAR ROUND GIFT BOOKS.

A series of entertaining and instructive volumes, profusely Illustrated with original Engravings by the first Artists, choicely printed on superfine paper, and elegantly bound in cloth and gold, and gilt edges, crown 8vo, price 3s. 6d. each.

1. Christian Osborne's Friends. By Mrs. Harriet Miller Davidson, Author of 'Isobel Jardine's History,' and Daughter of the late Hugh Miller.
2. Round the Grange Farm; or, Good Old Times. By Jean L. Watson, Author of 'Bygone Days in our Village,' etc.
3. Stories about Boys. By Ascott R. Hope, Author of 'Stories of School Life,' 'My Schoolboy Friends,' etc. etc.
4. George's Enemies: A Sequel to 'My Schoolboy Friends.' By Ascott R. Hope, Author of 'Stories about Boys.'
5. Violet Rivers; or, Loyal to Duty. A Tale for Girls. By Winifred Taylor, Author of 'Story of Two Lives,' etc.
6. Wild Animals and Birds: Curious and Instructive Stories about their Habits and Sagacity. With numerous Illustrations.
7. The Twins of Saint-Marcel: A Tale of Paris Incendie. By Mrs. A. S. Orr, Author of 'The Roseville Family,' etc. etc.
8. Rupert Rochester, the Banker's Son. A Tale. By Winifred Taylor, Author of 'Story of Two Lives,' etc.
9. The Story of Two Lives; or, The Trials of Wealth and Poverty. By W. Taylor, Author of 'Rupert Rochester.'
10. The Lost Father; or, Cecilia's Triumph. A Story of our own Day. By Daryl Holme.
11. Friendly Fairies; or, Once upon a Time.
12. The Young Mountaineer; or, Frank Miller's Lot in Life. The Story of a Swiss Boy. By Daryl Holme.
13. Stories from over the Sea. With Illustrations.
14. The Story of a Noble Life; or, Zurich and its Reformer Ulric Zwingle. By Mrs. Hardy (Janet Gordon), Author of 'The Spanish Inquisition,' 'Champions of the Reformation.'
15. Stories of Whitminster. By Ascott R. Hope, Author of 'My Schoolboy Friends,' 'Stories about Boys,' etc. etc.
16. Heroes of Ancient Greece: A Story of the Days of Socrates the Athenian. By Ellen Palmer, Author of the 'Fishermen of Galilee,' 'The Standard Bearer,' etc.

*** The object steadily kept in view in preparing the above series has been to give a collection of works of a thoroughly healthy moral tone, agreeably blending entertainment and instruction. It is believed this end has been attained, and that the several volumes will be found eminently suitable as Gift Books and School Prizes, besides proving of permanent value in the Home Library.

NIMMO'S HALF-CROWN REWARD BOOKS.

Extra foolscap 8vo, cloth elegant, gilt edges, Illustrated,
price 2s. 6d. each.

1. **Memorable Wars of Scotland.** By Patrick Fraser Tytler, F.R.S.E., Author of 'The History of Scotland,' etc.
2. **Seeing the World: A Young Sailor's own Story.** By CHARLES NORDHOFF, Author of 'The Young Man-of-War's-Man.'
3. **The Martyr Missionary: Five Years in China.** By Rev. CHARLES P. BUSH, M.A.
4. **My New Home: A Woman's Diary.**
5. **Home Heroines: Tales for Girls.** By T. S. Arthur, Author of 'Life's Crosses,' etc.
6. **Lessons from Women's Lives.** By Sarah J. Hale.
7. **The Roseville Family.** A Historical Tale of the Eighteenth Century. By Mrs. A. S. ORR, Author of 'Mountain Patriots,' etc.
8. **Leah. A Tale of Ancient Palestine.** Illustrative of the Story of Naaman the Syrian. By Mrs. A. S. ORR.
9. **Champions of the Reformation: The Stories of their Lives.** By JANET GORDON.
10. **The History of Two Wanderers; or, Cast Adrift.**
11. **Beattie's Poetical Works.**
12. **The Vicar of Wakefield.** By Oliver Goldsmith.
13. **Edgar Allan Poe's Poetical Works.**
14. **The Miner's Son, and Margaret Vernon.** By M. M. POLLARD, Author of 'The Minister's Daughter,' etc. etc.
15. **How Frank began to Climb the Ladder, and the Friends who lent him a hand.** By CHARLES BRUCE, Author of 'Lame Felix,' etc.
16. **Conrad and Columbine. A Fairy Tale.** By James MASON.
17. **Aunt Ann's Stories.** Edited by Louisa Loughborough.
18. **The Snow-Sweepers' Party, and the Tale of Old Tubbins.** By R. ST. JOHN CORBET, Author of 'Mince Pie Island,' etc. etc.
19. **The Story of Elise Marcel. A Tale for Girls.**
20. **A Child's Corner Book: Stories for Boys and Girls.** By RICHARD ROWE, Author of 'Episodes in an Obscure Life,' 'Jack Afloat and Ashore,' etc.
21. **The Lucky Bag: Stories for the Young.** By Richard ROWE, Author of 'The Tower on the Tor,' etc.

Books published by William P. Nimmo.

Nimmo's Two Shilling Reward Books.

Foolscap 8vo, Illustrated, elegantly bound in cloth extra, bevelled boards, gilt back and side, gilt edges, price 2s. each.

1. **The Far North**: Explorations in the Arctic Regions. By ELISHA KENT KANE, M.D.
2. **Great Men of European History.** From the Beginning of the Christian Era till the Present Time. By DAVID PRYDE, M.A.
3. **The Young Men of the Bible.** A Series of Papers, Biographical and Suggestive. By Rev. JOSEPH A. COLLIER.
4. **The Blade and the Ear**: A Book for Young Men.
5. **Monarchs of Ocean**: Columbus and Cook.
6. **Life's Crosses, and How to Meet them.** By T. S. Arthur.
7. **A Father's Legacy to his Daughters**, etc. By Dr. Gregory.
8. **Mountain Patriots.** A Tale of the Reformation in Savoy. By Mrs. A. S. ORR.
9. **Labours of Love**: A Tale for the Young. By Winifred Taylor.
10. **Mossdale**: A Tale for the Young. By Anna M. De Iongh.
11. **The Standard-Bearer.** A Tale of the Times of Constantine the Great. By ELLEN PALMER.
12. **Jacqueline.** A Story of the Reformation in Holland. By Mrs. HARDY (JANET GORDON).
13. **Afloat and Ashore with Sir Walter Raleigh.** By Mrs. Hardy (JANET GORDON), Author of 'Champions of the Reformation,' etc.
14. **Diversions of Hollycot; or, The Mother's Art of Thinking.** By Mrs. JOHNSTONE, Author of 'Nights of the Round Table,' 'Clan Albin,' etc.

Nimmo's Home and School Reward Books.

Foolscap 8vo, Illustrated, elegantly bound in cloth extra, bevelled boards, gilt back and side, gilt edges, price 2s. each.

1. **Lame Felix.** A Book for Boys. By Charles Bruce.
2. **Picture Lessons by the Divine Teacher; or, Illustrations of the Parables of our Lord.** By PETER GRANT, D.D.
3. **Nonna**: A Story of the Days of Julian the Apostate. By Ellen PALMER.
4. **Philip Walton; or, Light at Last.** By the Author of 'Meta Franz,' etc.
5. **The Minister's Daughter, and Old Anthony's Will.** Tales for the Young. By M. M. POLLARD, Author of 'The Miner's Son,' etc. etc.
6. **The Two Sisters.** By M. M. Pollard.
7. **A Needle and Thread**: A Tale for Girls. By Emma J. Barnes, Author of 'Faithful and True, or the Mother's Legacy.'
8. **Taken Up**: A Tale for Boys and Girls. By A. Whymper.
9. **An Earl's Daughter.** By M. M. Pollard.
10. **Life at Hartwell; or, Frank and his Friends.** By Katharine B. MAY, Author of 'Alfred and his Mother,' etc. etc.
11. **Stories Told in a Fisherman's Cottage.** By Ellen Palmer, Author of 'Nonna,' 'The Standard-Bearer,' etc. etc.
12. **Max Wild, the Merchant's Son**; and other Stories for the Young.
13. **Noble Mottoes**: Familiar Talks with Peter Glenville on the Mottoes of Great Families. By CHARLES BRUCE, Author of 'Lame Felix,' etc.
14. **Heroes of Charity**: Records from the Lives of Merciful Men whose Righteousness has not been Forgotten. By JAMES F. COBB, F.R.G.S., Author of 'Stories of Success,' etc.

London and Edinburgh.

NIMMO'S
Sunday-School Reward Books.

Foolscap 8vo, cloth extra, gilt edges, Illustrated, price 1s. 6d. each.

1. Bible Blessings. By Rev. Richard Newton.
2. One Hour a Week: Fifty-two Bible Lessons for the Young.
3. The Best Things. By Rev. Richard Newton.
4. The Story of John Heywood: A Tale of the Time of Harry VIII. By CHARLES BRUCE, Author of 'How Frank began to Climb,' etc.
5. Lessons from Rose Hill; and Little Nannette.
6. Great and Good Women: Biographies for Girls. By LYDIA H. SIGOURNEY.
7. At Home and Abroad; or, Uncle William's Adventures.
8. Alfred and his Mother; or, Seeking the Kingdom. By KATHARINE E. MAY.
9. Asriel; or, The Crystal Cup. By Mrs. Henderson.
10. The Kind Governess; or, How to make Home Happy.
11. Percy and Ida. By Katharine E. May.
12. Three Wet Sundays with the Book of Joshua. By Ellen PALMER, Author of 'Christmas at the Beacon,' etc. etc.
13. The Fishermen of Galilee; or, Sunday Talks with Papa. By ELLEN PALMER.

NIMMO'S
Sunday and Week-Day Reward Books.

Foolscap 8vo, cloth extra, gilt edges, Illustrated, price 1s. 6d. each.

1. The Sculptor of Bruges. By Mrs. W. G. Hall.
2. From Cottage to Castle; or, Faithful in Little. A Tale founded on Fact. By M. H., Author of 'The Red Velvet Bible,' etc.
3. Christmas at the Beacon. By Ellen Palmer.
4. The Sea and the Savages: A Story of Adventure. By HAROLD LINCOLN.
5. The Swedish Singer; or, The Story of Vanda Rosendahl. By Mrs. W. G. HALL.
6. My Beautiful Home; or, Lily's Search. By Chas. Bruce.
7. The Story of a Moss Rose; or, Ruth and the Orphan Family. By CHARLES BRUCE.
8. Summer Holidays at Silversea. By E. Rosalie Salmon.
9. Fred Graham's Resolve. By the Author of 'Mat and Sofie.'
10. Wilton School; or, Harry Campbell's Revenge. A Tale. By F. E. WEATHERLY.
11. Grace Harvey and her Cousins.
12. Blind Mercy; and other Tales. By Gertrude Crockford.
13. Evan Lindsay. By Margaret Fraser Tytler, Author of 'Tales of Good and Great Kings,' 'Tales of the Great and Brave,' etc.

Books published by William P. Nimmo,

Nimmo's One Shilling Favourite Reward Books.
Demy 18mo, Illustrated, cloth extra, price 1s. each; also in gilt side and edges, price 1s. 6d. each.

1. The Vicar of Wakefield. Poems and Essays. By OLIVER GOLDSMITH.
2. Æsop's Fables, with Instructive Applications. By Dr. CROXALL.
3. Bunyan's Pilgrim's Progress.
4. The Young Man-of-War's-Man: A Boy's Voyage round the World. By CHARLES NORDHOFF.
5. The Treasury of Anecdote: Moral and Religious.
6. The Boy's Own Workshop; or, The Young Carpenters. By JACOB ABBOTT.
7. The Life and Adventures of Robinson Crusoe.
8. The History of Sandford and Merton. A Moral and Instructive Lesson for Young Persons.
9. Evenings at Home; or, The Juvenile Budget Opened. Consisting of a variety of Miscellaneous Pieces for the Instruction and Amusement of Young Persons. By Dr. AIKIN and Mrs. BARBAULD.
10. Unexpected Pleasures; or, Left alone in the Holidays. By Mrs. GEORGE CUPPLES, Author of 'Norrie Seton,' etc.
11. The Beauties of Shakespeare. With a General Index by the Rev. WILLIAM DODD, LL.D.
12. Gems from 'The Spectator.' A Selection from the most admired Writings of Addison and Steele.
13. Burns' Poetical Works. With a Complete Glossary.
14. The Sketch Book. By WASHINGTON IRVING.

*** The above Series of elegant and useful books is specially prepared for the entertainment and instruction of young persons.

Nimmo's Popular Religious Gift Books.
18mo, finely printed on toned paper, handsomely bound in cloth extra, price 1s. each.

1. Across the River: Twelve Views of Heaven. By NORMAN MACLEOD, D.D.; R. W. HAMILTON, D.D.; ROBERT S. CANDLISH, D.D.; JAMES HAMILTON, D.D.; etc. etc.
2. Emblems of Jesus; or, Illustrations of Emmanuel's Character and Work.
3. Life Thoughts of Eminent Christians.
4. Comfort for the Desponding; or, Words to Soothe and Cheer Troubled Hearts.
5. The Chastening of Love: Words of Consolation for the Christian Mourner. By JOSEPH PARKER, D.D., Manchester.
6. The Cedar Christian, and other Practical Papers. By the Rev. THEODORE L. CUYLER.
7. Consolation for Christian Mothers Bereaved of Little Children. By A FRIEND OF MOURNERS.
8. The Orphan; or, Words of Comfort for the Fatherless and Motherless.
9. Gladdening Streams; or, The Waters of the Sanctuary. A Book for Fragments of Time on each Lord's Day of the Year.
10. Spirit of the Old Divines.
11. Choice Gleanings from Sacred Writers.
12. Direction in Prayer; or, The Lord's Prayer Illustrated in a Series of Expositions. By PETER GRANT, D.D.
13. Scripture Imagery. By Peter Grant, D.D., Author of 'Emblems of Jesus,' etc.

NIMMO'S ONE SHILLING ILLUSTRATED JUVENILE BOOKS.

Foolscap 8vo, Coloured Frontispieces, handsomely bound in cloth, Illuminated, price 1s. each.

1. Four Little People and their Friends.
2. Elizabeth; or, The Exiles of Siberia. A Tale from the French of Madame COTTIN.
3. Paul and Virginia. From the French of BERNARDIN SAINT-PIERRE.
4. Little Threads: Tangle Thread, Golden Thread, and Silver Thread.
5. Benjamin Franklin, the Printer Boy.
6. Barton Todd, and The Young Lawyer.
7. The Perils of Greatness: The Story of Alexander Menzikoff.
8. Little Crowns, and How to Win them. By Rev. JOSEPH A. COLLIER.
9. Great Riches: Nelly Rivers' Story. By Aunt FANNY.
10. The Right Way, and The Contrast.
11. The Daisy's First Winter. And other Stories. By HARRIET BEECHER STOWE.
12. The Man of the Mountain. And other Stories.
13. Better than Rubies. Stories for the Young, Illustrative of Familiar Proverbs. With 62 Illustrations.
14. Experience Teaches. And other Stories for the Young, Illustrative of Familiar Proverbs. With 89 Illustrations.

[Continued on next page.

Books published by William P. Nimmo,

NIMMO'S ONE SHILLING ILLUSTRATED JUVENILE BOOKS,
CONTINUED.

15. **The Happy Recovery.** And other Stories for the Young. With 26 Illustrations.
16. **Gratitude and Probity.** And other Stories for the Young. With 21 Illustrations.
17. **The Two Brothers.** And other Stories for the Young. With 13 Illustrations.
18. **The Young Orator.** And other Stories for the Young. With 9 Illustrations.
19. **Simple Stories to Amuse and Instruct Young Readers.** With Illustrations.
20. **The Three Friends.** And other Stories for the Young. With Illustrations.
21. **Sybil's Sacrifice.** And other Stories for the Young. With 12 Illustrations.
22. **The Old Shepherd.** And other Stories for the Young. With Illustrations.
23. **The Young Officer.** And other Stories for the Young. With Illustrations.
24. **The False Heir.** And other Stories for the Young. With Illustrations.
25. **The Old Farmhouse; or, Alice Morton's Home.** And other Stories. By M. M. POLLARD.
26. **Twyford Hall; or, Rosa's Christmas Dinner,** and what she did with it. By CHARLES BRUCE.
27. **The Discontented Weathercock.** And other Stories for Children. By M. JONES.
28. **Out at Sea, and other Stories.** By Two Authors.
29. **The Story of Waterloo; or, The Fall of NAPOLEON.**
30. **Sister Jane's Little Stories.** Edited by Louisa LOUGHBOROUGH.
31. **Uncle John's First Shipwreck; or, the Loss of the Brig 'Nellie.'** By CHARLES BRUCE, Author of 'Noble Mottoes,' etc.

NIMMO'S
NINEPENNY SERIES FOR BOYS AND GIRLS.

In demy 18mo, with Illustrations, elegantly bound in cloth.

This Series of Books will be found unequalled for genuine interest and value, and it is believed they will be eagerly welcomed by thoughtful children of both sexes. Parents may rest assured that each Volume teaches some noble lesson, or enforces some valuable truth.

1. In the Brave Days of Old; or, The Story of the Spanish Armada. For Boys and Girls.
2. The Lost Ruby. By the Author of 'The Basket of Flowers,' etc.
3. Leslie Ross; or, Fond of a Lark. By Charles Bruce.
4. My First and Last Voyage. By Benjamin Clarke.
5. Little Katie: A Fairy Story. By Charles Bruce.
6. Being Afraid. And other Stories for the Young. By Charles Stuart.
7. The Toll-Keepers. And other Stories for the Young. By Benjamin Clarke.
8. Dick Barford: A Boy who would go down Hill. By Charles Bruce.
9. Joan of Arc; or, The Story of a Noble Life. Written for Girls.
10. Helen Siddal: A Story for Children. By Ellen Palmer.
11. Mat and Sofie: A Story for Boys and Girls.
12. Peace and War. By the Author of 'The Basket of Flowers,' etc.
13. Perilous Adventures of a French Soldier in Algeria.
14. The Magic Glass; or, The Secret of Happiness.
15. Hawks' Dene: A Tale for Children. By Katharine E. May.
16. Little Maggie. And other Stories. By the Author of 'The Joy of Well-Doing,' etc. etc.
17. The Brother's Legacy; or, Better than Gold. By M. M. Pollard.
18. The Little Sisters; or, Jealousy. And other Stories for the Young. By the Author of 'Little Tales for Tiny Tots,' etc.
19. Kate's New Home. By Cecil Scott, Author of 'Chryssie Lyle,' etc.

14   Books published by William P. Nimmo,

NEW WORKS.

NEW EDITION OF THE EDINA BURNS.
In crown 4to, price 12s. 6d., elegantly bound in cloth, extra gilt and gilt edges, also in Turkey morocco antique, very handsome, 42s., the popular Drawing-room Edition of the

Poems and Songs by Robert Burns. With Illus-
trations by R. HERDMAN, WALLER H. PATON, SAM. BOUGH, GOURLAY STEELL, D. O. HILL, J. M'WHIRTER, and other eminent Scottish Artists.

Fifth Edition. Thirteenth Thousand.

In demy 8vo, cloth elegant, richly gilt, price 7s. 6d., or in Turkey morocco antique, 21s.,

Things a Lady would Like to Know, concerning
Domestic Management and Expenditure, arranged for Daily Reference. By HENRY SOUTHGATE, Author of 'Many Thoughts of Many Minds,' 'Noble Thoughts in Noble Language,' 'Gone Before,' 'The Bridal Bouquet,' etc. etc.

Twelfth Thousand.

In crown 8vo, beautifully bound in cloth extra, full of Engravings and Coloured Pictures, price 3s. 6d., or gilt edges price 4s.,

Three Hundred Bible Stories and Three Hundred
Bible Pictures. A Pictorial Sunday Book for the Young.

The Excelsior Edition of Shakespeare's Complete Works.

In large demy 8vo, with Steel Portrait and Vignette, handsomely bound, price 5s.,

Shakespeare's Complete Works. With a Bio-
graphical Sketch by MARY COWDEN CLARKE, a Copious Glossary, and numerous Illustrations.

The Excelsior Edition of Whiston's Josephus.

In large demy 8vo, with Steel Portrait and Vignette, handsomely bound, price 5s.,

The Whole Works of Flavius Josephus, the Jewish
Historian. With Life, Portrait, Notes, Index, etc.

THE
WAVERLEY NOVELS.
ENTIRELY NEW EDITION.

Crown 8vo, with Frontispiece and Vignette, in elegant wrapper printed in colours, price 1s. each. Also, in Twenty-six volumes, cloth extra, full gilt back, price 2s. per volume; and in Thirteen double volumes, roxburgh style, gilt top, price 3s. 6d. per volume.

Edited by the Rev. P. HATELY WADDELL, LL.D. With Notes, Biographical and Critical, and a Glossary of Scotch Words and Foreign Phrases for each Novel.

1. **Waverley; or, 'Tis Sixty Years Since.'**
2. **Guy Mannering; or, The Astrologer.**
3. **The Antiquary.**
4. **Rob Roy.**
5. **Old Mortality.**
6. **The Black Dwarf, and A Legend of Montrose.**
7. **The Bride of Lammermoor.**
8. **The Heart of Mid-Lothian.**
9. **Ivanhoe: A Romance.**
10. **The Monastery.**
11. **The Abbot: A Sequel.**
12. **Kenilworth.**
13. **The Pirate.**
14. **The Fortunes of Nigel.**
15. **Peveril of the Peak.**
16. **Quentin Durward.**
17. **St. Ronan's Well.**
18. **Redgauntlet.**
19. **The Betrothed.**
20. **The Talisman: A Tale of the Crusaders.**
21. **Woodstock; or, The Cavalier.**
22. **The Fair Maid of Perth; or, St. Valentine's Day.**
23. **Anne of Geierstein; or, The Maiden of the Mist.**
24. **Count Robert of Paris.**
25. **The Surgeon's Daughter, and Castle Dangerous.**
26. **The Highland Widow, and my Aunt Margaret's Mirror.**
    With an interesting summarized account of the Scott Centenary.

The above may also be had in substantial half-calf biudings.

NIMMO'S NATIONAL LIBRARY.

In crown 8vo, with Steel Frontispiece and Vignette, handsomely bound, cloth extra, price 5s. each; also in full gilt side, back, and edges, price 6s. each.

Seventh Thousand.

The English Circumnavigators: The most remarkable Voyages round the World by English Sailors. (Drake, Dampier, Anson, and Cook's Voyages.) With a Preliminary Sketch of their Lives and Discoveries. Edited, with Notes, Maps, etc., by DAVID LAING PURVES and R. COCHRANE.

The Book of Adventure and Peril. A Record of Heroism and Endurance on Sea and Land. Compiled and Edited by CHARLES BRUCE, Editor of 'Sea Songs and Ballads,' 'The Birthday Book of Proverbs,' etc.

The Great Triumphs of Great Men. Edited by JAMES MASON. Illustrated.

Great Historical Mutinies, comprising the Story of the Mutiny of the 'Bounty,' the Mutiny at Spithead and the Nore, the Mutinies of the Highland Regiments, and the Indian Mutiny, etc. Edited by DAVID HERBERT, M.A.

Famous Historical Scenes from Three Centuries. Pictures of celebrated events from the Reformation to the end of the French Revolution. Selected from the works of Standard Authors by A. R. HOPE MONCRIEFF.

The English Explorers; comprising details of the more famous Travels by Mandeville, Bruce, Park, and Livingstone. With Map of Africa and Chapter on Arctic Exploration.

The Book for Every Day; containing an Inexhaustible Store of Amusing and Instructive Articles. Edited by JAMES MASON.

The Book of Noble Englishwomen: Lives made Illustrious by Heroism, Goodness, and Great Attainments. Edited by CHARLES BRUCE.

A Hundred Wonders of the World in Nature and Art, described according to the latest Authorities, and profusely Illustrated. Edited by JOHN SMALL, M.A.

Other Popular and Standard Volumes in preparation.

www.ingramcontent.com/pod-product-compliance
Lightning Source LLC
Chambersburg PA
CBHW022021240426
43667CB00042B/1029